T0281070

SOFTWARE METRICS AND SOFTWARE METROLOGY

SOFTWARE METRICS AND SOFTWARE METROLOGY

Alain Abran

A JOHN WILEY & SONS, INC., PUBLICATION

Published by John Wiley & Sons, Inc., Hoboken, New Jersey.
Published simultaneously in Canada.

For general information on our other products and services or for technical support, please contact our Customer Care Department within the United States at (800) 762-2974, outside the United States at (317) 572-3993 or fax (317) 572-4002.

Wiley also publishes its books in a variety of electronic formats. Some content that appears in print may not be available in electronic formats. For more information about Wiley products, visit our web site at www.wiley.com.

Library of Congress Cataloging-in-Publication Data is available.

ISBN: 978-0-470-59720-0

Printed in the United States of America.

10 9 8 7 6 5 4 3 2 1

CONTENTS

FOREWORD

Software organizations must respond to increasingly demanding customers in a globally competitive market and must implement best industry practices. With services and products available from vendors the world over, customers are insisting that their software systems be of high quality and with support services that challenge those of the competition while costing as little as possible.

To satisfy these demands, software organizations must have the ability to develop and maintain software to meet the customer's needs, and it must have access to software that support the company's business processes.

- How do you know and how do you objectively demonstrate to your customers that your software organization is performing at the top of the industry?
- Can you leverage this knowledge to develop estimation skills as a competitive advantage?

Benchmarking and estimation is based on measurements. There is a tremendous need for software measures to support software performance measurement, benchmarking and software project estimation, even more so when software is contracted out to third party suppliers.

There is currently available a large number of software measures and quantitative models proposed to the practitioners' community for estimating software projects and measuring the quality of the software delivered. For instance, there are hundreds of measures proposed for software quality, software complexity, objects oriented as well as an impressive number of estimation models

But …

- How many software organizations today have in place software measurement programs and use these measures and models as a basis for decision-making?

There must be then something at work that impairs the use of quantitative data for decision making in software-base organizations.

- What is it?

Within the software measurement community that has produced this large inventory of measures and quantitative models, there is a presumption that the lack of use of software measures in industry is caused by the practitioners' and managers' resistance to change.

This book is based on a different analysis and understanding of this lack of use of software measures by industry: this chasm comes from a lack of credibility in the practitioners communities, and this lack of credibility comes from the immaturity and unreliability of the measures themselves proposed to date to the industry.

Up until recently, software 'metrics' have been most often proposed as the quantitative tools of choice in software engineering, and the analysis of these had been most often discussed from the perspective referred to as 'measurement theory'.

However, in other disciplines, it is the domain of knowledge referred to as 'metrology' that is the foundation for the development and use of measurement instruments and measurement processes.

In this book, we use as a foundation the sets of measurement concepts documented in the ISO VIM (International Vocabulary of Basic and General Terms in Metrology) to document and compare the state of maturity of measures in software with respect to classic domains of science and engineering.

- This helps in particular to document practical aspects with respect to the current design of software measures and to identify the strengths and weaknesses of their own design as measures.

What was still missing is the *know-how* about how to correctly design software measures, and how to recognize if a software measure is well designed, and worth using as a basis for decision-making. This book focuses precisely on these two issues.

It is up to you:

- to acquire such *know-how* about the design of a software measure and
- to run with it for the benefit of your organization.

PREFACE

A book on the design of software measures must be suited to software engineers, both practitioners and researchers.

This book presents a perspective on software measurement that, on the one hand, is new in software engineering and, on the other hand, is fairly classical in most domains of sciences, engineering, and even in all areas of business.

Here, we share years of experience in the design of software measures for their successful use as decision making tools by software managers.

Because measurement is a fundamental engineering concept, software organizations of all sizes can use this book, and managers will find in it effective strategies for improving software management, along with numerous illustrative examples.

Applying the best practices in software measurement will ensure that software engineers and managers are equipped to respond to the most demanding customers, feel supported by senior executives and are proud to be part of the software team.

In addition, this book introduces many of the theoretical concepts and references needed by professionals, managers and students to help them understand the fundamentals of the identification and evaluation of software development and maintenance processes, and of improvements to them.

This book is intended for those developing, maintaining and managing software as well as for those in software process improvements.

STRUCTURE AND ORGANIZATION OF THIS BOOK

This book is organized into four (4) parts and fourteen (14) chapters.

Part 1: Key Concepts for the Design of Software Measures

A number of the software measures proposed to the industry have deficiencies severe enough to make some of them useless to practitioners. Part 1 presents in chapters one through five the key concepts in measurement that are necessary to recognize whether the design of a software measure is sufficiently strong to be meaningful in practice. Part 1 introduces, as well, the measurement terminology that is common in most fields of science and engineering; that is, of the metrology and related ISO standards on software measurement.

Chapter 1: Introduction.
This chapter presents the current level of maturity of software measurement within the software engineering discipline.
Chapter 2: From Measurement Methods to Quantitative Models: A Measurement Context Model.
This chapter presents a model to understand the key concepts of software measurement as well as the measurement terminology that is consistent with measurement in all disciplines. This chapter also discusses the process necessary to design a software measurement method.
Chapter 3: Metrology and Quality Criteria in Software Measurement.
This chapter presents the set of classical concepts in metrology, and presents various definitions and quality criteria in classical measurement.
Chapter 4: Quantification and Measurement are not the Same.
This chapter presents some of the differences between quantification and measurement, and establishes a parallel with the ISO 15939 Measurement Information Model.
Chapter 5: The Design of Software Measurement Methods.
This chapter presents the key concepts and steps required to design and evaluate software measurement methods, including defining the measurement principle in software measurement up to post-design activities.

Part 2: Some Popular Software Measures: How Good Are They?

Some software measures are currently popular in the industry, often because they are easy to collect or because they appear to take into account a large number of the practitioners concerns. However, in software measurement, being popular and widely quoted is not synonym to being good. Part 2 uses in chapters six through ten the criteria from Part 1 to illustrate some of the major weaknesses in the design of a few of the software measures that are either widely used or widely quoted in the software industry.

Chapter 6: Cyclomatic Complexity Number: Analysis of its Design
Chapter 7: Hasltead's Metrics: Analysis of their Designs
Chapter 8: Function Points: Analysis of their Design.
Chapter 9: Use Case Points: Analysis of their Design.
Chapter 10: ISO 9126: Analysis of its Quality Models and Measures.

Part 3: The Design of COSMIC—ISO 10761

Part 3 illustrates in chapters eleven and twelve how the lessons learned from the analysis of the key concepts for the design of a software measure have been put into practice to design a software measurement method conformant to the ISO criteria for a measurement method of the functional size of the software, that is the COSMIC—ISO 19761. Part 3 focuses on the design process rather than on the details of this specific measurement method.

Chapter 11: COSMIC: Design of an Initial Prototype.

This chapter illustrates how this software measure of the functional size of software for real-time and embedded software was designed in response to an industry need. It describes in particular the process used to design the initial prototype of COSMIC, its field trials and its initial deployment.

Chapter 12: COSMIC—Scaling up and Industralization.

This chapter illustrates the additional effort to scale up COSMIC to increase its international acceptance and to bring it to be adopted as an international standard: ISO 19761. The key concepts of the COSMIC measurement method are also presented in this chapter.

Part 4: Other Issues in the Design of Software Measures

Part 4 illustrates in chapters thirteen and fourteen some additional issues that are traditional in measurement in day-to-day life, but that have not yet been seriously addressed in software measurement. Two specific examples are presented: convertibility across measurement design and measurement standard etalons.

Chapter 13: Convertibility across Measurement Methods

While numerous software measures are proposed for the same attributes, there is a scarcity of convertibility studies across alternative ways of measuring. This chapter presents a convertibility analysis across two functional size measurement methods: IFPUG Function Points and COSMIC Function Points.

Chapter 14: Design of Standard Etalons: The Next Frontier in Software Measurement

While measurement in science relies on well established standard etalons (such as for the meter and kilograms) to ensure the correctness and consistency of measurement results across contexts and countries, not a single standard etalon has yet been established for measuring software. This chapter looks at this next frontier in software measurement and reports on an initial attempt to design a first draft of a standard etalon for a referenced set of software requirements.

This book also contains three appendices:

Appendix A: List of Acronyms
Appendix B: Glossary of Terms in Software Measurement.
Appendix C: References

Additional material to complement the information contained in this book can be found at http://profs.logti.etsmtl.ca/aabran

If you are a software manager, you should:

Part of the book	Read chapters:	Why?	What to do with it?
1	1 & 2	Not all software measures have strong designs. These two chapters explain the quality criteria that should be expected from software measures.	Quality criteria your staff should look for when analyzing a software measure as a basis for decision making.
	3	Chapter 3 on Metrology: through a quick reading of this chapter, managers will get an understanding of why software measures are still far way from the maturity of other measures in science and engineering.	For information only.
	4	This chapter positions the key ISO standard on software measurement—ISO 15939—and clarifies the differences between measurement and quantitative models	For a better understanding of the subtleties in measurement and quantitative analysis
2	**One** of chapters 6 to 10	Select the chapter to read on the basis of which one of these measures are in use in your organization	For the measures in use in your organization, ask your software engineer to document the impact of the weaknesses identified in this book on the quality of the measures and models you use for taking decisions.

Part of the book	Read chapters:	Why?	What to do with it?
3	Chapter 12	For an example of a software measurement method that has been accepted as an ISO standard.	If your organization is using software measures that have not yet been standardized, you must be careful.
4	Chapter 13	To get an example of convertibility across two distinct measures of software.	If your organization is mixing together numbers from different measurement designs, you should get your software engineers to document the impact this has on your quantitative models for decision making.

If you are a software engineering practitioner or a software quality analyst *using or planning to use existing software measures* you should:

Part of the book	Read chapters:	Why?	What to do with it?
1	1 to 5	These chapters explain the quality criteria that should be expected from software measures. These chapters teach you what to look for when analyzing a software measurement method.	You should document the impact of the weaknesses identified in this book on the quality of the measures and models used in your organization for making decisions.
2	**One** of the chapters 6 to 10	For examples of major weaknesses in some of the popular measures proposed to the software industry.	If you are using one of these measures, you should review your actual interpretation and usage of the numbers you are getting out. If you are using other software measures, you should ask for similar analyses.
3	Chapter 12	Same as for managers	Same as for managers
4	Chapter 13	Same as for managers	Same as for managers

If you are in software process improvement or a researcher *planning to analyze existing software measures or to design new software measures* or **if you are taking an undergraduate or graduate course on software measurement** you should:

Part of the book	Read chapters:	Why?	What to do with it?
1	All chapters from 1 to 4	Same as in previous tables above and an in-depth discussion on the design of software measurement methods in Chapter 5.	Same as in previous tables. Use the design process described in chapters 2, 4 and 5, when you have to design a new measurement method for software or when you have to correct the design of an existing one.
2	All chapters from 5 to 10	For a good coverage of the analyses documented to date on the design of some of the popular measurement methods.	If you have to evaluate other software measures, these chapters will guide you on how to do such evaluations. If you have to design new software measures, these chapters will also teach you what mistakes to avoid.
3	Both chapters 11 and 12	For understanding the stages of developing a software measurement method, from its initial design up to its highest recognition in the field of measurement that is: an International Standard.	Use a process similar to the one in Chapter 11 for *introducing strengths* into the design of *new* measurement methods for software. Use a process similar to the one in Chapter 12 for *adding strengths* into the design of *existing* measurement methods for software.
4	Both chapters 13 and 14	For an understanding of two critical issues in software measurement: using distinct measurement methods for the same attributes and the lack of standard etalon in software measurement.	These issues still have to be tackled by researchers for the majority of measures proposed to practitioners.
	And All Advanced Readings sections	For an in-depth understanding of the issues presented in each chapter.	For detailed examples of concepts introduced in the various chapters.

This book is not about:

- A compendium of all software measures:
  - The purpose of this book is not to present an exhaustive list of measures of any type, or of a specific type (for instance on OO metrics).
  - There exists already on the market a number of books presenting inventories of alternative measures, as well as hundreds of research papers on emerging designs, which at this stage would still be fairly immature.
- A compendium of software estimation models:
  - This book does not list or discuss any of the estimation models for software.
  - For instance, COCOMO [Boehm 1981, 2000] is an 'estimation model' which attempts to predict the relationships across a large number of factors. COCOMO is not about measurement but a lot more about experimentation (as in science) to build prediction models. COCOMO, for instance, should be used and evaluated as an estimation model. This will be discussed in another book looking into the design and evaluation of estimation models.
- A compendium of analyses of all software measures:
  - This book presents from chapters six through ten analyses that have already been carried out in research and published at a number of international conferences.
  - A large number of software metrics, such as the ones in (or derived from) Chidamber & Kemerer metrics suite [Chidamber 1993], has not yet been analyzed from a metrology perspective. The analysis from a metrology perspective of these other measures still has to be done.

COSMIC Function Points

The COSMIC Function Points have been adopted in 2003 as an international standard—ISO 19761—for measuring the functional size of software. Having been designed to meet metrology criteria, COSMIC Function Points are at times used in this book to illustrate a number of measurement concepts. For more details on the design of COSMIC Function Points, see Section 5 of Chapter 12.

ACKNOWLEDGMENTS

A number of collaborators, including colleagues in industry and university as well as PhD students, have helped me over the years improve my understanding of many of the concepts presented in this book, in particular:

Chapter	Co-Contributor
2: From Measurement Methods to Quantitative Models: A Measurement Context Model	Dr. Jean-Philippe Jacquet (France)
3: Metrology and Quality Criteria in Software Measurement	Dr. Asma Sellami—University of Sfax (Tunisia)
4: Quantification and Measurement are not the Same.	Dr. Jean-Marc Desharnais—Ecole de technologie supérieure (Canada) & Bogaziçi University (Turkey)
5: The Design of a Software Measurement Method	Dr. Naji Habra—Facultés Universitaires Notre-Dame de la Paix—FUNDP, Namur (Belgium)
6: Cyclomatic Complexity Number: Analysis of its Design	Dr. Naji Habra—FUNDP (Belgium)
7: Halstead's Metrics: Analysis of their Designs	Dr. Rafa Al-Qutaish—Alain University of Science and Technology, Abu Dhabi Campus, United Arab Emirates
8: Function Points: Analysis of their Design	
9: Use Case Points: Analysis of their design	Joost Ouwerkerk—Expedia (Canada)
10: ISO 9126: Analysis of its Quality Models and Measures	Dr. Rafa Al-Qutaish—Alain University of Science and Technology, Abu Dhabi Campus, United Arab Emirates
11: COSMIC—Design of an Initial Prototype	D. St-Pierre, Dr. Desharnais, Dr. P. Bourque and M. Maya (École de technologie supérieure—University of Québec—Canada)

Chapter	Co-Contributor
12: COSMIC—Scaling up and Industralization	C. Symons, M. O'Neil, P. Fagg, and a number of the COSMIC members of the measurement practices committee
13: Convertibility Across Measurement Methods	Dr Desharnais—Ecole de technologie supérieure (Canada) & Bogaziçi University Turkey
14: Design of Standards Etalons: The Next Frontier in Software Measurement	Dr. Adel Khelifi—University Al Hosn (United Arab Emirates)

Above all, this book is dedicated to all those who provided me with feedback and insights on software measures over the years and who are contributing, each in his or her own way, to the improvement of software measures as a foundation for sound, quantitatively-based decision making.

ABOUT THE AUTHOR

Dr. Alain Abran is a professor and the director of the research group in Software Engineering Management at the École de Technologie Supérieure (ETS)—Université du Québec, Montréal, Canada (www.gelog.etsmtl.ca)

He is a co-editor of the *Guide to the Software Engineering Body of Knowledge* (www.swebok.org). He is actively involved with software engineering standards with ISO/IEC JTC1 SC7—Software and System Engineering—and has been its international secretary in 2001–2003. He is chairman of the Common Software Measurement International Consortium (COSMIC).

Dr. Abran has more than 20 years of industry experience in information systems development and software engineering and 15 years of university teaching. He holds a PhD in electrical and computer engineering (1994) from the École Polytechnique de Montréal (Canada) and Master's degrees in management sciences (1974) and electrical engineering (1975) from the University of Ottawa (Canada).

His research interests include software productivity and estimation models, software engineering foundations, software quality, software measurement, functional size measurement methods, software risk management and software maintenance management.

Most of his publications can be downloaded from: http://profs.logti.etsmtl.ca/aabran/Publications/index.html

PART 1

KEY CONCEPTS FOR THE DESIGN OF SOFTWARE MEASURES

1

INTRODUCTION

This chapter covers:

- Software measurement: is it mature or not?
- Software measurement as a new technology
- The designs of software measures must be verified
- Advanced Readings: Measurement within the Software Engineering Body of Knowledge

1.1. INTRODUCTION

In the field of software engineering, the term "metrics" is used in reference to multiple concepts; for example, the quantity to be measured (measurand[1]), the measurement procedure, the measurement results or models of relationships across multiple measures, or measurement of the objects themselves. In the software engineering literature, the term was, up until recently, applied to:

- measurement of a concept: e.g. cyclomatic complexity [McCabe 1976],
- quality models: e.g. ISO 9126—software product quality, and

[1]A measurand is defined as a particular quantity subject to measurement; the specification of a measurand may require statements about quantities such as time, temperature, and pressure [VIM 2007].

- estimation models: e.g. Halstead's effort equation [Halstead 1977], COCOMO I and II [Boehm, 1981, 2000], Use Case Points, etc.

This has led to many curious problems, among them a proliferation of publications on metrics for concepts of interest, but with a very low rate of acceptance and use by either researchers or practitioners, as well as a lack of consensus on how to validate so many proposals.

The inventory of software metrics is at the present time so diversified and includes so many individual proposals that it is not seen as economically feasible for either the industry or the research community to investigate each of the hundreds of alternatives proposed to date (for instance, to measure software quality or software complexity).

This chapter illustrates the immaturity of both the software measures themselves and the necessity to verify the designs of these measures.

1.2. SOFTWARE MEASUREMENT: IS IT MATURE OR NOT?

The IEEE Computer Society defines software engineering as:

*"(1) The application of a systematic, disciplined, **quantifiable** approach to the development, operation, and maintenance of software; that is, the application of engineering to software.*

(2) The study of approaches as in (1)" [IEEE 610.12]

From the IEEE definition of software engineering—see box; it is obvious that measurement is fundamental to software engineering as an engineering discipline.

But what is the status of measurement within software engineering, and how mature is the field of knowledge on software measurement?

In software engineering, the software *metrics* approach has, up to fairly recently, been the dominant approach to measurement in this new engineering discipline.

Over recent decades, hundreds of so-called software metrics have been proposed by researchers and practitioners alike, in both theoretical and empirical studies, for measuring software products and software processes [Boehm 2000, Chidamber 1993, Karner 1993, Halstead 1997, etc.]:

- Most of these metrics were designed based either on intuition on the part of researchers or on an empirical basis, or both, and they have most often been characterized by the ease with which some entities of the development process can be counted.
- In their analysis of some of them, researchers have most often used the concepts of measurement *theory* as the foundation for their analytical

investigation. However, while relevant, measurement theory deals with only a subset of the classical set of measurement concepts, and software metrics researchers, by focusing solely on measurement theory, have investigated mainly the representation conditions, the mathematical properties of the manipulation of numbers, and the proper conditions for such manipulations [Fenton 1997, Zuse 1997].

• In the scientific fields, including engineering, as well as in others, like business administration and a significant number of the social sciences, measurement is one of a number of analytical tools. Measurement in those sciences is based on a large body of knowledge built up over centuries, even millennia, which is commonly referred to as "metrology".

In the literature on software metrics, there is almost no reference to the classical concepts of metrology in investigations into the quality of the *metrics* proposed to the software engineering community.

Only recently have some of the metrology-related concepts been introduced in the software engineering community, including the selection of the ISO vocabulary on metrology [VIM 2007] as the basis for measurement terminology for all future ISO standards on software measurement.

One of the peculiarities of software engineering relative to other engineering and scientific disciplines is its lack of general use of quantitative data for decision making. Symptoms of this are:

• a very limited number of accepted software measures available to practitioners and recognized as mature enough to be recognized as international standards, and
• a very small number of rigorous experimental studies (which constitute general practice in the engineering and medical fields, for example).

In mature disciplines, there is:

• a large international consensus on measures, in addition to established measurement methods and an etalon for each, and
• a significant number of measuring instruments to be used in different contexts and under various constraints, many of them certified and calibrated against internationally recognized, and traceable, etalons.

In mature disciplines, measures are also recognized as a necessary cost of doing business and of carrying on engineering activities, as well as a must for improving decision making.

In the software domain, we have none of the above, with the exception of the recent adoption of ISO standards for the measurement of the functional size of software, and some works-in-progress for the measurement of software quality.

ISO Standards for Measuring the Functional Size of Software

— The ISO 14143-1 on the mandatory set of characteristics of software functional size (i.e. a meta-standard),

— Five (5) ISO recognized specific measurement methods to implement the quantification of these functional size characteristics: ISO 19761- COSMIC, ISO 20926-IFPUG, ISO 20968-MKII, ISO 24570-NESMA and ISO 29881-FISMA.

Note: The software functional size measurement process is not yet mature enough for there to be a single universal way of measuring software functional size.

ISO Standards for the Measurement of Software Quality

The set of models of software product quality in ISO 9126-1 constitutes an international standard.

The three catalogs of more than 250 "metrics" in Parts 2 to 4 of ISO 9126 are still only ISO technical reports: much work remains to be done to bring them up to ISO standard status.

What does this mean for software measurement?

- Many, if not most, of the software measures proposed to the industry have not been seriously analyzed, nor are they sufficiently mature.
- In contrast to other fields of science and engineering, these software measures lack the credibility to be used as a basis for decision making.
- Verification criteria for software measures should be comprehensive, carefully defined, and agreed upon.
- Designers of software measures should document how well their proposed measures meet these verification criteria.

Impact of Lack of Credibility of Software Measures

It is not until it can be demonstrated unambiguously that a proposed measure achieves a high level of measurement quality that it can be expected to reach a level of credibility in the practitioner and manager communities, and then be used in practice on a large scale.

Impact of the absence of software measure credibility: when objective and quantitative data are required for decision making in software engineering, software engineering researchers and practitioners must often design and develop their own individual software measures and measurement methods, whereas these already exist in other fields of knowledge.

1.3. SOFTWARE MEASUREMENT AS A NEW TECHNOLOGY

Technology is defined as the set of methods and materials used to achieve industrial or commercial objectives.

This definition does not limit technology to materials alone: it also includes processes and the knowledge related to them, referred to as "know-how."

From that perspective, software measurement is a technology.
While some technologies are quite mature and widely used by practitioners in industry, others are emerging and in need of significant improvement if they are to penetrate deeply into an industrial domain.

- Mature technologies: they typically have been fine-tuned over many years and they have been adapted with a number of features and tools to fit various contexts and to facilitate their use by non experts.
- Innovative and immature technologies: they require significantly more expertise for using them in their 'immature' status.
  - Innovative (and immature) technologies are used initially by innovators who try them, test them and invest in improving them to facilitate their use within their technical context. Innovators work at bypassing initial design weaknesses to facilitate their use and adoption by people with less expertise.

Software measurement is definitively a new technology, and, as such, it shares many of the characteristics of new technologies and as well as the constraints that must be tackled to facilitate its adoption by industry at large and by individual practitioners.

What does it take for a new technology to be adopted?

On the part of an *organization*:

- The new, initially unknown technology must promise enough benefits to overcome the pain of changing from a known one.
- The organization must have (or gain) the technological know-how to make it work.
- The organization must be clever enough, and enthusiastic enough, to harvest its benefits, which takes time.

On the part of an *industry*:

- The new technology must become integrated into the industry's technological environment.
- It must also become integrated into the business context (which includes its legal and regulatory aspects).
- It must have been proven to work well in a large variety of application contexts (that is, the technology must be mature, or maturing rapidly).

What does it take for an industry to promote a new technology?

- The industry must recognize that there is a direction that has been proven to work in similar contexts.
- It must recognize that current practices are not good enough.
- It must also recognize that the players will not, on their own, submit to the pain of change (unless the environmental-regulatory context forces such a change).
- It must want to speed up the transition to the new technology.

What does it take for software measurement to be adopted as a new technology?

On the part of a *software organization*:

- Software measurement must promise enough benefits to overcome the pain of changing to an initially unknown technology.
- The organization must have the technological know-how in software measurement to make it work.
- The organization must be clever enough, and enthusiastic enough, to harvest the benefits, which takes time.

On the part of the *software industry*:

- Software measurement must become integrated into the technological environment of the software industry.
- It must become integrated into the business context (which includes its legal and regulatory aspects).
- Software measurement must already have been proven to work well in a large variety of contexts (that is, it must be mature as a technology, or maturing rapidly).

What does it take for an industry to promote software measurement as a new technology?

- Software measurement must have been proven to work in similar contexts.
- Current software measurement practices must be good enough.
- The industry must recognize that the players will not, by themselves, submit to the pain of change (unless the environmental-regulatory context forces such a change).
- It should want to speed up the transition to quantitative support for decision making.

The software industry has yet to resolve many of these issues, and much work remains to bring software measurement to a high enough level of quality and maturity to meet market expectations.

1.4. THE DESIGNS OF SOFTWARE MEASURES MUST BE VERIFIED

Software measurement must play an increasingly important role in software engineering if it is to truly become an engineering discipline.

- Over the past twenty years, a significant number of software metrics have been proposed for better control and greater understanding of software development practices and products.
- Unfortunately, very few of these metrics have been looked at closely from a measurement method perspective, and it is currently difficult, because of a lack of agreed-upon frameworks of verification and validation procedures, to analyze their quality.

What constitutes a valid metrics, or even a valid measurement method? How can a measurement method be validated?

Various authors have attempted to address these questions in recent years, and from different points of view (mathematical, practical, etc.)[2].

The analytical perspective proposed in this book is complementary to previous works referred to above and discusses this issue from a measurement method point of view. Furthermore, to avoid the confusion generated by inconsistent terminology in previous studies on validation, the more precise set of concepts of *verification* criteria is preferred here over *validation* criteria.

In Part 1 of this book (Chapters 2 to 5) we will refer to *specific criteria for verification*, rather then to *generic concepts related to validation* in general.

Examples of Verification Questions that Need to be Investigated

— Does the measurement method really measure the concept intended to be measured?

— Has the measurement method been internally verified, i.e. in the sense that it can be shown that it gives a proper numerical characterization of the attribute to be measured?

— Is the measurement method usable? A measurement method which is as perfect as possible from a mathematical viewpoint would not be of any interest if it could not be applied (if it were far too time-consuming, for example).

---

[2] See Chapter 2, Section 6.

ADVANCED READINGS: HOW MUCH MEASUREMENT SUPPORT IS RECOGNIZED WITHIN THE SOFTWARE ENGINEERING BODY OF KNOWLEDGE (SWEBOK)?

Audience

This Advanced Reading section provides to readers an overview of how software measurement fits within the discipline of software engineering, and how much support software measurement provides to software from an engineering perspective.

Software engineering has only recently reached the status of a legitimate engineering discipline and a recognized profession.

- Up to 2003, there was no generally accepted body of knowledge in this new field.
- To address the issue, the IEEE-Computer Society initiated various task forces in the 1990s, including the SWEBOK (Software Engineering Body of Knowledge) project [Abran, Moore *et al.* 2005d], to develop an international consensus on a compendium of the body of knowledge that has been developing and evolving over the past four decades and a guide to that compendium.

Importantly, the SWEBOK is not static, and the Guide to it must, of necessity, develop and evolve as software engineering matures.

The SWEBOK was established with the following five objectives:

1. Promote a consistent view of software engineering worldwide;
2. Clarify the place and set the boundary of software engineering with respect to other disciplines, such as computer science, project management, computer engineering, and mathematics;
3. Characterize the contents of the software engineering discipline;
4. Provide a topical access to this body of knowledge;
5. Provide a foundation for curriculum development, and for individual certification and licensing material.

The material that is recognized as being within the realm of software engineering is organized into the 10 Knowledge Areas (KAs) listed in Table 1.1.

The topic of measurement was the subject of one of the editorial criteria for the initial write-up of the first draft of the SWEBOK Guide, that is, that the measurement "theme" be common to all KAs.

Measurement in engineering is an integral part of all engineering KAs, and therefore had to be incorporated into the proposed breakdown of topics in each KA for software engineering.

TABLE 1.1. The 10 SWEBOK Knowledge Areas

---

1. Software requirements
2. Software design
3. Software construction
4. Software testing
5. Software maintenance
6. Software configuration management
7. Software engineering management
8. Software engineering process
9. Software engineering tools and methods
10. Software quality

Since a criterion for the inclusion of knowledge in the SWEBOK Guide was that it be generally accepted, it is important to ask what did, in fact, gain approval on a consensual basis with respect to measurement, and what can be learned from this consensus, or the lack of it.

The SWEBOK Definition of "Generally Accepted"

Applies to most of the projects, most of the time, and widespread consensus validates its value and effectiveness
This definition is borrowed from the Project Management Institute (PMI).

Another tool used for the development of the SWEBOK, from an engineering viewpoint, was the Vincenti [1990] classification of engineering knowledge, including, of course, "quantitative data" as a category.

On the left-hand side of Table 1.2, the six categories of engineering knowledge are listed, while the next three columns present related sub-concepts identified in specific engineering disciplines for classification purposes.

At the beginning of the SWEBOK project, it was suggested to the specialists in charge of a particular software engineering KA that they use this classification for their initial draft.

This was, of course, a challenging assignment, because:

- the discipline of software engineering was not mature enough at the time, and
- the classification could not be *directly* implemented in most of the KAs of the software engineering taxonomy.

The Vincenti classification for engineering knowledge types is very useful for understanding the depth of coverage of some engineering topics (including measurement) within each KA.

TABLE 1.2. Classification of Engineering Knowledge—Vincenti

Vincenti Categories	Related sub-concepts		
Fundamental Principles	Operational principle: how the characteristic parts of an operation fulfill their special functions in combining into an overall operation.	Normal configuration: common arrangement of the constituent parts.	To be learned deliberately. Form an essential part of *design* knowledge.
Criteria & Specifications	Specific requirements (of operational principles). Limits (across an entire technology).	To translate general, qualitative goals couched in concrete technical terms Note: the "… ilities".	Key knowledge: selection of the appropriate set of criteria.
Theoretical Tools	*Design* concepts; intellectual tools for thinking about design.	Mathematical methods & theories for design calculations. Models: combinations of measures/ parameters.	Methods of value are micro-methods, closely tailored to the tasks of developing parts which are particularly well understood.
Quantitative Data	Represented in tables and graphs.	Obtained empirically or calculated theoretically,	Descriptive or prescriptive.
Practical Considerations	Theory: often insufficient —considerations from experience and practice. Trade-offs: resulting from general knowledge about the device, its use, and its context.	Structured procedures; Knowledge derived from practice, learned from on-the-job experience. Knowledge from an expert's skills set.	Ad-hoc assumptions about a phenomenon: not formally codified, but represented by rules of thumb.
Design Instrumentalities	Know-how: ways of thinking. Procedural knowledge.	Solutions can be sought where some element of novelty is required.	Judgment skills. Knowledge on how to carry out tasks: repeatable and documented.

For instance, it can be observed that, while the term "measurement" appears by design throughout all the SWEBOK KAs (that is, it was the subject of one of the editorial criteria), neither the KA editors nor the group of reviewers has pointed to key references providing generally accepted quantitative data for any of the topics identified in each KA.

In the 2004 version of the SWEBOK Guide, there is no reference to highly credible and documented quantitative data and relevant repositories of quantitative references.

This means, for instance, that, while there are a large number of chapters and books dedicated to estimation in the software engineering literature, the raw datasets available for study often lack engineering rigor in the data collection procedures on the one hand, and, on the other, the estimation models proposed usually have both poor explanatory power and significant limitations in generalization power.

Quantitative Data in Engineering

In engineering, quantitative data does not mean raw data, but rather descriptive or prescriptive data usually derived from controlled experiments using widely recognized measurement concepts, verified measurement instruments, documented measurement protocols, and extensive testing and replication procedures to ensure both the verification of data inputs and an in-depth understanding of the phenomena under study in order to identify both the range of operations and their limitations.

Data in Software Engineering Estimation Models

In both versions of the COCOMO models [Boehm 1981, 2000], many parameters are described by linguistic values, and their influence is determined by expert opinion rather than on the basis of information from descriptive and prescriptive engineering repositories.

Significant effort still needs to be invested by model builders in terms of incorporating engineering strength into these models.

EXERCISES

1. In every organization, there is a well-staffed and well-funded accounting department. An accounting department is basically a measurement program. Why is such measurement considered as essential to any organization, from the very small to the largest?

2. In software organizations, most consider measurement programs too expensive and too time-consuming. Why?

3. Business managers and engineers thrive on measurements and quantitative data. What about software managers?

4. In all areas of an organization, staff resources willingly collect all kinds of measures for management purposes. Why are software staff so reluctant to collect software measures?

5. In various business areas, many measures are collected manually and used for taking major business decisions. Why are manually collected measures regarded with such suspicion in software organizations?

6. In engineering organizations, significant efforts are devoted to measurement? What benefits are expected?

7. In engineering organizations, significant budgets are dedicated to acquiring or developing measuring instruments. By comparison, how much is spent in software organizations on acquiring or developing automated measurement systems?

8. In engineering and in the basic sciences, a great deal of research funding goes towards conducting experiments to collect "quantifiable data". How much of the research budget in software engineering goes into collecting such data?

9. Select three of the most often quoted "software metrics". For which of these does your organization have the technological knowledge to make them work.

10. Select two software measures collected in your organization. Identify business decisions which have been based on results from data collected with these two measures.

11. What is the ultimate recognition for a measure in most scientific fields?

12. Which criteria would you use to verify that the design of a software measure is sound?

13. Can you have engineering without measurement? Can you have software engineering without measurement?

14. Give examples of international consensus on some software measures.

15. How much quantitative data in software engineering are now recognized as generally accepted? Provide supporting evidence for your answer.

16. List five software measures and explain why you would consider them either mature or immature.

TERM ASSIGNMENTS

1. If you consider software measurement to be a new technology, what are the typical hurdles that must be overcome to implement software measures in an organization and in the software industry?

2. Of the software measures you are currently using in your organization, for which of them do you currently have documented evidence that they are based on a sound foundation?

3. Measurement and quantitative data are fundamental in engineering. Measurement is also important in the Guide to the Software Engineering Body of Knowledge—SWEBOK www.swebok.org. Identify recent sets of quantitative data which you would recommend for inclusion in the next release of the SWEBOK.

2

FROM MEASUREMENT METHODS TO QUANTITATIVE MODELS: A MEASUREMENT CONTEXT MODEL

This Chapter Covers:

- An overview of the differences across numbers, measures, and quantitative models
- A measurement context model
- A process model for the design of a software measurement method
- A discussion on the application of a measurement method and on the exploitation of measurement results in quantitative models
- Advanced Readings: Analysis of the ISO requirements for the designs of Functional Size Measurement methods

2.1. INTRODUCTION: NUMBERS, MEASURES, AND QUANTITATIVE MODELS

It is important to clarify, right from the start, the differences among:

- a number in its mathematical sense;
- a number obtained from a measurement exercise, and
- a number obtained from a quantitative decision making model.

Software Metrics and Software Metrology, by Alain Abran
Copyright © 2010 IEEE Computer Society

2.1.1   A Number in Its Mathematical Sense

As youngsters, we learn our numbers from one on. As we progress through school, we learn the mathematical rules governing how to combine the numbers through valid mathematical operations: comparison, addition, division, real numbers, equations, etc.

In this way, we learn to deal with numbers in a mathematical sense and, in so doing, to deal mostly with abstract concepts: there is no need to measure or assess anything in particular, or to take a decision.

Mathematics ≠ Decision Making

Mathematics: When we deal with numbers only in a mathematical sense, we implicitly make the following assumption: we consider that there is no uncertainty tied to these numbers.

Decision making: When we have to make a decision, we must explicitly verify the uncertainties in the numbers used in the decision making process: we cannot take for granted the quality-related characteristics attached to measures, such as: accuracy, repeatability, reproducibility.

2.1.2   A Number Obtained from A Measurement Exercise

A number derived from a measurement exercise on a specific entity is more than a number, as it includes:

- the measurement unit attached to that number; and
- the specific measurement procedure followed to obtain it.

This measurement result is the number assigned to the specific attribute of a specific entity:

- It is represented by a number and its measurement unit, and there is also a degree of uncertainty as to its value, in terms of the various types of potential errors inherited from the measurement procedure (such as random and/or systematic errors in the measurement process).
- Similarly, the number obtained from a measurement exercise is limited to the characteristic being measured.

Measurement of Temperature

A temperature measurement tells us specifically about the temperature, in a quantitative manner and relative to a measurement scale (such as the Celsius scale).

However, such a measurement result does not tell us whether or not it is windy, whether or not it is raining, or whether or not we can play golf!

2.1.3   A Number Obtained from a Quantitative Decision Making Model

Quantitative decision making models, and also evaluation models, are a combination of (quantitative) numbers and rules on how to interpret numbers of different types concurrently.

Decision Models

An informal model for deciding when to play golf will take into account not only the temperature (in degrees Celsius or Fahrenheit), but also other data, whether numerical or qualitative:

- What is the strength of the wind (does it exceed a threshold)?
- Is it raining?
- Is it a workday or not?
- Am I in shape today?
- Is there something important I should be doing today?

Software Decision Model

A model for deciding when to stop testing a piece of software will, for instance, take into account:

- the number of bugs,

as well as a number of additional parameters, such as:

- the size of the software,
- the number of tests,
- the testing period,
- the decreasing of number of bugs per period of time or per number of tests, and so on.

This chapter presents a measurement context model to highlight the differences between *measurement methods* and *quantitative models*.

Management is mostly interested in quantitative models; however, such models cannot be expected to produce a reliable basis for decision making if their inputs are of poor quality, that is, if the models use as inputs numbers derived from:

- unsound measurement methods, or
- sound but improperly applied measurement methods, which leads to unreliable measurement results.

Measurement methods and quantitative models are distinguished in this chapter by means of a measurement context model which clarifies the distinct steps from the design of a software measurement method to the exploitation of the measurement results in subsequent quantitative models, such as quality and estimation models.

Here, the focus is on the steps for designing a measurement method.

This chapter is organized as follows:

- Section 2 presents a measurement context model.
- Section 3 presents the steps for the design of a measurement method.
- Section 4 presents the steps for the application of a measurement method.
- Section 5 discusses the exploitation of measurement results in quantitative models.
- Section 6 discusses the differences across validation and verification of measurement methods.
- The Advanced Readings section at the end of this chapter presents the requirements imposed by ISO 14143-1 standard on the design of measurement methods for the functional size of software.

2.2. MEASUREMENT CONTEXT MODEL

2.2.1 Measurement Terms in Technical Texts

In day-to-day language and in literature in general, the term "measure" is used in different ways to mean different things. It can refer to:

1. a method allowing the assignment of a numerical (or symbolic) value to an object in order to characterize one attribute of this object;
2. the application of this method (e.g. the action of measuring);
3. the result of the application of a measurement method;
4. the use of the measurement result in describing *relationships across many different entities and attributes* (e.g. between size and effort in estimation models, between defects and maintainability in quality models);
5. the whole process from the design of a measurement method to its exploitation in quantitative models, whether the inputs to these models have been derived from:
   - a subjective judgment, or
   - rigorous application of a standardized measurement method.

However, in technical texts in engineering in general, as well as in mature disciplines in which quantitative data are used (such as physics and chemistry), the terms "measure" and "measurement" should never be used alone, but be accompanied by the qualifiers that specify which specific measurement concepts are involved.

In technical texts, the term "measurement" must only be used in expressions, such as:

- "measurement method",
- "application of a measurement method", and
- "measurement results".

2.2.2 Measurement Context Model

Actually, the three (3) uses of the term "measurement" listed above correspond to the three (3) steps in the measurement context illustrated in Figure 2.1:

Step 1: Before measuring, it is necessary to either select a measurement method if one already exists, or design one (if an existing method does not fit the need).

Step 2: Once the measurement method has been designed, its rules are applied to software or a piece of software to obtain a specific measurement result;

Step 3: The measurement result is exploited in a quantitative or qualitative model, usually in combination with other measurement results of different types (e.g. the productivity ratio for benchmarking purposes: output over input, O/I).

The arrows in Figure 2.1 illustrate the sequencing of these steps during the process of designing a measurement method. Of course, lessons learned in a subsequent step can be fed back to previous steps (in a feedback loop).

Now, managers are mostly interested in Step 3; they use either informal or formal models for making a decision, and the models they use can be based on either qualitative or quantitative data, or both.

In this book, we deal mostly with the quantitative aspects of measurement, preferably with numbers with a ratio scale to which the usual mathematical operations (addition, multiplication, division) apply. Qualitative models are out of scope in this book.

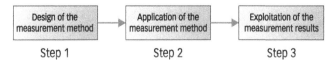

Figure 2.1. Measurement Context Model—The Design View

A Documented Quantitative Model for Decision Making

An estimation model based on an algorithm derived from a statistical regression on a set of completed projects.

An Informal Qualitative Model For Decision Making

A contractor proposes to develop software for a client at an incredibly low price.
  His decision model is not based on a published estimation model, but on some risk-taking, involving, for example:

- the opportunity to obtain more profitable contracts with this same client later on, or
- his ability (as he perceives it) to negotiate this price at a significantly higher level later, when the client will have no choice but to accept over-budget expenses.

Quantitative models can be very helpful in decision making, provided, of course, that their own designs are well structured and based on:

- sound theory,
- experimental or empirically verified foundations, and
- input parameters that meet a number of quality characteristics.

The manager's role is typically to use quantitative models in decision making (Step 3), rather than to carry the measurement application (Step 2) or design measures (Step 1). However, it is vital to the manager that the measurement application has sufficient controls that he can trust the inputs to his quantitative decision making model, and that the design of the measures used be sound. See Figure 2.2.
  In turn, it is the responsibility of the software engineer to ascertain that:

- the quantitative models themselves are sound and that they provide a sound basis for decision making, with known constraints and limitations;
- the inputs to these models are themselves sound (that is, the inputs can be trusted, and their levels of uncertainty and precision are known); and
- the designs of these measures are themselves sound and meaningful.

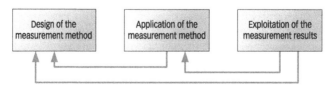

Figure 2.2. Measurement Context Model—The User/Manager View

Examples of unsound designs and unsound applications of a measurement method are provided in side boxes.

Unsound *Design* of A Measurement Method

Example 1: When the measurement method includes a design that incorrectly mixes the scale types of its sub-components, numbers are produced, but such numbers are meaningless and their use in measurement models can only be meaningless (that is, they lead to meaningless models, which in turn provide managers with a false sense of well-being—that is, they increase risks, rather than reducing them).

(See Part 2 of this book—Chapters six through nine)

Example 2: When the design of the measurement method is limited to a single algorithm without clear definition of the parameters of that algorithm, it cannot be expected that different measurers measuring the same piece of code or documentation will produce similar numbers as measurement results.

Unsound *Application* of A Measurement Method

It is unreasonable to expect the numbers obtained in the following examples to be of high quality and precision:

Example 1: If the numbers are derived from an analysis of incomplete and ambiguous documentation.

Example 2: If the number of lines of code is derived from the wrong version of the software (from a lack of configuration control).

In large software organizations, it is the responsibility of the software process improvement group to identify and address the specific weaknesses identified in software measures and in related quantitative models, and to develop improvement solutions.

While there exists a large body of knowledge on the development and use of quantitative models, including estimation models and quality models, and on how to recognize whether or not such models are good, very little has been published on how to design measures for software or on how to recognize whether or not a design is a good one, and if is not, how to improve it.

This book focuses on the foundation of this chain of measurement for decision making, that is, on the design of software measurement methods.

2.2.3 Inputs and Outputs in A Measurement Context Model

Figure 2.3 illustrates the various steps of the measurement context model, together with their inputs and intermediate steps and corresponding outputs, as well as the relationships between those steps. This model helps in understanding the measurement chain, and, later on, will help in identifying the verification criteria necessary at each stage to ensure that the outcomes (for instance, the design of the measurement method in Step 1) are sound.

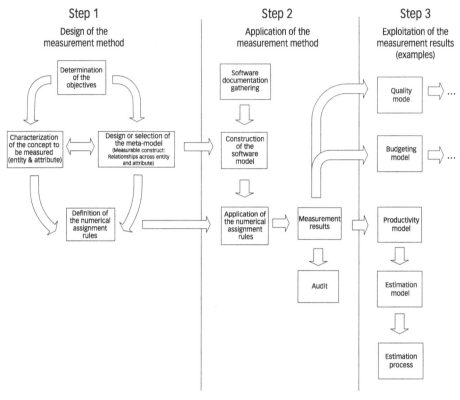

Figure 2.3. Detailed Measurement Context Model

Three (3) successive steps (or stages) in the measurement context model presented in Figure 2.2 can be clearly distinguished.

1. The first step refers to the *design* of a measurement method.
   - The input to this step is a description of the measurement objective, and the set of concepts and techniques required for designing a measure constitutes the resources.
   - The output is the identification of the measurable concepts and constructs, its measurement principle, and the description of its measurement method for the implementation of its numerical assignment rules.

   Of course, when a measurement method already exists, there is no need to design one. However, software practitioners and managers should know enough about the design of a measurement method to have the ability to recognize if an available design is adequate for their purposes.

2. The second step refers to the *application* of the measurement method in a specific context.

- The inputs to this step are the entity to be measured and the generic measurement method. Both are needed to set up a specific measurement procedure in a specific context to produce a measurement result.
- The outcome is not only the measurement result, but also the insights into the quality of that measurement result, such as an appreciation of the degree of uncertainty of the result and the factors that have influenced this uncertainty.

This step also includes the gathering and documentation of measurement information, which could be used in future applications for verification and auditing purposes.

3. The third step refers to the *exploitation* of the measurement result in an information context, often in relationship with other data, whether quantitative or qualitative, or both.
   - This includes analysis of the quantitative result of the model, usually for purposes of evaluation, statistics, comparison, or prediction.

The linear description of the above process as three (3) successive steps is aimed at providing a global structure for the activities involved.

In practice, the process can be more realistically be viewed as iterative as different kinds of verification activities are carried out throughout the three (3) steps, each activity could detect anomalies which would, in turn, lead to back-tracking to the previous activity, and so on.

These three steps are presented in greater detail in the following sections.

2.3. HOW TO DESIGN A MEASUREMENT METHOD

The left-hand side of Figure 2.3 shows the four (4) sub-steps required to *design* a measurement method:

1. Determination of the measurement objectives.
2. Characterization of the concept to be measured by specifying the entities to be measured and the characteristics (attributes) to take into account.
3. The setting up of the measurable construct, or of the meta-model, including the relationships across the concept to be measured (entity and attribute).
4. Definition of the numerical assignment rules.

The modeling of these sub-steps is based on a logical perspective and on the recognition that iterative and successive refinements are required to improve the initial design proposal of a measurable concept and of its corresponding measurement method. It should also be recognized that sub-steps 2 and 3 are usually performed in parallel, each influencing the other.

These four sub-steps are presented next in more detail.

Sub-step 1: Determination of the measurement objectives
Before designing a software measurement method, it is important to know:

- what we want to measure (what kind of software, which attribute, etc.),
- what the measurement point of view will be (software user, software designer, etc.), and
- who the intended users are of the measurement results.

All these criteria have a strong influence on the design of the measurement method, and, of course, on the corresponding verification criteria.

Sub-step 2: Characterization of the concept to be measured
In order to enable the measurable concept to be defined in a measurable construct, and, from that, to build the measurement method, the concept to be measured must be clearly defined.

Once the attribute (or concept to be measured) has been chosen in the design of a measurement method, an (empirical) operational definition of this attribute must be given, that is, the concept must be characterized.

This characterization can be made by first stating implicitly how the concept is decomposed into sub-concepts. This decomposition describes what role each sub-concept plays in the constitution of the concept to be measured, and how these sub-concepts are themselves defined.

In the concurrent sub-step 3, these interrelationships have to be organized into a measurable construct (e.g. a meta-model of the measurable attribute).

What Do We Measure: A Concept or An Object?

To measure distance, the concept of distance must be identified and a consensus developed and instantiated through a widely recognized definition: the concept of distance.

In our modern civilization, the concept of the distance between two points is now well defined. If we consider two distances, we are able to say whether these distances are equal or not, and, if they are not, which is bigger.

"Distance" is defined as the *direct path between two dimensionless points*.

A "point" is an abstract concept which is used as the foundation for the concept of distance.

Therefore, distance itself is indeed an abstract concept that is measured when we apply a measurement method to physical entities (or to models of these physical entities when they are represented, for instance, on geographical maps).

Software: An Object or A Concept?

Software is often referred to as an intangible product, that is, an *intellectual* product.

Notwithstanding this definition, software does exist in the physical world and is visible through multiple representations (e.g. a set of screens and reports for a user, a set of lines of code for a programmer, a set of software model representations for a software designer, etc.).

(Moreover, software is physically visible to the hardware through a series of *bits* in a computer, which have been created by a compiler or interpreter.)

For this physical software and its representations, measurable concepts are then defined, such as functional size, complexity, quality, etc.

To characterize the concept to be measured, two other types of concepts need to be determined:

1. the type of entity to be measured (that is, the measurand on which to apply the measurement rules—e.g. code), and
2. the attributes to be measured on this entity type (that is, the measurable concept itself—e.g. lines of code, as a representation of the size of the code).

Sub-step 3: Design (or selection) of the meta-model (e.g. measurable construct)

The set of characteristics selected to represent software or a piece of software, *together with the set of their relationships*, constitute the meta-model (e.g. measurable construct) of the software to which the proposed measurement method will be applied.

- The meta-model should be described *generically*, that is, it should not be specific to a particular piece of a software and should be independent of the context of measurement while meeting the objective of the measurement.
- The meta-model must also describe *how to recognize the attributes to take into account to measure the entities* involved in the measurement exercise.
- The meta-model must also describe what role each sub-concept plays in the make-up of the concept measured, and how these sub-concepts are themselves defined.

Example 1: Cyclomatic Complexity Number

For the Cyclomatic complexity number of the software:

- the entity to be measured is the control flow graph of the software program, and
- the characteristics to take into account are described through a set of identification rules defined to recognize those characteristics as valid for its measurement purpose; that is, the edges and nodes in the control flow graph.

See also Chapter 6.

Example 2: Function Points

In the Function Point measurement method, an internal logical file (ILF) is an entity-type part of the implicit Function Point meta-model of the size of the software.
   The Function Point Counting Practices Manual provides:

   • a definition of this ILF entity type, as well as
   • identification rules to ensure that each and every ILF can be clearly recognized within the software.

See also Chapter 8.

Example 3: COSMIC—ISO 19761

In the COSMIC functional size measurement method, an Entry is a piece of software of the entity type "data movement", as recognized by the COSMIC method. This entity type is defined according to the explicit COSMIC meta-model of the software.
   The COSMIC implementation Guide to ISO 19761 provides:

   • the definition to the Entry entity type, as well as
   • the identification rules that ensure that each and every Entry can be clearly recognized within the software and taken into account in the measurement procedure.

See also Chapters 11 and 12.

A note on sub-step 2 and sub-step 3: It is important to note that these two sub-steps, "definition of the concept to be measured" and "design of the meta-model," are strongly related:

   • the definition of a concept cannot be achieved without a representation of the type of entity to be measured, i.e. without a meta-model;
   • the design of meta-models is itself partly dictated by the way the concept will be characterized.

Because of the relationships between these two sub-steps, they are represented on the same level in Figure 2.3. Although different, they cannot effectively be performed separately.

Sub-step 4: Definition of the numerical assignment rules
The fourth step, the numerical and mathematical one, consists in defining an empirical relational set[1].

---

[1]See also Chapter 5.

From a mathematical viewpoint, to characterize a concept is to define an empirical relational set.

- This is achieved by defining numerical assignment rules.
- This sub-step should also include the selection (or design) of a measurement unit.

Measurement Unit(s) for Distance

The concept of distance is not specific to a context of measurement.

However, in practice and over centuries, different units have been used to measure distance, whether on land, at sea, or in the air.

Notwithstanding the above, the selection of measurement units may vary, for practical reasons:

— the *mile* in the British system for the measurement of distance on land, and
— the *nautical mile* for the measurement of distance at sea .

Of course, a single universal measurement unit for a measurable concept is much better, such as the *meter* for the measurement of distance.

The basis for these numerical assignment rules is the proposed meta-model and the characterization of the concept. A numerical assignment rule can be described through:

- a descriptive text (a practitioner's description), or
- mathematical expressions (a formal theoretical viewpoint).

The first type of description is used when the measurement method is applied in practice.

The second is required to allow a mathematical analysis of the mathematical properties of the measurement method.

This analysis (carried out by establishing the relationships between the characterization of the concept and the mathematical description of the measurement method) will, among other things, enable determination as to whether or not the measurement method has been built consistently and which mathematical operations can be used on the results.

The definition of numerical assignment rules must also specify the measurement unit(s).

The definition of units is related, among other things, to the way an attribute is measured. This means, of course, that some relationships exist between:

- the unit,
- the measurement method, and
- the measured attribute.

TABLE 2.1. Template for the Design of a Measurement Method

Step—Sub-step	Comments-Description
Step 1: Determination of the Measurement Objectives	
What do we want to measure? What attribute of which entity type? From what measurement point of view? (user, developer, etc.) Intended uses of the measurement result?	
Step 2: Characterization of the concept to be measured: the measurable construct	

Clear definition of the concept to be
  measured (entity & attribute)
The (empirical) operational definition of
  the attribute to be measured =
  characterization of the concept
How the concept is decomposed into
  sub-concepts
The definition of each sub-concept
The type of entity to be measured
  (=the measurand)	

Step 3: Design(or selection) of the meta-model (the measurable construct) **Meta-model = set the of characteristics selected and the set of their relationships**	

Generic description of the meta-
  model = independent of the context of
  measurement while meeting the
  measurement objective
Description of how to recognize the
  attributes to take into account to
  measure the entities involved
Relationships between the sub-concepts
  (i.e. The roles of each sub-concept)	

Step 4: Definition of the numerical assignment rules	

Define an empirical relational set = defining
  the numerical assignment rules
Selection of a measurement unit + The
  justification for this selection
How each sub-concept contribute to
  the numerical assignment rules:
  — A descriptive text (a practitioner's
    description)
  — Mathematical expression (a formal
    theoretical viewpoint)	

The justification for the decision as to what unit to use in a measurement method should be provided (for example, by reference to a standard, to a theory, etc.).

If this is not done, then the rationale for the interpretation of the unit is not provided. For instance, what is a Function Point?[2]

For those who need to design a measurement method, the various steps and sub-steps described in this section are listed in Table 2.1; this table can be used as a work-in-progress template for recording the outcomes of each step and sub-step.

End of the design step of a software measurement method
The four (4) distinct design sub-steps defined in Figure 2.3 should have been completed by the end of every measurement method design process, and all their deliverables should be available and documented, that is:

- objectives of the measurement
- characterized concept and its decomposition,
- the meta-model selected for the entities and attribute to be measured, and
- the numerical assignment rules,

all codified into a measurement method.

Is This Design Present in All Software "Metrics"?

The four necessary sub-steps for the design of a measure (and its corresponding measurement method) are in marked contrast to current practices with various software metrics proposals.

Quite often the design of a software "metrics" is incomplete, and limited to the definition of some numerical assignment rules through an equation and then attempts to analyze whether or not the resulting numbers bear some relationship to attributes other than the ones being measured!

In such a case, these software "metrics" can hardly be qualified as *bona fide* measurement methods.

2.4. APPLICATION OF A MEASUREMENT METHOD

Once the measurement method has been designed and all its design deliverables are available, it can be applied to measure specific software or a piece of software.

In the specialized terminology of measurement, the "application of the measurement method" to "a specific context of measurement" corresponds to the design of a *measurement procedure* for a specific measurement exercise.

The application of a measurement method is carried out through the following sub-steps (when the application of the measurement method is not automated):

1. Gathering of the software documentation;
2. Construction of the software model to be measured;

[2] See Chapter 8, Section 6.4.

3. Assignment of the numerical rules;
4. Presentation of measurement results;
5. Verification of measurement results.

These five sub-steps in the application of a measurement method are detailed below.

Measurement Method ≠ Measurement Procedure [VIM 2007]

Measurement method:
A measurement method is *a logical sequence of operations, described generically*, used in the performance of measurement.

Measurement procedure:
A measurement procedure is *a set of operations, described specifically*, used in the performance of *particular measurements* according to a given method.

Sub-step 1: Gathering of the software information
The information required for the application of the measurement method is collected:

- from the software to be measured, when the software is available;
- from the documentation of the software; for instance, when the software has not yet been built.

This information gathering process allows the second sub-step to be carried out, the modeling of the software (if the appropriate model of this software is not readily available in the documentation).

Sub-step 2: Construction of the software model to be measured
Once this documentation has been gathered, the software model is built according to the rules of the measurable construct. This model describes how the software to be measured is represented by the measurement method.

The basis for the construction of the model is, of course, the proposed meta-model or measurable construct, and the rules to model it are the rules identifying the relevant components (entities and attributes) that will take part in the measurement.

If the appropriate model has already been built and is available from the previous sub-step, this second sub-step is bypassed.

Sub-step 3:
The numerical assignment rules are next applied to the software model derived from Sub-steps 1 and 2.

Sub-step 4: Presentation of the measurement results
Applying the measurement rules makes it possible to obtain a measurement result. In order to be evaluated, this result should generally be documented with the following:

- the measurement unit,
- a description of the intermediate measurement steps,
- a description of the measurement process,
- the measurers,
- the measurement procedure, etc.

Standards of Measurement Reporting

ISO 14143-1 states very precisely how to document the measurement results of an ISO recognized Functional Size Measurement method.

Sub-step 5: Verification and audit of the measurement results
The measurement results should now be verified and audited, using various methods, to ascertain their quality. For example, the tricky parts of mathematical calculations should be checked.

The results can also be compared with other well-known results in order to evaluate their correctness [Desharnais and Morris 1996].

Verification of Measurement Results

Example 1. For lines of code: Verification that all lines of code within the scope of the measurement have been included.

Example 2. For the COSMIC measurement method: Verification that all triggering events have been identified.

2.5. EXPLOITATION OF MEASUREMENT RESULTS IN QUANTITATIVE MODELS

The results of the application of the measurement method can be used in many different ways, many of which might not have been foreseen at the design stage of the measurement method.

The right-hand column of Figure 2.3 illustrates a few potential uses of a software measurement result:

- in evaluation models, such as quality models,
- in budgeting models,

- in an estimation process, which is itself is based on a productivity model, and an estimation model.

This fourth sub-step is much better known. It is not discussed here, but is discussed in a second book on *Productivity and Estimation Models*.

Evaluation models

A quality model requires both the measurement results of the entity being evaluated and an interpretation scale and context for these results (e.g. a reference model).

CMMi Capability Model

The CMMi is an evaluation model for a software development organization.

If an organization obtains a measurement result of 3, how can this value be interpreted?

- If the organization had been evaluated at level 2, then a measurement result of 3 represents a significant organizational achievement; however, if the previous assessment result was 4, then the result of 3 represents a significant degradation in the capabilities of the organization.
- Similarly, a level 3 result represents a significantly better level of achievement when all the organization's competitors are at level 2, but certainly an under-achievement if a number of its competitors have achieved a level of 5.

It must be noted that, in the CMMi instance, the numbers of the levels 1, 2, 3, 4, and 5 are not numbers in a mathematical sense, but only simple ordered labels which represent the following corresponding concepts: ad hoc, structured, managed, quantified, and optimized.

If the CMMi is considered as a maturity model, then each increasing level corresponds to a more *mature* organization.

If the CMMi is considered as a capability model, then each increasing level corresponds to a more *capable* organization.

2.6. VALIDATION OR VERIFICATION?

The validation problem has been addressed from many different points of view. For example:

- Schneidewind [1992] proposes a validation process based mainly on the analysis of the uses of the results of measurement methods, for example in prediction systems (Step 3 in Figure 2.3: Exploitation of the measurement results).
- Fenton and Kitchenham [1991] suggest that, in order to be valid, a measurement method must satisfy the representation condition of measurement theory.

In other words, a validation process is proposed which addresses mostly the relationships between the two sub-steps, "characterization of the concept to be measured" and "definition of the numerical assignment rules," of Step 1 in Figure 2.3.

- Kitchenham *et al.* [1995] propose a validation process addressing some parts of the three steps in Figure 2.3, but does not cover the full spectrum of the process model of measurement methods proposed here.

For example, it does not tackle the verification of the meta-model and of its relationships with the various components of measurement methods.

Verification or Validation?

- **Verification:** provision of objective evidence that a given item fulfills specified requirements [ISO VIM 2007].
- **Validation:** verification, where the specified requirements are adequate for an intended use [ISO VIM 2007].

In this book, use of the term *valid measurement* in a general sense is avoided, because of the diversity of the validation approaches in the literature which cover a wide spectrum of criteria at different levels. To be as general as possible and to take into account the diversity of existing approaches, this book proposes instead a list of criteria which should be verified throughout the measurement context life cycle.

Verification activities are thus viewed as a continuous process taking place during the phases of the measurement life cycle; in particular, several verification criteria are to be identified during the design phase.

The rationale is that, in software engineering, most research is carried out on the use of numbers in software measures, and not enough on their design or on how to create them, even though the design of software measures is the fundamental phase of measurement.

Different kinds of verification activities should be applied in order to obtain verified measurement results with a sufficient degree of confidence, i.e. relying on quality results criteria such as accuracy, repeatability, reproducibility, etc.

An overview of verification activities is presented in Table 2.2.

- For Step 1: verification of the design of a measurement method should ideally be performed only once, when the design in proposed.
- For Step 2: verification of the application of the measurement procedures should be performed every time a measurement exercise is carried out to ensure that the measurements results are accurate and to determine their degree of uncertainty when required.

TABLE 2.2. Verification Activities for Each Step

1—Design Step	2—Application Step	3—Exploitation Step
Verification of the design of a measurement method (with respect to the objective and measurement principle).	Verification of a practical application of the measurement procedures, including the measurement instruments or steps, and of results obtained.	Verification of the quality of the models of relationships across multiple measurement results.

In particular, Step 2 starts with the application of the measurement method on some chosen sample, followed by the detection, by the method, of one or more anomalies.

These anomalies, when encountered, will lead a measurer to reconsider the measurement instrument and its calibration, rework a part of the measurement procedure, or even alter the choice of the basic definitions of the measurement method if it is not mature enough.

· For Step 3: the quality of the models across multiple measurement results should not be verified every time a model is used; however, the users of these models should have a good understanding of the strengths and weaknesses of the models they use.

The approaches of the various authors, as well as the *validation* concepts being differently addressed by these authors, can be categorized depending on whether or not they addressed *verification* issues related to Steps 1 to 3 of the high level measurement context model—Figures 2.1, 2.2, and 2.3.

ADVANCED READINGS: ANALYSIS OF THE ISO REQUIREMENTS FOR THE DESIGNS OF FUNCTIONAL SIZE MEASUREMENT METHODS

Audience

This Advanced Reading section is of most interest to the readers puzzled by the large number of metrics proposed to measure the same concept (such as for the measurement of software complexity or software coupling, for instance), and interested in knowing how ISO has developed its set of requirements for the designs of functional size measurement, and how well ISO has performed in tackling this challenge.

1. Overview

The ISO 14143-1 standard is the first in a set of six documents on the design of functional size measurement methods for software. The ISO 14143 series corresponds, therefore, to a meta-standard, which is a standard that sets out rules for other standards (in this context, the standards for the measurement methods for the functional size of a software).

This case study analyzes ISO 14143-1 using the measurement context model presented in this chapter. This analysis is from the perspective of the intended users of this ISO standard, that is:

- users of functional size measurement (FSM) methods;
- designers of functional size measurement (FSM) methods.

The Advanced Readings section is organized as follows:

- Section 2 presents the background on the ISO 14143 series and discusses the scope of ISO 14143-1.
- Section 3 presents the scope of ISO 14143-1 with respect to the measurement method context model.
- Section 4 presents a comparison at the design requirements level.
- Section 5 presents a summary, including the strengths and weaknesses identified in this analysis.

2. Background for ISO 14143-1

In the mid-1990s, over 30 variants of Function Points (FP) had been published in an attempt to address some of the weaknesses of the initial FP method.

At that time, the international standardization community recognized the need to address the issue of such a large variety of functional sizing proposals, and agreed to commit resources to staff a new ISO working group to tackle it.

Soon after the ISO working group began its activities, it became clear that a choice had to be made between two alternative strategies for standardization:

- Alternative 1: proceed quickly to accept Function Point Analysis as the single standard for functional size measurement in spite of a number of documented deficiencies.
- Alternative 2: recognize that no known single functional size measurement method could at that time adequately meet all the requirements for all types of software, and that some methods had strengths others did not have.

It was also perceived that progress towards a single functional size measurement method would be slow and quite challenging, in terms of effectively defining one integrated Functional Size Measurement (FSM) method which would suit all circumstances. It was also felt in this working group that, for the foreseeable future, multiple functional size measurement methods would coexist.

Alternative 2 was judged to be the best for the long term. The strategy then evolved towards the identification of sets of criteria that any proposed FSM method would have to meet to be recognized as an international standard. This ISO working group subsequently developed a six-document series, including ISO IS 14143-1—"Definition of concepts." This international ISO standard specifies a list of mandatory concepts that must be present in an FSM method; it provides the basis for assessing whether or not a particular method conforms to the ISO definition of an FSM method.

3. The scope of ISO 14143-1 within the Measurement Context Model
The scope of ISO 14143-1 is twofold:

- to define the "… *fundamental concepts of Functional Size Measurement (FSM)*," and
- to describe the "… *general principles for applying an FSM Method.*"

It is also specified in the scope section of the standard that it does NOT provide detailed rules on how to:

- *measure the Functional Size of software using a particular method;*
- *use the results obtained from a particular method;*
- *select a particular method.*

It also states that the standard is not aimed at addressing "quality" criteria with respect to measurement methods; that is, it does not provide requirements for qualifying them as either "good" or "effective" FSM methods. Some of these quality-related issues are addressed in subsequent technical reports (ISO 14143, Parts 3 to 5).

ISO 14143-1:

- focuses on defining requirements for the design of FSM methods for software; that is, the first step of the model of measurement context described in this chapter.
- provides a few requirements for the application of a measurement method (that is, Step 2), when it specifies how measurement results must be reported.
- describes the exploitation of the FSM results; for example, Step 3 of the measurement context model (discussed only in the Informative Appendix to this ISO document).

In this ISO standard, the typical mistake made by the software engineering industry and academic communities of using the terms (nouns) "measure" and "measurement" indiscriminately to refer to many distinct concepts concurrently has been avoided. In ISO 14143-1, the terms are never used alone, but always within expressions such as:

1. Functional size measurement—FSM: *The process of measuring Functional Size.*

2. Functional size measurement method: *A specific implementation of FSM defined by a set of rules, which conforms to the mandatory features of this part of ISO 14143.*

4. Comparison of the design requirements for an FSM

Does ISO 14143-1 require that all four sub-steps for the design of software measurement methods be addressed to recognize a proposed FSM as an ISO one?

Sub-step 1: Definition of the measurement objectives
ISO 14143-1does not impose any constraints on objectives, but recommends that they be addressed in every FSM method proposed: *an FSM Method should describe the purposes for which the FSM Method can best be used such that the users of the FSM Method can judge its suitability for their purpose.*

Sub-step 2: Characterization of the concept to be measured
What is the concept to be measured?
The concept to be measured (or the attribute) is, of course, functional size, and this is embedded within the definitions of "functional size."

Functional Size: *A size of the software derived by quantifying the Functional User Requirements.*

Functional User Requirements: *A sub-set of the user requirements. The Functional User Requirements represent the user practices and procedures that the software must follow to fulfill the users' needs.*

What is the measurand? (That is, what entities will be measured?)

Software is visible in a number of ways (e.g. for a user: a set of reports, screens etc.; for a programmer: a set of lines of code). The measurement process will therefore be applied to these measurands.
ISO 14143-1 does not specifically identify the entities on which the measurement method will be applied, but rather the *type* of entities, that is, the Functional User Requirements.

What attribute, or characteristics, of the entity will be measured?

ISO 14143-1 does not specify any requirement, nor does it provide any directive or specification as to the characteristics comprising the concept of functionality. It specifies only criteria that "shall not" take part in the characterization of the concept of functional size:

1. *it is not derived from the effort required to develop the software being measured;*

2. *it is not derived from the effort required to support the software being measured;*
3. *it is independent of the methods used to develop the software being measured;*
4. *it is independent of the methods used to support the software being measured;*
5. *it is independent of the physical components of the software being measured;*
6. *it is independent of the technological components of the software being measured.*

ISO 14143-1 specifies some other characteristics in a negative way in the following requirement: *It expresses only Functional User Requirements; it does not express Technical Requirements, and it does not express Quality Requirements.*

That this ISO document does not specify requirements about the characterization of the concept can be explained by the lack of consensus about what makes up the concept of functionality or about the properties of this concept.

ISO 14143-1 requires that an FSM method specify what kind of software can be measured using their design: *An FSM Method shall describe the Functional Domain(s) to which the FSM Method can be applied.*

ISO 14143-1 refers to guidelines on the concept of "Functional Domain" provided in ISO TR 14143-5, but it is not mandatory to respect guidelines.

Sub-step 3: Design of the meta-model (measurable construct)
The set of characteristics selected to represent software or a piece of software and the set of their relationships constitutes the meta-model proposed for the description of the software to which the proposed measurement method will be applied. The meta-model must therefore describe the entity types to be used to describe the software and the rules allowing identification of the entity types.

In short, when considering meta-models, three main elements have to be examined:

1. The entity types of the meta-models (i.e. the different types of components taking part in the modeling of the software).
2. The relationships among entity types.
3. The entity (type) identification rules.

This sub-step specifies the requirements relating to these three main elements of the design of a measurement method:

1. Entity types of the meta-model—ISO 14143-1 does not identify the entity types to be measured for functional size, but it states that the FSM method specifies them, using the following vocabulary:

- *Base Functional Component (BFC): An elementary unit of Functional User Requirements defined, and used, by an FSM Method for measurement purposes*
- *BFC Type: A defined category of BFCs*
- *Boundary: A conceptual interface between the software under study and its users*

Some examples are provided, but only for illustrative purposes and not as requirements.

2. Relationships among entity types—A requirement about relational entity types is specified. *An FSM method shall define the relationship, if any, between the BFC Type and the boundary.*
3. Entity identification rules—ISO 14141-1 also specifies that requirements about entity identification rules be addressed. *An FSM method shall:*

   - *describe how to identify BFCs within the Functional User Requirements;*
   - *define how to classify BFCs into BFC types, if there is more than one BFC type.*

For the sake of generality, this ISO document does not impose a specific meta-model. However, ISO 14143-1 clearly addresses the design sub-step of the meta-model for proposals of FSM methods, but it imposes few constraints on the answers to be provided.

Sub-step 4: Definition of the numerical assignment rules
ISO 14143-1 lists some requirements concerning the way the numerical assignment must be achieved. The requirements specified deal with:

1. Assessment of BFCs. This ISO document specifies that calculation of an FSM must be based on the evaluation of each BFC. ISO 14143-1 requires, therefore, that FSM methods shall:

   - *define the rules used to assess the BFCs;*
   - *define how to assign a numeric value to a BFC according to its BFC Type;*
   - *derive the functional size through the assessment of BFCs.*

However, ISO 14143-1 does not require a statement of the full rationale for the selection of the rules for assigning a numerical value to the software according to the BFC assessment. Therefore, the list of requirements provided for this step does not seem complete without this last requirement.

2. Units of the measurement method. ISO 14143-1 contains only one requirement for the units of a measurement method: *An FSM method shall define the units in which Functional Size is expressed.*

TABLE 2.3. Summary of Measurement Design Findings in ISO 14143-1

Measurement Method Context Model	Topics addressed in ISO 14143-1	Topics not addressed in ISO 14143-1
Steps (and sub-steps)		
Step 1: Design of the measurement method.		
Definition of the objectives	Prescribes that all required sub-steps be addressed (what is going to be measured, what the measurement viewpoint is, etc.).	Prescribes specific requirements only on the viewpoint to be stated, that is, the user viewpoint.
Design or selection of the meta-model	Prescribes the three main elements of meta-models: the entity types (BFCs, BFC types, and the boundary), the relationships among entity types, and the entity type identification rules.	No specific requirements are specified. Distinct measurement methods could therefore even measure distinct objects, thereby rendering convertibility across methods quite challenging.
Characterization of the concepts	Describes what MUST NOT be included in the characterization of the concept of functionality.	Does not provide requirements on characteristics that should be included in this characterization, i.e. measuring the same objects differently, could lead to different sizes according to each method proposed.
Definition of the numerical assignment rules	Requires the numerical assignment rules and the definition of the measurement units.	Does not require the rationale for the assignment rules.
Step 2: Measurement method application.		
Software documentation gathering	The document acknowledges "Software documentation gathering".	
Construction of the software model		Not addressed explicitly
Application of the numerical assignment rules	The document acknowledges the "application of the numerical assignment rules" sub-steps, and describes a list of activities for carrying them out.	
Presentation of the Measurement Results	The document provides specifications on how a measurement result must be documented.	
Verification of the measurement results		Outside the scope of the document—addressed in ISO 14143-3
Step 3: Exploitation of the measurement results in a quantitative model		
		Outside the scope of ISO 14143-1 (mentioned only in the Informative Appendix)

5. Summary

Using the structure of the three steps of the measurement context model, Table 2.3 presents a summary of the topics addressed and not addressed in the ISO 14143-1 standard.

This analysis of the content of the ISO standard, carried out using the measurement process model, confirms that, from a measurement method perspective, this ISO document specifies that most of the measurement method concepts have to be addressed, but imposes very few constraints on how they are to be addressed.

However, a key issue has not been adequately addressed, which is how the concept of functionality has to be characterized. This ISO document does not specify the mandatory requirements imposed on the functionality concept to be measured. It does not provide:

- any direction or specifications as to the subconcepts comprising the concept of functionality, or
- any direction on the role each subconcept plays in the constitution of the concept measured and how these subconcepts are themselves defined.

It specifies mostly criteria which "shall not" take part in the characterization of the concept of functional size.

The weaknesses identified mean that compliance will not ensure that the functional size of a piece of software has been adequately measured.

By not providing specific requirements as to the characteristics that should be included in the characterization of functionality, measuring the same objects differently could lead to different sizes according to each method proposed, even though they would have been, and recognized as being, in compliance with this ISO standard.

Even more serious is the fact that distinct measurement methods could even measure the same measurand by using different views of the attributes, thereby rendering convertibility across methods quite challenging for both users and designers of FSM methods.

EXERCISES

1. When you deal with numbers in a mathematical sense only, what assumptions do you implicitly make about these numbers?

2. If you measure temperature only, what does that tell you? Does temperature alone provide enough information for a decision to be taken?

3. What are some of the differences between a number in a mathematical sense and a quantitative model for decision making?

4. Managers are interested in using quantitative models. From a measurement perspective, what must be verified before such models are used?

5. Explain the three steps of the measurement context model presented in this chapter.

6. Explain the controls implemented in your organization (e.g. the measurement procedures) for the collection of effort in software projects. What is the precision of the effort collected: for each person, and overall?

7. What are the differences between Sub-step 2 and Sub-step 3 in the design of a software measure?

8. Why are Sub-step 2 and Sub-step 3 in the design of a software measure performed concurrently and iteratively?

9. Take a software measure that you know, and discuss its resulting measurement unit.

10. Is the definition of a numerical assignment rule sufficient for defining a software measure? Justify your answer.

11. What is the difference between a measurement method and a measurement procedure?

12. Is the application of a measurement method a one-step process? Justify your answer.

13. Provide five examples of the exploitation of measurement results in the management of software projects.

14. What is the average maturity level of two organizations at Level 2 and two organizations at Level 4 as defined in the CMMI model? Justify your answer.

TERM ASSIGNMENTS

1. Select a software attribute, and use the template presented towards the end of Section 2.3 to design a measure for the attribute you selected.

2. A very large number of measures have been proposed for coupling. Design a metamodel (i.e. a measurement construct) about the design of measures of coupling.

3. A very large number of measures have been proposed for software complexity. Design a metamodel (i.e. a measurement construct) for the design of measures of complexity.

4. A very large number of measures have been proposed for reliability. Design a metamodel for the design of measures of reliability.

5. A very large number of measures have been proposed for usability. Design a metamodel for the design of measures of usability.

6. Design a template of verification criteria to analyze the design of a software measurement method.

7. Design a template of verification criteria to analyze the application of a measurement procedure for a software measurement method.

8. Design a template of verification criteria to analyze the design of a quantitative evaluation model.

9. Design a template of verification criteria to analyze the design of a prediction model.

3

METROLOGY AND QUALITY CRITERIA IN SOFTWARE MEASUREMENT[1]

This chapter introduces the readers to a number of classic concepts in measurement derived from the domain of metrology:

- A model of a measuring device
- Quality criteria for the design of a measurement method
- Quality criteria for the application of a measurement method
- Quality criteria for the measurement results

Advanced Readings: Measuring Chain & Measuring System

3.1. INTRODUCTION TO METROLOGY

Measurement is one of a number of analytical tools used in the scientific fields, including engineering, as well as in other fields such as business administration and a significant number of the social sciences.

[1]A more extensive discussion of the topics addressed in this chapter (but using the 1994 version of the ISO VIM) can be found in the following reference:

Alain Abran and Asma Sellami, "Initial Modeling of the Measurement Concepts in the ISO Vocabulary of Terms in Metrology," International Workshop on Software Measurement—IWSM 2002, Magdeburg, Germany, Oct. 8–9, 2002, pp. 9–20.

Software Metrics and Software Metrology, by Alain Abran
Copyright © 2010 IEEE Computer Society

The basis of measurement in these fields is a large body of knowledge, built up over centuries and millennia, which is the domain commonly referred to as **"metrology."**

- This domain is supported by government metrology agencies, which are found in most industrially advanced countries.
- The ISO document, "International Vocabulary of Basic and General Concepts and Associated Terms", often referred to as the **VIM**, represents the international consensus on a common and coherent terminology for the set of concepts of metrology.

The term "metrology" is defined in the VIM as **"the science of measurement and its application."**

Metrology underlies all measurement-related concepts in the natural sciences and engineering, and to each of the different interpretations of a *software metrics* is associated a related distinct metrology term with related metrology criteria and relationships with other measurement concepts.

History of the VIM

In 1984, the ISO published the 1st edition of the international consensus on the basic and general terms in metrology (VIM), along with other participating organizations (BIPM, IEC, and OIML[2]).

In 1993, the VIM was reviewed, and then the ISO published the 2nd edition of the VIM, in collaboration with six participating organizations (BIPM, IEC, OIML, IUPAC, IUPAP, and IFCC).

In 2007, the ISO published its 3rd edition of this document, to integrate, in particular, concepts related to measurement uncertainty and metrological traceability, and nominal properties. This 3rd edition has been approved by the eight organizations represented in the Joint Committee for Guides in Metrology—JCGM.

The VIM 2007 edition on metrology presents 144 terms in five categories and in increasing order of complexity (in parentheses, the number of terms in each category):

- Quantities and Units (30 terms),
- Measurements (53 terms),
- Devices for measurement (12 terms),
- Properties of measuring devices (31 terms), and
- Measurement Standards—Etalons (18 terms).

[2]See Appendix A—List of acronyms.

While metrology has a long tradition of use in physics and chemistry, it is rarely referred to in the software engineering literature. Notable exceptions are the following:

- Carnahan *et al.* [1997] are among the first authors to identify what they referred to as "IT metrology."
  - They highlight the challenges and opportunities arising from the application of the metrology concepts to information technology.
  - In addition, they proposed logical relationships between metrology concepts, specifically four steps to be followed to obtain measured values: defining quantities/attributes, identifying units and scales, determining the primary references, and settling the secondary references.
- Gray [1999] discusses the applicability of metrology to information technology from the software measurement point of view.

This key ISO document is widely known in the sciences and in engineering; however, it is almost unknown in the software engineering community. Consequently, most of its concepts are not being used, either by those proposing new software measures to the software engineering community, or by the users of these proposed measures.

This chapter is based on this ISO document, which represents the official national and international consensus on the vocabulary of basic and general concepts and associated terms in metrology [VIM 2007].

The objective of this chapter is, therefore, to introduce that set of metrology concepts to the software engineering community [Abran 2003; Sellami 2003], so that they can be used for:

- the design of new software measurement methods and related measuring systems and measuring devices,
- the evaluation of current *metrics* proposals, and
- the design of improvements to current software *metrics* to give them the strengths of *bona fide* measurement methods.

The chapter is organized as follows:

- Section 3.2 presents a model for measuring devices, using the set of concepts from metrology.
- Section 3.3 presents quality criteria for the design of measurement methods.
- Section 3.4 presents quality criteria for the application of measurement methods.
- Section 3.5 presents quality criteria for the measurement results.

3.2. A MODEL FOR MEASURING DEVICES

A measurement process can be entirely automated, partially automated, or entirely manual.

Examples of Types of Measurement Processes

Entirely automated: a measurement process, and the corresponding measuring device, to measure radioactivity in a nuclear power plant

Partially automated: a surveyor who uses a laser-guided device to measure the distance across a river
    (This includes a number of procedures to position his laser-guided device correctly, to carry out various verification tasks and controls, to record readings, etc.)

Entirely manual: the counting of apples in a shopping bag

How do you describe a measurement process, and what constitutes a measuring device?

The classical representation of a production process is used here (see Figure 3.1) to identify the necessary elements of a device for measuring and the relevant relationships across these elements, where:

- the input is labled "Measurand,"
- the output is labeled "Measurement result,"
- the process itself is labeled "Measurement," in the sense of measurement procedure, and
- the control variables are "Etalons" and "Quantities and Units."

The set of concepts is represented as the "Devices for measurement," and the measurement operations are themselves influenced by the "Properties of the measuring devices."

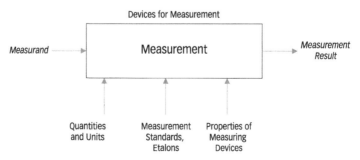

Figure 3.1. Process model of a device for measurement

Note that, in the VIM, the term "measurements," when used as a single term, corresponds to the process for measuring. That is: having the object of experimentally obtaining one or more quantity values, representing a measurement result that can reasonably be attributed to a quantity intended to be measured—a measurand.

In this chapter, the presentation of the quality criteria is organized in accordance with the measurement context model presented in Chapter 2.

3.3. QUALITY CRITERIA FOR THE DESIGN OF A MEASUREMENT METHOD

The criteria for a "good" design of a software measurement method will refer to the following three (3) sets of metrology concepts:

1. Measurement foundation
2. Quantities and units
3. Measurement standards—Etalons

3.3.1 Measurement Foundation

Figure 3.2 positions a measurement method within a hierarchy of concepts, which constitute the measurement foundation. In this figure, the hierarchy is defined top-down, from the most general to the specific:

Level 1: Metrology, which includes all the theoretical and practical aspects of measurement, refers to the science of measurement in the VIM, whatever the measurement uncertainty and field of application (science or technology).

Level 2: Measurement principle, which is specific to the measurement of a particular concept to be measured and represents the phenomenom serving as a basis of a measurement.

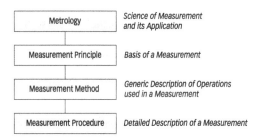

Figure 3.2. Measurement foundation levels

Level 3: Measurement method, defined in the general sense as a logical organization of operations used in a measurement.

Level 4: Instantiation of the measurement method in a measurement procedure as a detailed description of a measurement, and based on a measurement model, and including any calculation to obtain a measurement results.

The hierarchy of measurement-related concepts in Figure 3.2 is referred to as the *measurement foundation*.

Measurement Principles for Determining Temperature

A method for measuring temperature (and for building a corresponding measuring device) may depend on:

- the principle of the expansion of lead (for a lead-based thermometer)
- the principle of the difference in the coefficient of expansion of two metals (for thermometers in a sauna)
- other principles for other types of measuring devices.

3.3.2   Quantities

Metrology specifies that quantities (typically expressed as numbers) are not sufficient as measures *per se*. Additional concepts must also come into play in order for a quantity (or a number) to be recognized as a measure in metrology.

In particular, metrology requires the following properties (or criteria when analyzing the quality of the design of a measurement method)—see Figure 3.3:

A—a measurement unit,
B—the quantity value,
C—the quantity dimension,
D—a system of quantities,
E—kind of quantity,
F—the quantity calculus.

Table 3.1 presents sub-elements relevant to each of these 6 elements.

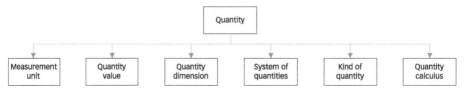

Figure 3.3. The elements of a quantity in metrology

TABLE 3.1. Characteristics of the Six Elements of a Quantity in Metrology

	Quantity				
Measurement unit	Quantity value	Quantity dimension	System of quantities	Kind of quantity	Quantity calculus
Base unit	Numerical	Quantity of	Base	Ordinal	Quantity
Derived unit	quantity	dimension	quantity	quantity	equation
Coherent derived	value	one	Derived	Nominal	Unit equation
unit	Quantity-		quantity	property	Conversion
System of units	value scale		International		factor
Coherent system of	Ordinal		system of		between
units	quantity-		quantities		units
Off-system	value scale		(ISQ)		Numerical
measurement unit	Conventional				value
International system	reference				equation
of units (SI)	scale				
Multiple of a unit	Ordinal value				
Submultiple of a					
unit					

3.3.2.1 *Measurement Unit.* Within a measurement unit, there is:

- a base unit (e.g. a meter with the symbol "m" in the SI)
- a derive unit (e.g. the meter per second, symbol m/s, of speed in the SI)
- a multiple and a sub-multiple of a unit, etc.

The Measurement Unit—Indispensable in Measurement & Metrology

In metrology, a quantity (i.e. a number) requires a reference, such as a unit, in order to be meaningful:

- the quantity 4 is meaningless in measurement (unless its unit is specified as one)
- 4 cm and 4 kg are well recognized, and meaningful, as measurement results.

Summary
A number can only be recognized as a measure if it is accompanied by a unit specified by convention.

Challenge

List software metrics for which:

- units are not specified
- units are specified

3.3.2.2 Quantity Value. In metrology, a number of concepts are associated with the quantity value, in addition to the purely numerical value obtained from a device, such as a measuring instrument.

For example, a numerical value on a thermometer is obtained by reading that value off a conventional reference scale on the thermometer. This reading might be subject to a measurement error of 0.5 degree relative to the measured quantity value of the temperature at that time, had the thermometer been calibrated perfectly and no errors made in reading the quantity-value scale on the thermometer.

3.3.2.3 Dimension of a Quantity. The VIM 2007 defines the dimension of a quantity as an expression of the dependence of a quantity on the base quantities of a system of quantities as the product of the powers of the factors corresponding to the base quantities, omitting any numerical factors.

The VIM indicates that a quantity of dimension one (e.g., a dimensionless quantity) might also exist. For example:

- Some quantities of dimension one are defined as the ratios of two quantities of the same **kind**.
- Numbers of entities are quantities of dimension one.

3.3.2.4 System of Quantities. A system of quantities may include both *base quantities* and *derived quantities (and the international system of quantities—ISQ)* where:

- A **base quantity** is defined as a conventionally chosen subset of a given system of quantities, where no subset quantity can be expressed in terms of the others.
  - Example: The set of base quantities in the **International System of Quantities** such as: time in seconds, length in meters, etc.
- A **derived quantity** is defined as a quantity, in a system of quantities, defined in terms of the base quantities of that system
  - Example: mass density is a derived quantity defined as the quotient of mass and volume (where volume is itself = length to the third power).

See also Section 4.4 of Chapter 4 for a discussion and additional examples of base and derived quantities.

3.3.2.5 Kind of Quantity. The kind of quantity is defined as the aspect common to mutually comparable quantities.

3.3.2.6 Quantity Calculus. The quantity calculus is a set of mathematical rules and operations applied to quantities other than ordinal quantities.

3.3.3 Measurement Standards—Etalons

Also required in the design of a measurement method in the sciences, and in engineering in particular, is a measurement standard, or etalon (from the French, "étalon"), which metrology defines as follows:

Measurement Standard—Etalon: realization of the definition of a given **quantity**, with stated **quantity value** and associated **measurement uncertainty**, used as a reference.

It is noted in the VIM 2007 that:

1. A "realization of the definition of a given quantity" can be provided by a **measuring system**, a **material measure**, or a **reference material**.
2. A measurement standard is frequently used as a reference in establishing **measured quantity values** and associated measurement uncertainties for other quantities of the same **kind**, thereby establishing **metrological traceability** through **calibration** of other measurement standards, **measuring devices**, or measuring systems.
3. The term "realization" is used in the VIM in the most general meaning. It denotes three procedures of "realization."

   - The first one consists in the physical realization of the **measurement unit** from its definition and is realization *sensu stricto*.
   - The second, termed "reproduction," consists not in realizing the measurement unit from its definition but in setting up a highly reproducible measurement standard based on a physical phenomenon, as it happens, e.g., in case of use of frequency-stabilized lasers to establish a measurement standard for the metre, of the Josephson effect for the volt or of the quantum Hall effect for the ohm.
   - The third procedure consists in adopting a material measure as a measurement standard. It occurs in the case of the measurement of the measurement standard of 1 kg.

Examples of Measurement Etalons

- 1 kg mass standard
- 100 Ω standard resistor
- cesium frequency standard
- reference solution of cortisol in human serum having a certified concentration

---

Many additional concepts are directly related to the measurement etalon, and presented in Table 3.2 in two groups:

1. different levels of measurement standards:
   - requiring an official status (national or international measurement standard—first example in the box above)

TABLE 3.2. Quality Characteristics of a Measurement Standard/Etalon

(Measurement) Standard/Etalon	Conservation of a (Measurement) Standard
International (Measurement) Standard	Calibrator
National (Measurement) Standard	Reference Material (RM)
Primary Measurement Standard	Certified Reference Material (CRM)
Secondary Measurement Standard	Commutability of a Reference Material
Reference Measurement Standard	Reference Data
Working Measurement Standard	Standard Reference Data
Transfer Measurement Standard	Reference Quantity Value
Traveling Measurement Standard	
Intrinsic Measurement Standard	

- a widely recognized basis (primary or secondary measurement standard—last example in the box above)
2. criteria for the conservation of a measurement standard:
  - calibrator
  - reference material
  - certified reference material
  - commutability of a reference material
  - reference data
  - standard reference data
  - reference quantity value.

Examples:

- A "transfer measurement standard" is used as an intermediary to compare standards, for example, to compare a British national measurement standard kept in London with the corresponding US national standard.
- Gasoline pumps must be calibrated to a national measurement standard to ensure that the customer receives the volume of gasoline for which he has paid. This is achieved through a "working measurement standard" used by a federal agency to monitor and certify all gas pumps at every gasoline station in the country.

3.4. QUALITY CRITERIA FOR THE APPLICATION OF A MEASUREMENT METHOD

The application of a measurement method requires:

1. a measurement procedure
2. devices for measurement

3. operations with devices such as a measuring system

4. properties of such measuring devices.

3.4.1 Measurement Procedure

Measurement presupposes the description of a quantity commensurate with the intended use of a measurement result, a measurement procedure and a calibrated measuring system operating according to the specified measurement procedure, including the measurement conditions, in order to experimentally obtain one or more quantity values (Table 3.3).

The application of a measurement procedure requires a number of elements and processes to ensure that the measurement result is of high quality. This section identifies the necessary elements (i.e. the criteria that must be verified to ensure that a measurement procedure is applied correctly).

Figure 3.4 presents a process representation of a measurement procedure with its corresponding elements described in the VIM (again represented as a process model having several inputs, many control variables, and an output representing the measurement results).

TABLE 3.3. Description of the Measurement Elements

Measurement				
Measurement result	Measurement procedure	Measuring device	Measurement conditions	Measurement error
Measured quantity value True quantity value Conventional quantity value	Reference measurement procedure Primary reference measurement procedure	Measuring system	Repeatability condition of measurement Intermediate precision condition of measurement Reproductibity condition of measurement	Systematic measurement error Measurement bias Random measurement error

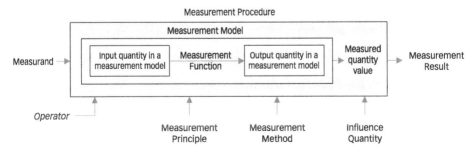

Figure 3.4. The elements of a measurement procedure

To carry out a measurement exercise, an operator should design and follow a measurement procedure, which consists of a detailed description of a measurement, specifically described, according to one or more measurement principles and to a given measurement method, based on a measurement model and including a measurement function to obtain a measured quantity value, representing a measurement result.

The instantiation of a measurement procedure handles a measurement model representing the mathematical relation among all quantities involved in a measurement.

This measurement model can involve one or more equations.

In turn, the instantiation of a measurement model handles a measurement function, which can be symbolized as an algorithm, and produces the value of which, when calculated using known quantity values for the input quantities in a measurement model, is a measured quantity value of the output quantity in the measurement model. This is the value which represents the measurand given in input.

Finally, the measurement result can be expressed either:

- by a measured quantity value and a measured uncertainty or
- by a single measured quantity value if the measurement uncertainty is considered to be negligible for some purpose.

The measurement result can have been influenced by:

- The operator—For example, when an operator is an inexperienced surveyor and has never executed a measurement procedure with a laser-guided distance measuring device, he may make many more mistakes than an experienced surveyor.
- The measurement principle—For example, thermoelectric effect applied to the measurement of a temperature.
- The measurement method selected—For example, there are now five ISO-recognized methods for measuring the functional size of software[3].
- A quantity which influences the measurement process—For example, the temperature of the micrometer may need to be taken into consideration during the measurement of the length of an object.

In each case, there is an element which can influence the application of the measurement procedure.

3.4.2   Devices for Measurement

A measuring system may consist of only measuring instrument (see Figure 3.5), which can include:

---

[3]See also the second side-box in chapter 1.

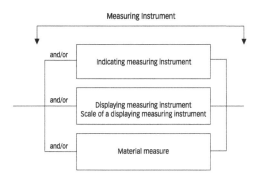

Figure 3.5. A typical measuring device

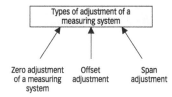

Figure 3.6. Operations on measuring devices

- an indicating measuring instrument
- a displaying measuring instrument (a measuring device may or may not store the measurement results):
  - A household thermometer typically does not record the temperature.
  - An industrial thermometer must often record the temperature (at specified time intervals).
- a scale of a displaying measuring instrument, and
- a material measure.

Again, the quality of the displaying, recording, and integrating devices may impact the quality of the measurement results.

3.4.3 Operations on a Measuring Device

While reading a household lead thermometer typically only involves checking the mark on the thermometer's scale, the use of a more complex measuring system might require a number of other operations, such as an adjustment of a measuring system—see Figure 3.6.

Many types of adjustment of a measuring system include:

- zero adjustment of a measuring system,
- offset adjustment, and
- span adjustment (called gain adjustment).

TABLE 3.4. Characteristics of Measuring Devices

Selectivity of a measuring system
Stability of a measuring instrument
Step response time
Accuracy class

TABLE 3.5. Detailed Quality Criteria for a Measurement Result

Measurement Precision	Measurement Uncertainty	Calibration	Metrological traceability
Measurement accuracy	Definitional uncertainty	Calibration hierarchy	Metrological traceability chain
Measurement trueness	Type A evaluation of measurement uncertainty	Verification	Metrological traceability to a measurement unit
Measurement repeatability	Type B evaluation of measurement uncertainty	Validation	
Intermediate measurement precision	Standard measurement uncertainty	Correction	
Measurement reproducibility	Combined standard measurement uncertainty		Metrological comparability of measurement results
	Relative standard measurement uncertainty		Metrological compatibility of measurement results
	Uncertainty budget		
	Target measurement uncertainty		
	Expanded measurement uncertainty		
	Coverage interval		
	Coverage probability		
	Coverage factor		

3.4.4 Properties of Such Measuring Devices

A measuring device (such as a measuring instrument or a measuring system) has an indication that can be presented in visual or acoustic form or can be transferred to another device, a blank indication and a measuring interval, which represents a set of values of the same kind within which the instrumental uncertainty can be expected i.e. within defined conditions, such as indication interval, nominal indication interval, range of a nominal indication interval, and nominal quantity value.

The quality of the measurement results will also depend on a number of properties related to the measuring devices, each of which corresponds to a quality criterion. Table 3.4 lists a number of the characteristics described in the VIM.

3.5. QUALITY CRITERIA FOR MEASUREMENT RESULTS

In metrology, the quality criteria for measurement results can be classified into the following four (4) categories (Table 3.5):

- Measurement precision
- Measurement uncertainty
- Calibration
- Metrological traceability

3.6. SUMMARY

The domain of knowledge referred to as metrology is the foundation for the development and use of measuring devices and measurement processes. The ISO International Vocabulary of Metrology: Basic and General Concepts and Associated Terms—VIM—contains the international consensus on the set of metrology terms, which describes:

- the elements of a measurement procedure and of measuring devices, and
- the characteristics necessary to ensure the quality of the measurement results, quality which must itself be analyzed along with a number of criteria.

While this set of metrology-related criteria might look impressive to software engineers, to the point of giving the impression that it is next to impossible to tackle all of them at once, we must remind ourselves that all are typically verified (and controlled) in traditional science and engineering environments.

That they are not currently used in the measurement of software does not preclude their relevance to the measurement of software. Rather, it is a very strong indication that the measurement of software still has a great deal of maturing to do.

The Advanced Readings section at the end of this chapter presents the use of a measuring system within a measuring chain.

In this chapter on Metrology, the measurement concepts have been presented as defined in classical metrology and used throughout the sciences and in engineering. However, software has defined its own measurement terminology:

- For instance, while the widely "quantity," "base quantity," and "derived quantity" are the terms adopted in metrology, the corresponding terminology in software would be "attribute," "base attribute," and "derived attribute."
- To help practitioners and researchers in the software engineering and metrology communities bridge the cultural gap between them, Appendix B presents the terms, and their definitions, that would be the most familiar to each culture.

ADVANCED READINGS: MEASURING CHAIN AND MEASURING SYSTEM

Audience

This Advanced Reading section is of most interest to those interested in building measuring system for software measurement programs as well as to those developing commercial tools for software measurement.

When we measure for our own purposes, such as looking at one's watch or measuring the length of one's desk, we typically use a simple measuring device.

By contrast, in industrial usage, where measurement is more complex and must be performed precisely and with traceability (i.e. for credibility or security purposes), a measuring chain must be in place to ensure that the measurement results meet the quality targets required by the industrial context.

This section uses the VIM to illustrate what constitutes a measurement chain and a measuring system. Functionality tests (i.e. quality criteria) that should be in place, verified, and controlled to ensure the quality of the measurement results are also presented.

Figure 3.7 presents the concept of the *measuring chain*. It includes

- the sensor (e.g. carrying a quantity to be measured as a signal to the measuring system), and
- the output of the measuring system (that is, the measured quantity values).

This measuring chain is further detailed in Figure 3.8: the set of instruments and other devices assembled for measurement constitute the *measuring system*.

- Following a stimulus or an input signal, the detector (or sensor) will detect the presence of the signal. If there is a signal, the device will indicate the value of a quantity associated with it.
- Following a reading, the measuring transducer provides an output quantity having a determined relationship to the input quantity.

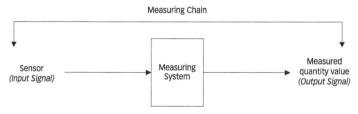

Figure 3.7. Measuring chain

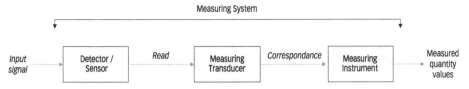

Figure 3.8. Measuring system

- The output of the measuring transducer will correspond to the input of the measuring instrument, that indicating the generated measured quantity values as result—indicated on a displaying measuring device—see Figure 3.5.

The measuring device may also make use of a material measure, defined as follows: *a measuring instrument reproducing or supplying, in a permanent manner*

Material Measures Used in Measuring Devices

- a weight
- a measure of volume (of one or several values, with or without a scale)
- a standard electrical resistor
- a gauge block
- a standard signal generator
- a reference material

TABLE 3.6. Functionality Tests on Measuring Devices

Use	Verify
Steady-state operating condition	Sensitivity of a measuring system
Rated operating conditions	Resolution
Limiting operating conditions	Resolution (of a displaying device)
Reference operating conditions	Discrimination (threshold)
	Dead band
	Detection limit
	Instrumental bias
	Instrumental drift
	Variation due to an influence quantity
	Instrumental measurement uncertainty
	Maximum permissible measurement error
	Datum measurement error
	Zero error
	Null measurement uncertainty
	Calibration diagram
	Calibration curve

during its use, quantities of one or more given kinds, each with an assigned quantity value.

Table 3.6 presents the properties of functionality tests that can be carried out on a measuring device:

- at the moment of use (whenever a specific measurement procedure is performed).
- to verify a measuring device (for instance, to verify the intrinsic instrumental measurement uncertainty).

EXERCISES

1. What is metrology?

2. Provide three examples from your day-to-day life showing how metrology impacts you directly.

3. Which organizations contribute to the development and updating of the VIM?

4. Take two software measures in use in your organization and identify the characteristics of the measurement device used to collect data for these measures. Which characteristics of a classical measuring device have not been implemented?

5. Take two software measures proposed in the literature, and identify what you would need to do to design a measuring device to use these measures in an organization.

6. What is the principle of measurement for each of the above two software measures?

7. Take two devices to measure temperature and identify their principle of measurement.

8. Take two software measures, and identify their principle of measurement.

9. Take five software measures, and identify their units of measurement. What is the precise definition of the measurement unit of each of these five measures?

10. Can you have a measure without a measurement unit? Explain.

11. List software "metrics" which do not have a specified measurement unit of a value of one.

12. Identify a software measure with a standard etalon.

13. What is the use of working or transfer standards?

14. What is the difference between a measurement method and a measurement procedure?

15. What can influence a measurement procedure?

16. Take two software measures and identify their scale.

17. Take two software measures and identify their scale type.

18. List four characteristics of measuring devices. Explain.

19. Which types of errors can be observed in measuring devices?

20. List three verification criteria for measurement results.

21. How can you express measurement uncertainty?

TERM ASSIGNMENTS

1. Implement a measure of coupling in your organization. Describe the measuring system you put in place and compare it to a measuring system as described in metrology.

2. Measure the coupling of a design. Discuss the metrology criteria involved in your measurement procedure, and which ones you did not address. What does the measurement result tell you?

3. Select a functional size measurement method. Ask three friends or colleagues to measure the functional size of the *same software application which has been completed*. Use the metrology quality criteria for measurement results to compare the functional size obtained by three friends or colleagues.

4. Select a functional size measurement method. Ask three friends or colleagues to measure the functional size of the *Software Requirements Specifications (SRS) document* of the *same software application*. Use the metrology quality criteria for measurement results to compare the functional size obtained by your three friends or colleagues.

5. If your organization has implemented an automated or semi-automated software measure, which metrology characteristics of measuring devices can you identify in that tool and document? Which characteristics are absent (and, of course, not taken care of) in this automated or semi-automated software measurement tool?

6. Analyze the Time Reporting System (TRS) of your software organization. Document, from a metrology perspective, the quality of the *measurement procedures* in your Time Reporting System.

7. Analyze the Time Reporting System (TRS) of your software organization. Document, from a metrology perspective, the quality of the *measurement results* produced by your Time Reporting System.

8. Carry out a survey of object-oriented software measures, and analyze how they manipulate scale types and units of measurement. Comments on their validity from a metrology perspective.

4

QUANTIFICATION AND MEASUREMENT ARE NOT THE SAME!

This chapter covers:

- The difference between a number and an analysis model.
- The Measurement Information Model in ISO 15939, together with its metrology-related perspective and its analysis perspective for the quantification of relationships.
- Examples of these differences within a Measurement Information Model.
- Examples of the designs of the measurement of a single attribute and of the quantification of relationships across attributes and entities.

4.1. INTRODUCTION: NUMBERS ARE NOT ALL CREATED EQUALS

Software practitioners and researchers alike often forget that numbers are not all created equal. For instance:

- A number derived from the result of a measurement process which meets the metrology requirements[1] is a quantity expressed with a measurement unit. A number with a measurement unit obtained through the proper

[1] See chapter 3 on metrology.

Software Metrics and Software Metrology, by Alain Abran
Copyright © 2010 IEEE Computer Society

application (manual or automatic) of its corresponding measurement method will have many more measurement qualities (in the metrology sense) than a number derived from opinion only.

- A number derived from a mix of mathematical operations without consideration of measurement units and scale types will still be a number, but it could be a meaningless one. Practitioners may feel good about models which appear to take into account a large number of factors (i.e. as in many estimation models and quality models). However, feeling good does not add validity to mathematical operations that are inadmissible in measurement.
  - For example: some of the Halstead's metrics—see Chapter 7.
  - For example: see the Use Case Points in Chapter 9.

In practice, various types of quantitative models produce numbers in outputs (i.e. the outcomes of the models) which do not have the same qualities as numbers which meet the requirements of metrology:

- An estimation model will provide a number as an estimate. However, to every such estimated number is associated a (potentially large) range of variations, depending on the number of input parameters and their corresponding uncertainties, as well as on the uncertainties about the relationships across all such input parameters; and these estimated numbers are not meaningful without a knowledge (and understanding) of the corresponding uncertainties.
- A quality model will provide a number which typically depends on a specific selection among a (potentially large) number of alternatives; the assignment of a percentage to each contributing alternative, which assignment is based on the opinion of one person (or a group of persons) and; comparison of each contributing alternative with distinct threshold values, which themselves are often defined by opinion as well.

In many instances, in these analysis models:

- some, if not all, of the numbers used as inputs to these models are obtained by opinion, rather than from precise measurements (with measurement instruments or from the application of detailed measurement procedures);
- these numbers are combined without explicitly describing the admissible mathematical operations and treatment of the corresponding measurement units; and
- the outcomes of such models are indeed numbers, but they do not have metrological properties[2], and should be handled very cautiously.

---

[2]See chapter 3.

Analysis models like these are quantitative models, but they are not measurement models in the metrological sense. Such differences between quantitative analysis and measurement are not generally discussed in the software engineering literature.

This chapter is organized as follows:

- Section 4.2 presents the ISO 15939 Measurement Information Model.
- Section 4.3 clarifies the scope of ISO 15939 Measurement Information Model.
- Section 4.4 presents its metrology related perspective in ISO 15939.
- Section 4.5 presents its analysis perspective for the quantification of relationships.
- Section 4.6 illustrates these concepts by using as an example the differences between a productivity ratio and a productivity model as a Measurement Information Model.
- Section 4.7 presents examples of designs from a metrology perspective for a single attribute and from an analysis perspective for the quantification of a relationship across multiples entities and multiples attributes.

4.2. ISO 15939 MEASUREMENT INFORMATION MODEL

The Measurement Information Model from ISO 19539 (Figure 4.1) sets out the various steps necessary for the design an *information product* when a measurable concept has to be designed and used in practice. In the illustration of this model in Figure 4.1, ovals represent activities and rectangles represent the input and output of an activity.

Figure 4.1, when read from the bottom up, shows the following:

1. A specific *measurement method* has to be designed to obtain a *base measure* for a specific attribute.
2. The values of two or more base measures can be used next in a computational formula (by means of a measurement function) to construct a specific *derived measure*.
3. These derived measures are used next in the context of an *analysis model* of relationships to construct an *indicator*.
4. Then, the indicator (i.e. the number from point 3 above) is used for interpretation purposes to build the information product to meet the information needs. This means that the indicator's value is interpreted within the prescribed context as describing, in the language of the measurement user, an information product for his information needs [ISO 15939].

It is to be noted that, in numbers 2 and 3 above, both the derived measures and the indicator inherit the properties of the mathematical operations on which they are built:

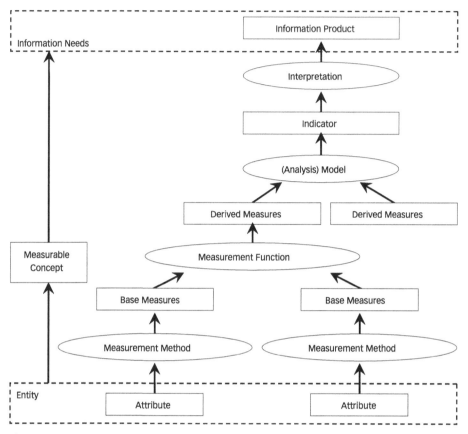

Figure 4.1. Measurement Information Model from ISO 15939. This figure was adopted from Figure A.1 (p.21) of ISO/IEC 15939:2007(E). This figure is not to be considered an official ISO figure nor was it authorized by ISO. Copies of ISO/IEC 15939:2007(E) can be purchased from ANSI at http://webstore.ansi.org.

- These numbers are meaningful when derived from admissible mathematical operations.
- These numbers are meaningless when derived from inadmissible mathematical operations, or when the measurement units and measurement scale types are not considered correctly within the mathematical operations.

The direction of the arrows in Figure 1 has been added to the ISO 15939 Measurement Information Model to highlight the sequence of steps required to implement an already well defined Information Product, i.e. from the detailed measurement of the base measures up to the interpretation of the information, that is, the end Information Product.

Example: When an organization already collects measures of project effort and software size, it uses then such measures to build its own productivity models of past projects and next, uses such models to prepare estimates for its selection of future projects.

When the Information Product structure does not yet exist, an organization would typically work in top-down fashion, by:

- starting with specification of the information product it needs, and
- working top-down to define the detailed analysis and measurement processes required to fulfill its information needs.

ISO 15939 Definitions Adapted from the VIM

The terminology of the ISO International Vocabulary of Basic and General terms in Metrology (VIM) has been adopted in ISO 15939 as the agreed-upon measurement terminology for software and system engineering-related ISO standards (with a few adaptations to facilitate its use within the software engineering community, which was previously using a variety of non standardized terms).

The VIM defines *base quantity* and *derived quantity*, while ISO 15939 uses the expressions *base measure* and *derived measure* for the corresponding VIM concepts.

This adaptation of terms was designed to facilitate the adoption of ISO 15939 in the software engineering community. See also the measurement definitions in Appendix B.

4.3. SCOPE OF THE ISO 15939 MEASUREMENT INFORMATION MODEL

To better understand the Measurement Information Model in ISO 15939, it is useful to identify what in the model is related to metrology concepts and what is not.

4.3.1 Metrology-Related: Measurement of the Attribute of an Entity

The bottom portion of the ISO 15939 Measurement Information Model can be mapped to the metrology concepts in two steps—see Figure 4.2:

1. **Data Collection**: when a measurement method is used to measure an attribute[3], the corresponding output is the base measure of the specific entity being measured. This then corresponds to the **data collection** of the base measure for each entity being measured;
2. **Data Preparation**: when a number of the base measures of the data collected are combined through a measurement function (using agreed-upon mathematical formula and related labels), then the combined units are

---

[3]Of course, the attribute must be well defined; if not, it is pretty challenging to design an adequate measurement method.

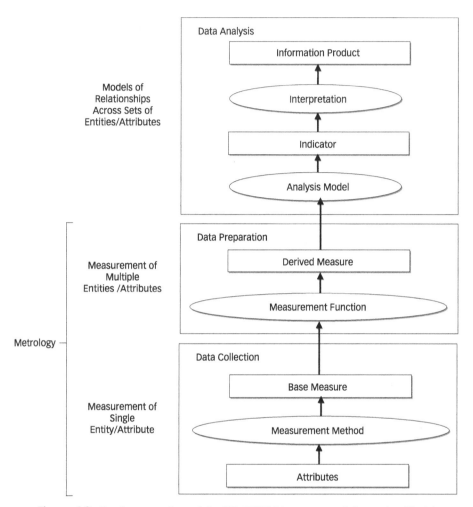

Figure 4.2. The 2 perspectives of the ISO 15939 Measurement Information Model

considered as derived measures. This corresponds, then, to **data preparation**, prior to the analysis phase.

4.3.2 Non Metrology-Related: Quantification of Relationships Across Attributes and Entities

The top portion of the ISO 15939 Measurement Information Model deals with the analysis (through quantification) of relationships across entities and attributes.

This analysis part of the ISO 15939 Measurement Information Model includes two activities (i.e. ovals in the figure):

1. Analysis model: refers to the modeling of the relationships across entities and attributes[4] to derive an indicator of the value of such relationships.
2. Interpretation: the indicator would then be interpreted to produce the Information product that would typically be used next in an evaluation or decision making process.

The metrology-related bottom part of the Measurement Information Model is supported by the set of metrology concepts, as described in Chapter 3.

The upper part of the Measurement Information Model is outside the scope of the VIM, since it deals with the use of the measurement results from the lower part of the model. This analysis is not extensively described in ISO 19539, except through a few complex definitions tailored to that specific standard.

These two perspectives are discussed in more details in the next two sections.

4.4. THE METROLOGY PERSPECTIVE IN THE ISO 15939 MEASUREMENT INFORMATION MODEL

This section describes the metrology-related perspective of the ISO 15939 Measurement Information Model—i.e. the bottom part of Figure 4.2.

4.4.1 Data Collection: Base Measures[5]

Every base measure must correspond to a single, distinct, software attribute (i.e. a property of an object or concept). So, identifying the attribute of the entity to be measured and quantifying it through its measurement method corresponds to the data collection step—see Figure 4.3.

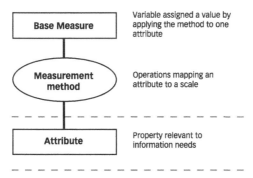

Figure 4.3. The data collection of a base measure for an attribute (ISO 15939). This figure was adopted from Figure A.1 (p.21) of ISO/IEC 15939:2007(E). This figure is not to be considered an official ISO figure nor was it authorized by ISO. Copies of ISO/IEC 15939:2007(E) can be purchased from ANSI at http://webstore.ansi.org.

[4]See Section 4.5 and Figure 4.4 of this chapter for more details.
[5]See section 3.3.3 in Chapter 3 for the VIM definitions of base quantities and derived quantities.

4.4.2   Data Preparation: Derived Measures[6]

Depending on the Information Needs, some of the base measures already collected for an entity can be assembled according to a measurement function (e.g. a computational formula) defined for each derived measure—see Figure 4.2 in the Data Preparation step.

A derived measure is therefore the product of *a set of measurement units* properly combined (through a measurement function).

Addition of the Same Units ≠ Derived Measure

The addition of houses (of the same types or of different types) gives a total number of "houses": the addition of base measures *of the same type* does not lead to derived measures.

Similarly, the additions of "numbers of points" (however "points" have been defined) lead to a total number of "points": this does not represent a derived measure.

If a derived measure is designed bottom-up, the name assigned to this combination of units should correspond to the concept representing the particular combination of measurable attributes.

The accuracy of a derived measure (together with the corresponding measurement errors) is directly related to the accuracy of each of its base measures, and how these base measures are mathematically combined[7].

Stated differently, the qualities of the corresponding measuring device(s) of the base measures impact the quality of the derived measures.

Example: Accuracy Depends on Base Measures

The accuracy of a measurement of velocity will directly depend on the accuracy of its two base measures: distance and time.

When their corresponding base measures are not sufficiently well defined, standardized, and instrumented to ensure the accuracy, repeatability, and repetitiveness of measurement results, then, when the same entity (software) is measured by different measurers, the results can potentially be significantly different.

It must be noted that a derived measure is *descriptive*. It does not explain a relationship, nor does it say anything about the strength of such a relationship across distinct attributes.

---

[6]See section 3.3 in Chapter 3 for the VIM definitions of base quantities and derived quantities.
[7]See chapter 5.

Example of a Derived Measure: Velocity

The combination *distance traveled over a period of time* (e.g. km/hour) is associated with the concept of velocity.

Such a derived measure (i.e. velocity) is typically measured by a measuring device which:

- captures both base measures simultaneously (that is, distance and time, measured in meters and seconds on a car's speedometer, for instance),
- has an integrating feature which divides the base measures to produce a ratio (time/distance) to represent the velocity concept, and
- has a display feature which shows up the measurement results using a standardized display convention:

For example, converting meters per second into the universally adopted standard for cars, which is "kilometers per hour."

It must be observed that the result of the mathematical operations must also lead to the combination of the measurement units of its corresponding base measures.

The Productivity Ratio: A Derived Quantity

The ratio of the outputs of a process to the inputs to this specific process (such as the number of cars produced by 1,000 work-days, or number of function points per person-month) is associated with the productivity concept.

This productivity ratio is entirely descriptive: it does not attempt to express why a given production process has such a value (i.e. such a ratio).

4.5. THE QUANTIFICATION OF RELATIONSHIPS IN ISO 15939

This section looks at the "Analysis of Relationships" in the ISO 15939 Measurement Information Model—the top part of Figure 4.2.

4.5.1   Quantitative Elements of the ISO 15939 Analysis Model

While the bottom part of the ISO 15939 Measurement Information Model deals with metrology-related concepts and refers to the VIM terminology for measurement (data collection & data collection), the top part of it is outside of the scope of the VIM:

It deals in particular with the third step of the Measurement Context Model presented in Chapter 2, that is, *the use of measurement results* in various evaluation or decision making models.

This use of measurement results is represented very succinctly in ISO 15939 using only two activities (the ovals in Figures 4.1 and 4.2) (Analysis) Model and Interpretation and one number: Indicator (the rectangle in Figure 4.1).

In practice, however, this use of measurement results typically involves:

- **analysis of the relationships across different measurement results** with respect to various conditions within a context, and
- **assessment against reference contexts** for evaluation and/or decision making.

The intricacies and subtleties of the above are not graphically represented in the Measurement Information Model in Figure 4.1, but are to be found in the textual descriptions of the following three expressions in ISO 15939—see the related box, where some of the terms not represented in the model are underlined:

- Indicator
- (Analysis) Model
- Decision criteria.

A number of concepts within these descriptions do not appear in the Measurement Information Model of ISO 15939, such as:

- Decision criteria
- Assumptions
- Expected relationships
- Estimates or evaluation
- Numerical thresholds or targets
- Statistical confidence limits, etc.

The ISO 15939 Definitions for the Use of Measurements Results

Indicator

An indicator is a measure providing *an estimate or evaluation* of specified attributes derived from a model with respect to defined information needs. Indicators are the basis *for analysis and decision making*. These are what should be presented to measurement users.

(Analysis) Model

An algorithm or calculation combining one or more base and/or derived measures with associated *decision criteria*.

It is based on an understanding of, or assumptions about, the expected *relationship between the component measures* and/or their behavior over time. Models produce estimates or evaluations relevant to defined information needs.

The scale and measurement method affect the choice of analysis techniques *or models* used to produce indicators.

> **Decision Criteria**
>
> Decision criteria are numerical thresholds or targets used to determine the need for action or further investigation, or to describe the level of confidence in a given result. Decision criteria help to interpret the results of measurement. Decision criteria may be calculated or based on a conceptual understanding of expected behavior.
>
> Decision criteria may be derived from historical data, plans, and heuristics, or computed as statistical control limits or statistical confidence limits.
>
> NOTE: Some of the terms not represented in the model in Figure 4.1 are in italics above in the descriptions.

4.5.2   Refined Representation of the Analysis Model

It was observed in the previous subsection that a number of the concepts mentioned in the three descriptions in the side box are not directly modeled in Figure 4.1.

To facilitate an understanding of the relationships across the many concepts embedded within the ISO 15939 Measurement Information Model, the set of key concepts has been extracted from these three descriptions and modeled in Figure 4.4.

The refined representation of the Analysis Model represented in Figure 4.4 includes two additional major blocks:

1. *A standard reference model (Figure 4.4, bottom left)*, which can include, for instance, an accepted model of the relationships across distinct types of objects of interest. When such a reference model exists, this can be:
   - an industry model
   - an ISO model
   - a generally accepted statistical technique (and related mathematical model).

   This standard reference model would include:
   - the set of formal (or informal and assumed) individual relationships, together with the base or derived measures to be considered as evaluation or decision criteria
   - the algorithm (mathematical or implied) that combines them in an (implied) criterion.

2. *An organizational reference context (Figure 4.4, upper left)*, ideally aligned with the standard reference model, with a set of selection criteria and values specific to the organization: this organizational reference would contain the reference values necessary for interpretation:
   - a set of reference values specified for this context
   - evaluation or decision criteria with either: target values, or specific evaluation scales.

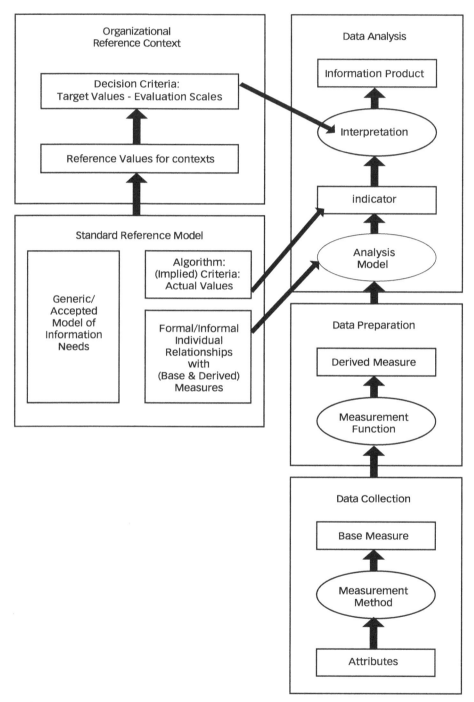

Figure 4.4. Refined Analysis Model of the ISO 15939 Measurement Information Model

Chapter 10 will present an illustration of a standard reference model represented by the ISO 9126 quality models.

4.5.3   The (Implicit) Link between Measurement and Quantitative Analysis of Relationships

In the Measurement Information Model of ISO 15939, the link between the two major parts illustrated in Figure 4.2 (that is, the Metrology-related bottom part of measurement and the Analysis-related upper part of quantification) are not explicitly described:

- ISO 15939 makes the assumption that this link exists and that it is complete on its own.
- In practice, the issue might be more complex, in particular in domains where measurement and quantification (or either one) are not yet mature.

The next section presents an example of analysis models and illustrates with the example of a productivity model the mapping to the corresponding analysis concepts within this refined representation of the ISO 15939 Measurement Information Model.

In practice, there is no guarantee that what can be measured adequately at the level of base and derived quantities does indeed represent the concepts and relationships that the analysis part of the Measurement Information Model attempts to quantify.

An example of this is the *maintainability* characteristic in ISO 9126, which is:

- not strictly limited to the software entity itself, but is
- implicitly related to the entity "effort required to maintain such software at a later time".

Chapter 10 will present an example with the ISO 9126 quality models whereas such a link is not yet mature and where much work remain to clarify the links between its measurement part and the quantitative analysis.

4.6. A PRODUCTIVITY MODEL: AN ISO 15939 MEASUREMENT INFORMATION MODEL

This section illustrates the differences between the metrology and non-metrology related part of the ISO 15939 Measurement Information Model by looking at the differences between a productivity ratio and a productivity model.

This section also illustrates how statistical techniques propose "standard reference models" to facilitate the analysis of relationships embedded in software production and estimation models.

4.6.1   A Productivity Model is More Than a Productivity Ratio

There are major differences between a productivity ratio and a productivity model.

A *productivity ratio* is related to the *metrology-related part* of the ISO 15939 Measurement Information Model: the productivity ratio is strictly defined as composed of two base measures (Output over Input):

- This productivity ratio is based strictly on the measurement, from a metrology perspective, of the respective distinct attribute of the corresponding two (2) distinct entities representing the output and the input (for example: Output = Function Points and Input = work-hours).
- This *productivity ratio is strictly descriptive and limited to what is being measured*.

If we move now from a *productivity ratio* to a *productivity model*, a number of additional elements are added, since the purpose of this analysis model becomes:

- the analysis of relationships across many entities (e.g. many projects) that have been measured, and often
- an estimation of what would happen should this production process (which has been quantified *indirectly* through the measurement of its output and input) be used again to estimate the next project.

To explore this, let us look at Figure 4.5, which illustrates a production process in its simplest form:

- The Input is on the left.
- The Process is in the middle.
- The Output is on the right.

It is to be noted that, while the productivity ratio has two *explicit* dimensions (Input and Output) that are explicitly present in a productivity ratio, the produc-

Figure 4.5. A (Software) Production Process

tion model has another (implicit) dimension as well, that is, the production process itself.

The objective is now **to quantify** this production model, typically using a productivity model (more commonly referred to as an estimation model in software engineering) rather than to measure it.

This quantitative representation of the production process is typically built by:

A) collecting the base measures of the production process over a number of completed projects, for example: Input = Effort (in work-hours or work-days).

See Table 4.1 for the information required to ensure consistency in the measurement of the "effort" variable in a multi-organizational data repository.

Similar rules must of course apply within a single organization to ensure that the effort recorded is recorded consistently across individuals and work groups— Output = Functional Size of the completed software (in Function Points).

B) Quantitatively modeling the relationships across Input and Output is based on:
- effort as the dependent variable, and
- functional size as the independent variable.

Statistical techniques can be considered as **standard reference models** for modeling these relationships, each with a distinct mathematical representation (and corresponding strengths, constraints, and limitations).

The productivity model, in its simplest form with a single dependent variable (x), could be expressed as: $x = f(y)$, where:

- the dependent variable "x" would be in work-hours, and
- the independent variable "y" would represent the size of the software (in Function Points).

The quantification of the productivity ratio is the outcome of the measurement of two entities (that is, Inputs and Outputs), while the meaning of the division of these two numbers represents something different, that is, the performance (in the sense of productivity) of a third entity, the process itself. This means that the measurement of the productivity of the process is derived not from a direct measurement of the process, but from an indirect measurement of two other entities (the Inputs and Outputs of the process).

The Analysis Model is expected to consider a number of distinct dimensions and combine them, in some manner, into a single number. This corresponds to the definition in ISO 15939 that a model is an algorithm combining one or more base and/or derived measures, along with their associated decision criteria.

TABLE 4.1. Recording Rules for the "Effort" Variable—Source: www.isbsg.org

TIME RECORDING METHODS	WORK EFFORT BREAKDOWN
Method-A: Staff Hours (Recorded) The daily recording of all of the WORK EFFORT expended by each person on Project related tasks. As an example, where a person who works on a specific project from 8am until 5pm with a 1 hour lunch break will record 8 hours of WORK EFFORT. **Method-B:** Staff Hours (Derived) It is possible to derive the WORK EFFORT where it has not been collected on a daily basis as in Method-A. It may have only been recorded in weeks, months or years. **Method-C:** "Productive" Time Only (Recorded) The daily recording of only the "productive" effort, (including overtime), expended by a person on project related tasks. Using the same example as used in Method-A above, when the "non-productive" tasks have been removed, (coffee, liase with other teams, administration, read magazine, etc.), only 5.5 hours may be recorded.	Data collected about the people whose time is included in the project work effort. **Level 1: Development Team** Those responsible for the delivery of the application under development. The team or organization, which specifies, designs and/or builds the software. It typically also performs testing and implementation activities. It comprises: Project Team Project Management Project Administration Any member of IT Operations specifically allocated to the project **Level 2: Development Team Support/IT Operations** Those who operate the IT systems that support the end-users and are responsible for providing specialist services to the Development Team, (but not allocated to that team). Support comprises: Data Base Administration Data Administration Quality Assurance Data Security Standards Support Audit & Control Technical Support Software Support Hardware Support Information Centre Support **Level 3: Customers / End Users** Those responsible for defining the requirements of the applications and sponsoring/championing the development of the application. Also the software's end users. The relationship between the project customer and the software's end users can vary, as can their involvement in a software project. It comprises: Application Clients Application Users User Liaison User Training

Finally, it must be observed that, while a derived measure gives a combination of units (e.g. Function Points per work-hour), the productivity model produces as output a single quantity with its corresponding single unit of the dependent variable. Here, the output of the $F(x)$ analysis model is strictly in work-hours (Effort), even though many additional independent variables would have been taken into account in more comprehensive productivity models (i.e. estimation models).

4.6.2 A Productivity Model Built with an Averaged Productivity

This subsection gives an example of a productivity model built with the average productivity from a set of completed projects. This average statistical function can be considered as the algorithm of a standard reference model.

A productivity model built using an averaged productivity is presented in Figure 4.6. An average is a well-known mathematical function, with corresponding properties (and limitations as well).

This average productivity is built by:

- calculating the productivity ratios of each single project within a sample, then
- adding them up, and
- dividing by the number of projects in the sample.

It is to be noted that this average describes the full sample, and not the individual projects in the sample.

In addition, a number of related characteristics are typically provided with the standard average function, such as:

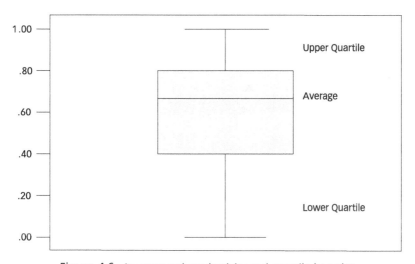

Figure 4.6. An averaged productivity and quartile box-plot

- minimum
- maximum
- first quartile, last quartile
- 1-standard deviation
- 2-standard deviation, etc.
- skewness
- kurtosis, etc.

Some of these are represented graphically in Figure 4.6, which presents both the average of a sample (i.e. the horizontal line within the grey box), as well as the box-plot of a quartile.

4.6.3   A Productivity Model Built with a Linear Regression

This subsection presents a second example of a productivity model built with the linear regression technique from a set of completed projects. This linear regression statistical function can be considered as the algorithm of a standard reference model.

A- The standard reference model—linear regression
A productivity model built using the linear regression technique is presented in Figure 4.7.

The quantitative representation from the linear regression statistical technique is of the following form: the dependent variable of Effort is a function of the independent variable of functional Size, that is: *Effort = f(Functional Size)*

In the linear regression model, this equation takes the following quantitative form: *Effort = a × Functional Size + b*

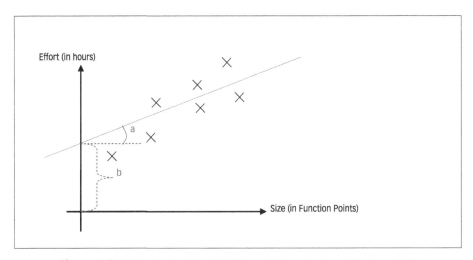

Figure 4.7. A Production Model with variable costs a) and fixed costs b)

In practical terms, in this equation from the linear regression model (the straight blue line):

- a represents the slope of the linear regression line
- b represents the point at the origin (that is, when the independent variable is $= 0$)

Stated differently, The slope a represents the increase of unit(s) of effort for an increase of 1 unit of functional size.

In terms of measurement units, this equation then corresponds to:

$$\text{Effort (in hours)} = a\,(\text{hours/Function Point}) \times \text{Functional size (in Function Points)} + b\,(\text{hours at the origin when the functional size} = 0).$$

When the mathematical expression is worked out with its measurement units, then the end result is, indeed, in hours. Therefore, both the left- and right-hand sides of the equation have the same measurement unit, which is "hours."

Finally, there is also a practical interpretation of this production model:

- The slope a represents the **variable cost** of the production process (that is, the variation due to an increase in functional size).
- The b value at the origin represents the **fixed cost** (that is, the portion of effort that is independent of the variation of the functional size).

For such a standard reference model (i.e. the linear regression model), a number of the well-known evaluation criteria of such statistical models are available in the literature, such as:

1. *Coefficient of determination (R^2)*—The coefficient of determination (R^2) describes the percentage of variability explained by the predictive variable in the linear regression models. This coefficient has a value between 0 and 1: an R^2 close to 1 indicates that the variability in the response to the predictive variable can be explained by the model, i.e. there is a strong relationship between the independent and dependent variables.
2. *Error of an estimate—Error*—The effort of an estimate (i.e. Error = Actual − Estimate) represents the error of the estimation model on a single project. For example, the difference between the known effort of a project completed (i.e. Actual) versus the value calculated by the model (i.e. Estimate).
3. *Relative Error (RE)*—The relative error (*RE*) corresponds to the Error divided by the Actual.
4. Magnitude of relative error:

$$MRE = |RE| = \left| \frac{Actual - Estimate}{Actual} \right|$$

5. Mean magnitude of relative error:

$$MMRE = \overline{MRE} = \frac{1}{n}\sum_{i=1}^{n} MRE_i$$

6. The root of the mean square error:

$$RMS = \left(\overline{SE}\right)^{1/2} = \sqrt{\frac{1}{n}\sum_{i=1}^{n}\left(Actual_i - Estimate_i\right)^2}$$

7. The relative root of the mean square error:

$$RRMS = \overline{RMS} = \frac{RMS}{\dfrac{1}{n}\sum_{i=1}^{n} Actual_i}$$

8. *Predictive quality of the model*—The prediction level of an estimation model is: $PRED(l) = \dfrac{k}{n}$ where k is the number of projects in a specific sample of size n for which MRE $\le l$.

Some interpretations of the values of these evaluation criteria

- The smaller the *RMS* or RRMS, the better the prediction level.
- In the software engineering literature, an estimation model is generally considered good when:
  - the MRE (Mean Relative Error) is within +/–25% for 75% of the observations, or
  - PRED(0.25) = 0.75.

B- The organizational reference context

A specific productivity model built within an organization with the set of completed projects from this organization would then become the organizational reference context.

Such a productivity model built from the organization's own past projects can then be used for estimating the next project for this organization. This productivity model will then: provide a specific estimate that would be directly on the linear regression line, as well as provide various elements of information on the quality characteristics of this model (such as its R^2, MMRE, etc.), which could be used as additional elements to make a decision on whether or not the selected estimate for the specific project would be:

- above the regression line (i.e. more costly)
- on the regression line
- below the regression line (i.e. less costly).

With respect to the ISO 15939 Measurement Information Model:

- the regression model would correspond to the "Analysis Model,"
- the specific outcome of the regression model would be the "Indicator," and
- the set of information from the specific productivity model built by this organization would correspond to the "Interpretation" context, while
- the standard statistical technique of linear regression, which forms the basis for the *organizational* reference context would also be part of the Interpretation context.

4.7. EXAMPLES: A METROLOGY DESIGN AND A QUANTIFICATION MODEL OF RELATIONSHIPS

In ISO 9126, there are close to 80 attributes identified as required to be measured as necessary for the more than 250 derived measures proposed to quantify the three ISO 9126 quality models, the 10 corresponding quality characteristics and the 27 quality sub-characteristics.

The measurement of one of these attributes, the "function," is necessary for 38 different derived measures, while another one, the "user pauses," is needed only in a single derived measure.

This section presents now the outcomes of an exercise carried out in a graduate course where it was required to select an attribute from any of the 80 attributes in ISO 9126 and to design a corresponding measurement method.

Using the measurement design methodology presented in Chapter 2, and in particular the Design template presented in Section 2.3, the graduate students came up with two very distinct types of design:

- A design corresponding to the metrology related part of ISO 15939,
- A design which, instead, took the perspective of the analysis of relationships and came up not with the design of a base measure, but with a quantification model of relationships across entities and attributes.

An example of each type of designs are presented next, not because these two designs are complete and finalized, but only to illustrate that designers of software measures must be aware that measurement and quantification are very distinct concepts, and have different properties.

4.7.1 Example 1: Design of a Base Measure

In ISO 9126 the "number of cases" is necessary in 38 distinct derived measures. To obtain the "number of cases" as a measurement result, it is necessary to have a well defined attribute of what is a "case," and this definition should preferably

TABLE 4.2. Characteristics and Sub-Characterictics Requiring Measurement of "Cases"

Characteristic	Subcharacteristic	Sample Measurable Attributes
Reliability	Recoverability	Availability
Functionality	Interoperability	Data exchangeability
Usability	Understandability	Demonstration Accessibility in use
	Learnability	Help frequency
	Operability	Customizability
Maintainability	Analyzability	Status monitoring capability
	Changeability	Parameterized modifiability
	Stability	Change success ratio
	Testability	Availability of built-in test function
Portability	Installability	Ease of installation

be the same for each of the 38 distinct derived measure. This design has been described in more details in (Ozcan Top, 2009).

4.7.1.1 Step 1: Determination of the Measurement Objectives. The specific objective selected was the design of a measurement method for the size of a "case".

The results of the measurement method were intended to be used in the derived measures for the ISO 9126 characteristics and sub-characteristics listed in Table 4.2.

4.7.1.2 Step 2: Characterization of the Concepts to be Measured. The characterization of the concept to be measured requires the definitions and the decomposition of such a concept.

The characterization of a concept should initially be based on the findings from a literature review. The literature review started with the definition of "cases" in ISO standards as well as with related definitions in the Use Cases literature. Twenty nine relevant references were identified in the literature review, including:

- ISO FCD 24765 Systems and software engineering—Vocabulary.
- ISO 26514 Systems and Software Engineering—Requirements for Designers and Developers of User Documentation.
- ISO 19761:2003: Software Engineering—COSMIC-FFP: A Functional Size Measurement Method

4.7.1.2.1 DEFINITION AND DECOMPOSITION OF THE CONCEPT. A number of concepts were identified from the literature review. Some of these definitions are presented in the side box. From these, the concept of "action" was identified as the central one from a measurement perspective.

Definitions from the Literature Review (Ozcan Top, 2009)

  Case is defined by ISO 24765 as: "A single-entry, single-exit multiple-way branch that defines a control expression, specifies the processing to be performed for each value of the control expression, and returns control in all instances to the statement immediately following the overall construct."

  Use Case is the description of the interaction between an Actor (the initiator of the interaction) and the system itself. It is represented as a sequence of simple steps. Each use case is a complete series of events, described from the point of view of the Actor.

  Actor, Main scenario, Alternative Paths (Extensions), and Exceptions are the concepts that will be used as a basis of the measurement:

  An Actor is "someone or something outside the system that either acts on the system—a primary actor—or is acted on by the system—a secondary actor. An actor may be a person, a device, another system or sub-system, or time. Actors represent the different roles that something outside has in its relationship with the system whose functional requirements are being specified."

  Preconditions define all the conditions that must be true before the initiation of the use case.

  Main Scenario is the description of the main success scenario in a sequential order.

  Action is the element of a step that a user performs during a procedure.

  Post-Conditions "describe what the change in state of the system will be after the use case completes. Post-conditions are guaranteed to be true when the use case ends."

  Alternative Paths; "Use cases may contain secondary paths or alternative scenarios, which are variations on the main theme. Each tested rule may lead to an alternative path and when there are many rules the permutation of paths increases rapidly. Sometimes it is better to use conditional logic or activity diagrams to describe use case with many rules and conditions."

  Exceptions, is the place "what happens when things go wrong at the system level are described, not using the alternative paths section but in a section of their own." An example of an alternative path would be: "The system recognizes cookie on user's machine," and "Go to step 4 (Main scenario)." An example of an exception path would be: "The system does not recognize user's logon information," and "Go to step 1 (Main path)."

  4.7.1.2.2 DEFINITION OF THE SUB CONCEPTS. Three key sub concepts were identified next as follows:

- **Input action:** "Any item, whether internal or external to the project that is required by a process before that process proceeds." "Data received from an external source."
- **Output action:** "Data transmitted to an external destination." "A product, result, or service generated by a process."
- **System action:** "Set of interrelated or interacting activities which transforms inputs into outputs."

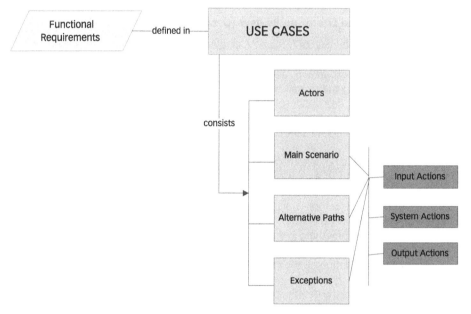

Figure 4.8. Meta-model of the concepts and sub-concepts for the size of a "case" (Ozcan Top, 2009)

4.7.1.3   Step 3: Design of the Meta-Model. Figure 4.8 presents the meta-model proposed to illustrate the relationships across the concepts and sub-concepts selected to characterize the size of "cases."

4.7.1.4   Step 4: Assignment of Numerical Rules.

4.7.1.4.1   THE EMPIRICAL DESCRIPTION (AND MEASUREMENT UNIT). The size of a "case" was defined as the addition of the Input Actions, System Actions and Output Actions. According to this measurement function, each action type (Input Action, System Action, and Output Action) is assigned next a numerical size of one Action Unit (AU).

4.7.1.4.2   MATHEMATICAL EXPRESSION(S). The above empirical description can now be expressed as a mathematical expression:
Size of a Case = (Input Actions) + (System Actions) + (Output Actions)

4.7.1.4.3   MEASUREMENT SCALE TYPE. AU (Action Unit = 1) has a ratio scale type which means it can be used in statistical analysis and mathematical calculations.
These numerical assignment rules are presented in Figure 4.9.
It must be noted that the example presented here has been designed by a single person, and should therefore be considered strictly as a first draft which

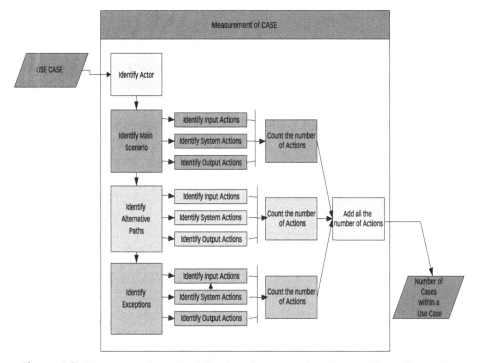

Figure 4.9. Measurement model of the size of cases within a Usecase (Ozcan Top, 2009)

should go through a number of iterations before reaching a certain level of maturity as a measurement method. Part 3 of this book presents in Chapters 11 and 12 the full design process of a measurement method that has gained an international consensus as a software measurement method that is, ISO 19761: COSMIC.

4.7.2   Example 2: Design of a Quantification Model of Relationships (Across Entities and Attributes) (Dikici 2009)

In ISO 9126, the number of "error messages" is necessary to measure the "Efficiency" and "Resource Utilization."

4.7.2.1 Step 1: Determination of the Measurement Objectives. The specific objective selected was the design of a measurement method for the efficiency of "error messages." The measurement results are intended to be used in the derived measures for the following ISO 9126 characteristics and sub-characteristics:

- Usability
- Operability

- Understandability
- Learnability

4.7.2.2 Step 2: Characterization of the Concepts to be Measured Definition and Decomposition of the Concepts. A number of concepts were identified from the literature review. Two of the main concepts identified were:

- Message Appearance
- Message Content.

In turn, each of these concepts can be decomposed in a number of sub-concepts—see Figure 4.10 and Table 4.3.

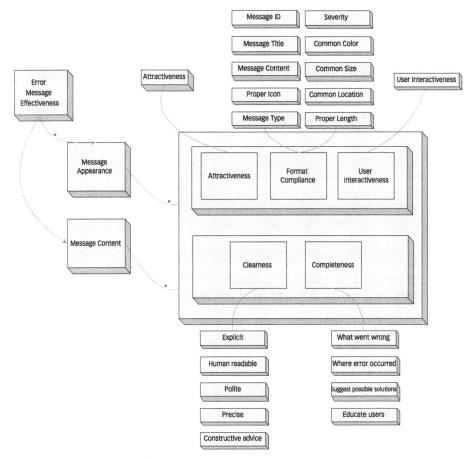

Figure 4.10. Attributes and Relationships (Dikici 2009)

TABLE 4.3. The Numerical Assignment Structure with Weights and Ranges of Ranking (Dikici 2009)

Concept	Sub-concept	Weight	Rank ranges
	Message Appearance		
Attractiveness		10	
	Attractiveness		0-10
Format Compliance		40	
	Message ID		0/4
	Message Title		0/4
	Message Content		0/4
	Proper Icon		0/4
	Message Type		0/4
	Severity		0/4
	Common Color		0-4
	Common Size		0-4
	Common Location		0-4
	Proper Length		0-4
User Interactiveness		5	
	User Interactiveness		0-5
	Message Content		
Clearness		25	
	Explicit		0-5
	Human-readable		0-5
	Polite		0-5
	Precise		0-5
	Constructive advice		0-5
Completeness		20	
	What went wrong		0-5
	Where error occurred		0-5
	Suggest possible solutions		0-5
	Educate users		0-5
Total **Effectiveness %**			

4.7.2.3 Step 3: Design of the Meta-Model. The identification of the relationships across the concepts and sub-concepts are illustrated in Figure 4.10.

4.7.2.4 Step 4: Assignment of Numerical Rules.

4.7.2.4.1 EMPIRICAL DESCRIPTION. The "effectiveness" of an error message was defined as the quantification of both the appearance and the content or error message, on the basis of the quantification of each of their own sub-concepts, as illustrated in the meta-model presented in Figure 4.10.

All of these sub-concepts were themselves quantified individually using their own set of rankings assigned by the person in charge of evaluating the effectiveness of the error message. For some of these sub-concepts, the ranking selected were from 0 to 4, others from 0 to 5 and for some other ones, from 0 to 10.

4.7.2.4.2 MATHEMATICAL EXPRESSION(S). The "effectiveness" of an error message is calculated based on measuring the sub-concepts presented in Figure 4.10.

The sub concepts are to be measured based on the rules specified in Table 4.3.

- The four concepts are each assigned a relative weight (as a percentage).
- The 21 sub-concepts (within these four concepts) are next assigned a range of rankings, starting at 0, and up to 4, 5 and 10—see Table 4.3. In this specific numerical assignment rule, each sub-concept has an equivalent range within a concept (e.g. from 0-4 for the 10 sub-concepts participating to the upper concept which itself was assigned a weight of 40).

4.7.2.4.3 MEASUREMENT SCALE TYPE. The numerical structure above is often used in practice in the evaluation of software quality based on a number of concepts and sub-concepts. However, being used often in practice is no guarantee that this is the most appropriate mathematical structure.

In particular, the scale type of the end results of this set of numerical assignment rules is challenging to determine without ambiguity:

- The intervals are in increments of one (from 0 to 4, for example), but there is no explicit definition of what is an interval of one, and no explicit and rigorous definitions that subsequent intervals from 2 to 4 are indeed equal intervals.
- Next, in practice, the selection of an interval is typically judgmentally based, and such a selection would often vary across people selecting a specific value, and may even vary if he same person was to select again a value let us say a week later.
  - In practice the corresponding values can certainly be considered as ordering values. But considering them as being on a ratio scale type would be somewhat far stretched.
  - It must be observed that each of the 21 sub-concepts in Table 4.3 is different, and if they were measured with an adequate design, they would each have their distinct measurement units and measurement scales: you would not then be able to add them up (since they do not have the same measurement units).

Therefore, adding up the values assigned to any one of the 21 sub-concepts does not correspond to a measurement exercise, whether or not they have been multiplied by a "weight" (or "points" as in a number of software "metrics").

Adding them up is a quantification, but without the rigor and meaningfulness of measurement with the rigor of metrology.

This is typical of any quantification whereas weights and "points" are somewhat arbitrarily assigned. This will be illustrated in more details in Chapter 8 in the analysis of the Function Points method and in Chapter 9 in the analysis of the Usecase Points.

4.8. SUMMARY

Numbers are not all created equal:

- A number derived from the result of a measurement process which meets the metrology requirements is a quantity expressed with a measurement unit.
- However, when a number is derived based on an attempt to quantify a set of relationships across a number of distinct entity types and attributes, such a number is not derived from a measurement process in the metrology sense, but from a quantification attempt. Such a quantitative model will provide a number which typically depends on a specific selection among a (potentially large) number of contributing concepts, the assignment of a percentage to each contributing concepts, which assignment is based on the opinion of one person (or a group of persons) and comparison of each contributing alternative with distinct threshold values, which themselves are often defined by opinion as well.

In many instances, in these quantitative models

- some, if not all, of the numbers used as inputs to these models are obtained by opinion, rather than from precise measurements (with measurement instruments or from the application of detailed measurement procedures);
- these numbers are combined without explicitly describing the admissible mathematical operations and treatment of the corresponding measurement units; and
- the outcomes of such models are indeed numbers, but they do not have metrological properties (see Chapter 3), and should be handled very cautiously.

A number derived from a mix of mathematical operations without consideration of measurement units and scale types will still be a number, but it could be a meaningless one:

- Practitioners may feel good about such a potpourri of numbers from models which appear to take into account a large number of factors (i.e. as in many quality models and estimation models).

- However, feeling good does not add validity to mathematical operations that are inadmissible in measurement.
- Analysis models like these are quantitative models, but they are not measurement models in the metrological sense.

Such differences between quantitative analysis and measurement are not generally discussed in the software engineering literature.

In Sections 4.2 to 4.5 of this chapter, we discussed these differences using in particular the ISO 15939 Measurement Information Model which contains a metrology related perspective as well as an analysis perspective. Section 4.6 has illustrated these concepts by using as an example the conceptual differences between a productivity ratio (built based on measures from a metrology sense) and a productivity model as an Analysis Model of relationships across attributes and entities.

Finally, section 4.7 has presented examples of the design process for:

- the measurement of a single attribute,
- the quantification of a relationship across multiple distinct entities and attributes.

Chapter 10 contains additional information on the measurement designs of ISO 9126, as well as a discussion on the identification of the missing links between the metrology basis and the analysis models in ISO 9126 for the measurement of the quality of software products.

EXERCISES

1. Explain some of the differences between a number obtained from a measurement instrument and a number derived from an analysis model.

2. In the Measurement Information Model from ISO 15939, what is the difference between:
   a. a base measure and a derived measure?
   b. measurement method and a measurement function?
   c. an analysis model and a measurement function?
   d. a derived measure and an indicator?

3. In the Measurement Information Model from ISO 15939:
   a. which part(s) of this model describe concepts with metrology characteristics?
   b. which other part(s) of this model address relationships across multiple attributes?

4. Will you use the same criteria to assess the "goodness" of a base measure and that of the estimate produced by an estimation model? Explain.

5. Provide five examples of base measures in software engineering.

6. Provide five examples of derived measures in software engineering.

7. What are the differences between a productivity ratio and a productivity (or estimation) model?

8. What are the differences between a standard reference model and an organizational reference context?

9. What standard reference models are available for measurement in software engineering?

10. Which relationship(s) is (are) modeled in a productivity model?

11. What is the practical interpretation of the regression line produced by an estimation model using the linear regression statistical technique?

12. Do you evaluate an estimation model with the same quality criteria used to verify the quality of a measuring instrument?

TERM ASSIGNMENTS

1. Build an estimation model based on 10 completed projects from your organization and determine the variable costs and fixed costs of those projects.

2. Identify a dataset of software projects, either from a publicly available repository of completed projects or from a published research paper, build an estimation model based on a selection of completed projects, and determine the variable costs and the fixed costs of these development projects.

3. Take the design of the size of a "case" presented in this chapter and test this design with a set of requirements documents with Use Cases. Comment on your measurement of this set of requirements and recommend improvements to the design of the measurement method proposed.

4. Take the design of the "efficiency of error messages" presented in this chapter, using it to measure software already implemented and to propose improvements to the design used above.

5

THE DESIGN OF SOFTWARE MEASUREMENT METHODS[1]

This chapter covers:

- Some of the links between software measurement and metrology
- The activities for the design (and evaluation) of software measurement methods, including:
  - Defining the measurement principle
  - Determining the measurement method
- Post design activities: the measurement procedures
- Advanced Readings 1: Verification criteria
- Advanced Readings 2: Relational structures

5.1. INTRODUCTION

It has been mentioned in previous chapters that researchers in software measurement had, until recently, approached the issue of the design, analysis, and validation of software measures using concepts from measurement theory, investigating

[1]See also: Naji Habra, Alain Abran, Miguel Lopez, and Asma Sellami, "A Framework for the Design and Verification of Software Measurement Methods," Journal of Systems and Software, Elsevier, Vol. 81, No. 5, May 2008, pp. 633–648.

mostly the relational structures, both numerical and empirical. Borrowing from the set of concepts from metrology, this chapter presents a broader view for the design of software measurement methods.

This chapter presents, at a detailed level, the activities and related products required for the design, analysis, and verification of measurement methods. Its goal is to contribute to a better understanding of the stages of software measurement design, as it integrates the various perspectives of existing measurement proposals presented in the software engineering literature [Habra 2008]. The approach presented here also integrates the concepts and vocabulary of metrology presented in Chapter 3:

- It provides definitions of the concepts as applied to the measurement of software, as well as the activities and products related to the design of a measurement method;
- It gives an integrated view, involving both the practical side and the theoretical side of software measurement.

The chapter is organized as follows:

- Section 5.2 presents the linkages between software measurement and metrology.
- Section 5.3 presents the activities to be performed to define a measurement principle for software.
- Section 5.4 presents the activities to be performed to define a measurement method.
- Section 5.5 presents the products of such a design.
- Section 5.6 presents briefly post-design activities in terms of measurement procedures.

Also included are two Advanced Readings sections:

- Verification criteria for software measurement methods.
- Relational structures in assigning a numerical value.

5.2. LINKING SOFTWARE MEASUREMENT AND METROLOGY

5.2.1 The Measurand: A Physical Object or a Model?

It is commonly believed that software engineering should be viewed as fundamentally different from engineering and other sciences. This is because software products are considered as intellectual products, while software engineers believe that the products of engineering and other sciences deal with physical objects.

The idea of making a distinction between software entities and engineering and scientific entities oversimplifies the nature of both software objects and engineering and scientific objects:

- On the one hand, by no means all modern scientific entities are physical and tangible, and capable of being comprehended through direct perception. Many more scientific entities than one might expect are related to the *models* scientists build to explain the physical world (e.g. modern physics models and laws related to light, atoms, electricity, etc.) and these scientific entities are usually comprehended through instruments.
- On the other hand, although software products are most often viewed as intellectual artifacts, they are also, in a broader sense, representations, through particular models, of physical phenomena occurring inside a computer which can be comprehended (e.g. sensed) by the human eye.

Therefore, a central notion at the core of any measurement activity is that the model used represents the entity for which a given attribute is to be measured.

- The choice of model for highlighting the target attribute is a determinant for the whole measurement life cycle, and this seems to be true for any engineering discipline, including software engineering.
- Generally speaking, it appears that an attribute to be measured is comprehended through models that, at times, can vary from very simple to quite complex.

Examples of Models for Measurement Purposes

- The undulatory model of light is the determinant for the measurement of the speed of light, and the corpuscular model of light is the determinant for the measurement of the photoelectric characteristics of light.
- The modeling of a program as a flow graph is the determinant for the measurement of software complexity, according to [McCabe 1976].

So, it is worth investigating such models. However, it is particularly important in the software domain because of the lack of consensual views about the models of software artifacts.

5.2.2   What is Measured: The Measurand or a Model of It?

In the physical sciences, is it the measurand that is measured directly, or one of its models?

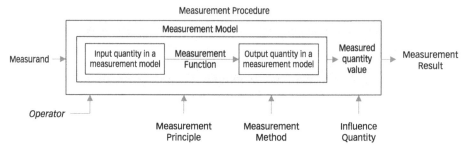

Figure 5.1. The measurement procedure in the VIM

- In practice, it is often not the measurand itself that is measured, but one of its model.
- In the VIM 2007, this is referred to as an "input quantity in a measurement model"—see Figure 5.1.

What is Measured by a Thermometer?

A thermometer does not measure temperature directly, but rather the *impact* of the temperature on something else captured by a measurement signal:

- The signal can be the expansion of lead, caused by a change in the ambient temperature (e.g. The input quantity in a measurement model), and this input quantity is next compared visually against a graduated scale on the thermometer (the output quantity in this measurement model).
- The signal can be derived from the distinct expansion rates of two metals on the same rod (e.g. a thermometer in an oven); that is, a distinct measurement model in input.

When, then, is the software the measurand?

- Can it be measured directly?
- Can it be measured indirectly through a measurement signal and a transformed value?

If the answer to either question is yes, how can this be integrated into the design of a measurement method?

5.2.3   How to Measure Software

The measurement context model, which was presented in Chapter 2, is reproduced in Figure 5.2.

To recap, the design step consists of a set of design activities performed through various sub-steps, from the definition of what we are measuring to an

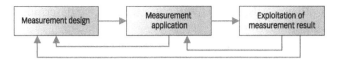

Figure 5.2. Measurement Context Model

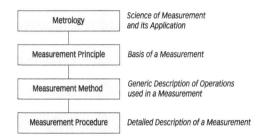

Figure 5.3. The levels in the measurement foundation in the VIM

operational description of the procedure(s) to be used. It involves all the activities needed to prepare the next step in Figure 5.2: the Application of the Measurement Method.

- Of course, if a measurement method already exists, this design step is skipped or considerably abbreviated. This is what happens in mature disciplines.
- But, if a measurement method does not exist at all, as is frequently the case in the software domain, then this step must be performed prior to specifying a measurement procedure for a particular measurement context.

The design activities are described next, along with the corresponding design *products* involved, and then a list of the associated verification criteria.

In practice, viewing measurement as a mapping between two structures (the real world and the numerical world) does not give sufficient information about how to measure and how to have a sufficient degree of confidence in the measurement results. To obtain that information, it is necessary to move beyond the theoretical definition of the mapping to an operational procedure.

The VIM describes this as the transition through three levels: measurement principle, measurement method, and measurement through a measurement procedure—see Figure 5.3.

1. The definition of the **measurement principle** should embody our knowledge or our understanding of the concept to be measured, that is, according to the vocabulary above, the entity and the attribute under consideration.

In other words, this activity gives the precise description of *what* we are going to measure.

For software entities (products), the measurement principle involves the model(s) used as a basis on which to describe the entity for which a given attribute is intended to be measured.

The idea is that modeling, as a central notion in software products, should be considered at the same level as scientific principles in other sciences and in engineering.

Accordingly, the modeling activity (e.g. the activity that consists of describing the entity under consideration to highlight the attribute to be measured) corresponds clearly to the activity of defining the measurement principle.

2. The **measurement method** is defined on the basis of that principle. It is a generic operational description, i.e. a description of a logical sequence of operations, of the way to perform a measurement activity (that is, to move from the attribute of an entity to be measured to the number representing the measurement result). This activity gives a general description of *how* we are going to measure.

3. A measurement method should, in turn, be implemented concretely by a **measurement procedure**, which describes a measurement according to one or more measurement principles and to a given measurement method. It consists of concrete operations performed by means of measuring instruments and/or practical actions such as selection, counting, calculation, comparison, etc.

It is more specific, more detailed, and more closely related to the environment and to the measuring instruments (e.g. tools) than the method, which is more generic.

Determination of an operational measurement procedure, that is, an implementation of the method in a particular context, is not considered as part of the design step, but is carried out with every measurement exercise to ensure both the accuracy of the measurement results and the traceability of the measurement exercise.

Each of these three activities is described in the following three sections.

5.3. DEFINING THE MEASUREMENT PRINCIPLE

5.3.1 Context

In the ISO metrology vocabulary, the measurement principle is defined as the phenomenon serving as the basis of a measurement. In mature disciplines, the output of this phase is the information obtained experimentally and referenced to well-established theories and laws, on top of which measurement methods have to be designed.

> **Example in Electricity**
>
> Electrical theories define concepts (e.g. voltage, current, resistance and power induc-tance, capacitance, impedance) and propose their relationships through laws (e.g. Ohm's law).
>
> Measurement methods in electrical engineering are based on similar theories and laws.

Thus, laws are general hypotheses judged by users to be sufficiently confirmed by experimentation to be accepted like descriptions of regular behaviors of enti-ties, although there are some exceptions. Some laws are quantitative, others are qualitative.

Measurement methods based on a particular scientific theory are not only useful for practical needs (e.g. building engineering devices), but also for the observation and experimentation that allow the theory itself to be either con-firmed or disproved.

The software domain is not nearly as mature and terms such as *theory* and *hypothesis* are frequently, and incorrectly, employed interchangeably.

To summarize, a theory is a unified and interrelated set of hypotheses and laws, those elements being coherent and organized in such a way that each complements the others.

In the software domain, a measurement method can seldom be designed directly from a well-established theory, which means that measurement design is a more challenging phase, involving not only:

- the design of an operational method and procedures, but also
- clarification of the theory behind the concepts to be measured, which could necessitate building and validating a brand new theory beyond the mea-surement process itself.

The question now is to determine what a measurement principle would look like in the software engineering domain.

Classical works in software measurement generally follow the *representa-tional measurement theory* in [Fenton 1994, 1997; Zuse 1997], where measurement is viewed as a mapping between:

- an empirical world (i.e. what we are going to measure) and
- a numerical world (i.e. the world of numbers from which we expect the measurement results).

This representational view is not sufficient, by itself, as a theory:

- It does not impose any particular way of characterizing these three parts: the empirical world, the numerical world, and the mapping;

- Consequently, such a characterization remains a fundamental part of the measurement principle.

Also, the representational view says nothing about how to obtain an operational view of this mapping, i.e. an operational process.

We consider that the rigorous characterization of the empirical world and the numerical world fits at the measurement-principle level, where the theoretical basis of the measurement has to be set. Characterizing the mapping between those worlds fits at the next level, i.e. the measurement method.

5.3.2 Describing the Empirical World: Characterization and Modeling

The attribute to be measured should be defined in a clear and precise way so that it is characterized sufficiently clearly and unambiguously. This characterization is referred to as the **attribute model**. The definition activity determines what is really about to be measured.

In other sciences and in engineering, the attributes to be measured have long been defined, and methods to measure them have long been established on the basis of precise and widely accepted definitions.

A definition of an attribute delimits the description of that attribute by specifying what it means and what it does not mean.

In Software Measurement: Often Immature Definitions of Attributes

In the software domain, it is not unusual to encounter measurement approaches (e.g. software metrics), where the attribute and/or the entity to be measured are unclear, or even not specified at all. See Chapters 6 to 9 for examples.

There is usually a lack of agreement on the definitions of the attribute, and, consequently, on the related measurement methods and procedures.

The measurement of software complexity is a typical example of this.

Another very important aspect of measurement is the development of consensus; such a consensus widens progressively, ultimately to universal adoption of its object as an international standard.

Measurement = Consensus

Measurement is also about deriving a broad, documented consensus on:

- what will be included in the measurement, and
- what will be excluded.

Measurement is not only an aggregation of practitioners' knowledge, but also a consensual agreement on a set of definitions and on a measurement scale.

In the software domain, the need to understand and characterize the attribute to be measured leads to the necessity of precisely determining the entity under consideration. One of the main distinctive features of software products is that they are initially perceived as abstract products, which:

- are sometimes difficult to delimit clearly; and
- can be changed from one form to another.

Examples in Software: Attributes and Entities

In the software measurement literature, there is frequently talk of a single attribute which can qualify different software products (entities):

- The software attribute "size" can be related to a program and to its requirements document.
- The software attribute's complexity can be related to a piece of code, to the algorithm that it implements, and to the graph representing it, etc.

Therefore, it is important to explicitly refer to the entity concerned.

To generalize as much as possible, one specific form is not imposed on the characterization of the attribute under consideration, i.e. the attribute model.

According to Fenton [1994], models come in many different forms:

- equations,
- mappings, and
- diagrams.

These models lead to an understanding not only of how the measurement results are obtained, but also how to interpret them.

To summarize, description of the empirical world involves:

1. determining the entity under consideration,
2. determining the attribute to be measured, and
3. building an adequate model to characterize that attribute.

Of course, if there are already existing models of entities and attributes, and there is agreement on them, this step is skipped.

The main issue is thus to characterize the attribute for which a measurement method is to be built. The issue is to determine what the criteria should be for a model to constitute an adequate basis for a measurement method.

An adequate model of an aspect of the empirical world should fulfill different kinds of requirements:

- On the one hand, the model should have a sound theoretical basis, in that it should be precise, complete, and consistent.
- On the other, it should be practical, in that it should be simple to understand, coherent with respect to practitioners' views, consensual, and facilitate operational implementation of the methods.

Many technical and theoretical difficulties related to that modeling activity arise, e.g.:

- the choice of an adequate modeling language and/or technique,
- the model's precision and completeness,
- the model's adequacy with respect to the measurement goal,
- the extraction of practitioners' knowledge about the entity and the attribute,
- the selection of representative practitioners, and perhaps dealing with their conflicting viewpoints, etc.

5.3.3   Modeling Techniques for Describing the Empirical World

Many modeling techniques can be used to characterize aspects of the empirical world. Two kinds of approaches are presented here:

- A- Mathematical: these approaches use equations, or, more generally, logical axioms to characterize the attribute concerned [Whitmire 1997; Zuse 1997], and
- B- Conceptual modeling: these approaches are based mainly on graphics-based modeling languages.

The mathematical approaches derive from the formal view of software, while the conceptual approaches derive from conceptual modeling techniques (e.g. UML), which are very frequently used in software engineering.

5.3.3.1   Mathematical Techniques. The empirical world can be modeled as a mathematical structure, including:

- a set of entities, say A,
- a collection of binary ordering relations, say $R_1, \ldots R_n$, representing the order according to the different attributes of the entity considered, and
- a collection of operations, say $O_1, \ldots O_m$, representing different possible compositions of entities from the universe of A.

Example of a Mathematical Structure

- A could be the set of all object-oriented programs,
- R_1 could be the relation "more complex than,"
- R_2 could be the relation "more maintainable than," and
- O_1 could be the operation for adding classes of the program $a_1 \in A$ to the classes of program $a_2 \in A$, etc.

Mathematical axioms describe some properties of entities; in particular, they express properties of the order induced by the attribute being measured, like transitivity or symmetry. Mathematical axioms could also express the properties of some composition operation(s), like, for example, the additivity of operations on the entities.

The advantage of mathematical axioms lies in their potential use as a basis for a formal reasoning about the attribute being measured, and hence about the measurement method based on that model.

Axioms in Measurement

Axioms allow formal reasoning about some verification criteria according to the representational view of measurement [Whitmire 1997].

More precisely, the representational view requires correspondence between:

- the empirical world structure, as defined here, and
- the numerical world structure.

This correspondence could be expressed mathematically as the *homomorphism* of the mapping.

Correspondence—Homomorphism

This allows formal expression of:

- the criteria to be verified by the chosen scale types, as well as
- the operations allowed on the measurement result.

However, such a mathematical description is not sufficient for the whole of the measurement life cycle.

In particular, it does not provide, by itself, a practical way to determine the entities to be measured, to identify them, etc.

Mathematical Axioms

Mathematical axioms describe the properties of entities (in particular, the ordering properties like transitivity or symmetry induced by the attribute), but they do not define them by extension—entity population models are usually infinite sets.

5.3.3.2 *Conceptual Modeling Techniques.* Conceptual modeling techniques are used frequently in software engineering, to model:

- (initially) data and data-centric systems (e.g. the basic entity-relationship diagrams [Chen 1976]),
- (then) objects and object-based systems (e.g. UML diagrams), and,
- (more recently) generically, to model the so-called ontology (i.e. any structural knowledge about a domain [Gruber 1993]).

Roughly speaking, the idea is to identify a few basic concepts and a few possible relationships between them, and to build a representation of the system/domain/knowledge/etc. on the basis of those concepts and relationships.

Graphical representations are used extensively:

- as a practical way to model the knowledge we have about an entity type for which one (or more) attributes are to be measured; and
- as a structural representation of the knowledge, in particular with a graphical view, which makes it easy understand the concept under consideration.

Consequently, graphical representations can facilitate the reaching of that consensus, clearly identifying the building tools, as well as the concept under consideration.

Though some popular modeling techniques are limited to ad hoc graphical notation, conceptual modeling techniques could also have precise semantics associated with them, bringing them to the same level of precision as mathematical descriptions—see [Harel 2000] for a discussion on the semantics of graphical notations.

Example of Conceptual Modeling in Software Measurement

The key concepts for a functional size measurement method have been defined by international consensus at the ISO level in ISO 14143—see Chapter 2—Advanced Readings.

  Measuring the functional size attribute in the COSMIC measurement method is based on the modeling of software functional user requirements, in that:

- it highlights concepts like functional processes (e.g. data movements—entry, exit, etc.), and
- it defines their relationships with one another.

In particular, the designers of the COSMIC measurement method analyzed a great deal of software to capture the knowledge about such a concept:

- by figuring out what was common across multiple contexts (and not what was specific to a particular context), and
- by defining what would be taken into account (data movements) and what would not be taken into account (data transformations).

The consensual definition and the characterization of functional size measurement constitute a fundamental part of the definition of the COSMIC measurement method. See also Chapters 11 and 12.

It is to be noted that conceptual modeling is aimed at describing the attribute to be measured, and the model built represents a particular abstraction of the entity under consideration.

Abstraction and Measurement

The aim of the abstraction is to:

- highlight the attribute(s) to be measured,
- while ignoring others.

If the attribute to be measured is a person's height, a line will be an adequate abstraction (another geometrical abstraction would also be suitable, but only one dimension is needed).

So, even though we have to take into account the entity, we should keep in mind the goal of the modeling, i.e. to make the abstraction that is to represent the attribute to be measured.

In the design of a measurement method, it is important to keep in mind what is going to be measured (i.e. which attribute of which entity).

5.3.4   Representative Elements

Further complementary knowledge about the attribute to be measured can be given through a representative set of entities, such knowledge being useful mainly for verification purposes.

A Representative Set of Entities

The idea is to ask experienced staff:

- to determine a set of entities that is representative of the attribute to be measured, and
- to rank those entities according to the value they would assign to that attribute.

Of course, the ranking should be consistent with the other knowledge available.

This knowledge corresponds to a very rough approximation based on subjective observations.

Therefore, it should be viewed only as a way to remedy the impossibility of giving an explicit ranking for an infinite set of entities.

The implicit hypothesis is that the order on the infinite set of entities could be approximated by an ordering on the equivalence classes represented by the representative set. Of course, this complementary knowledge is not sufficient by itself, but it can be helpful in quickly detecting problems arising during the design phase.

Testing Measurement Designs with a Representative Set

This is done if the measurement results obtained through the candidate measurement method are inconsistent with the ranking given by experienced staff.

Any problem with the candidate measurement method, or with the measurement principle itself, for example, must be identified and analyzed.

It can be noted that characterizing the empirical world can be achieved using different kinds of modeling approaches in a complementary way to take into account theoretical and practical needs.

The characterization of the empirical world makes it possible to combine knowledge expressed by means of various techniques, typically:

- representing the attributes to be measured by a conceptual model, obtained by consensus, which includes base definitions of the concept under consideration, as well as the characteristics that must, or must not, be taken into account;
- the properties of the ordering relation induced by the attribute(s) to be measured and of the possible composition operations are described mathematically; and
- using a representative ordered set as complementary knowledge for verification.

5.3.5 Describing the Numerical World: Scale Types and Units

Measurement is also viewed as a mapping of the empirical world to the numerical world. It is important in this case to define the numerical world to which the attribute description is to be mapped.

A Reminder of What a Mathematical Structure Is

A mathematical structure is:

- a set, along with
- a collection of defined relations on it.

Example
The target set could be:

- the Naturals, **N**, or the Reals, **R**, or a subset of one of these, along with
- operations on it (e.g. + <, ≤, etc.).

Describing the numerical world is related to the concept of scale type used in the classical measurement literature [Fenton 1997].

- It is to be noted that the scale type indicates the type of admissible operations to be accomplished.
- Actually, a scale type corresponds to one category of mathematical structures, the individuals in which can be mapped to one another by a homomorphic transformation (e.g. transforming a length scale in centimeters into a length scale in inches).

Convertibility as An Homomorphic Transformation

The intuitive idea behind convertibility is to consider a family of measurement targets (a family of numerical structures) which are structurally identical and which are related to one another by a so-called scaling transformation or a conversion between units.

It is to be noted, too, that scale types are closely dependent on measurement units.

In software engineering, the scale types currently used are "nominal," "ordinal," "interval," "ratio," and "absolute."

Some arithmetic operations are clearly inappropriate in some scales; for example, it is inappropriate to add two values on an interval scale because the result is not significant.

The scale type as a characterization of a numerical world is a part of the measurement principle on the basis of which a measurement method is to be designed:

TABLE 5.1. Scale Type and Mathematical Structure

Scale Type	Mathematical Structure (See also Tables 3.3 and 3.4 in Section 5.5 of Chapter 5)
Nominal	The mathematical structure of a nominal scale includes a finite set of values with no operations at all, since there is no magnitude associated with those values. The nominal scale corresponds to a very simple kind of measurement, and some authors consider that it is not a measurement at all. As it corresponds to a set on which we do not have even a weak order, there is no possible ordering at all for the elements of such a set; they can only be compared using the symbols = and ≠.
Ordinal	The mathematical structure of an ordinal scale includes a set of values with a weak ordering relation.
Interval	The mathematical structure of an interval scale is characterized by a weak ordering relation, and also includes an operation reflecting a notion of distance between elements (e.g. the operation of addition has meaning with this scale).
Ratio	The mathematical structure of a ratio scale is like that of an interval scale, but also includes a zero element (e.g. with this scale, measurement averages can be calculated).
Absolute	An absolute scale is like a ratio scale, except that an absolute scale is unique, in the sense that it does not admit any transformation into another structurally equivalent scale [Whitmire 1997].

- Associating one specific scale type to a particular attribute is not correct, as it is possible to measure the same attribute with different units belonging to different scale types (temperature, for example).
- Therefore, the scale type of a measurement result should be considered in the context of a particular measurement method.

To generalize as much as possible, the numerical world is considered as a mathematical structure, that is, a set, along with a collection of defined relations on it, without restriction, necessarily, to the scale types defined above.

This leaves open the possibility of another way of ordering relations, one that may be useful for software attributes which have not yet been sufficiently investigated (e.g. some software attributes could appear to be multidimensional and would necessitate more complex structures).

Defining the numerical world is:

- not only about the kind of numerical structures we seek as a target (e.g. a particular scale type),
- but also about the choice of the actual quantity values to be used, which also include the underlying units.

The Unit in Measurement

According to the VIM, the value of a quantity—the value of the attribute in our termi-nology—is not only a number, but also a number and a reference, where a reference could be a unit, the Unit 1 (which is generally not written) or a measurement procedure and an ordinal number.

To summarize, a numerical world involves the set of actual numbers to be used with the ordering relation on them. In addition, it could involve (according to the scale chosen and the structure underlying it) some particular operations and/ or particular elements, e.g. the definition of a so-called *distance* function, a *unit* element, or a *zero* element.

5.4. DETERMINING THE MEASUREMENT METHOD

According to the representational view, measurement is, by definition, consid-ered to be a mapping between the empirical world and the numerical world. A precise definition of those two worlds has been referred to as the measurement principle.

A measurement method corresponds to a mapping between those two (2) worlds.

So, after precisely determining both the numerical and the empirical world with their properties, what information about the mapping should be considered in terms of the measurement method?

5.4.1   A Mathematical View of the Mapping

Mathematically, a minimum of information about the mapping is the property ensuring that the mapping preserves the structure of the empirical world in the numerical world. This corresponds to the requirement that the mapping be a homomorphism.

At the other extreme, a maximum of (very hypothetical) information about the mapping would involve having a complete, extensive definition of the mapping (i.e. as a list of couples, each empirical element along with one number represent-ing its measurement result). Of course, this is not practicable, as the set of empiri-cal elements, i.e. the entity population, is usually infinite.

On a more practical level, some other properties about the mapping can be given as a complement to the minimal requirement that the mapping be a homomorphism.

Determining a Reference—Etalon

When a representative set of entities is defined, it could be given with the numbers representing the measurement values of the attribute for those entities.

To be significant, these numbers should be related to a reference standard.

(This corresponds to the general concept of the etalon in the ISO VIM 2007)

The simplest way to give such reference information is to assert that one particular entity, (i.e. the etalon in the restricted sense, as defined in the VIM) should have (by definition) the number 1 as the value of its measurement result.

Etalon: Consistency & Traceability

It is worth noting that the concept of the etalon has a more general purpose, which is to ensure the consistency and traceability of measurement.

The challenge is to produce measurement results which are consistent with both the scale and the etalon.

For the sake of clarity, measurement scales are defined, by convention, with regard to the circumstances in which the measurement is carried out.

Determining a measurement scale type is important, in order to highlight arithmetic operations applicable on the values of that scale, if a scale is associated with multiple and sub-multiple units (to give more precision to the measurement operation).

5.4.2   An Operational View: The Numerical Assignment Rules

According to the ISO metrology vocabulary of the VIM, a measurement method is defined as a generic description of a logical sequence of operations used in a measurement.

Therefore, it should give a first operational definition of the mapping described above, that is, an operational description:

- of how to map a given empirical entity to its corresponding value;
- corresponding to the *numerical assignment rules* in the measurement context model presented in Chapter 2.

More precisely, these rules define how to find, in practice, the values associated with a particular attribute of an empirical entity (remember that a value is a number with a reference). At this level, the description of the method should be given as a set of operations.

The declarative properties of the level above (e.g. the measurement principle) characterize the mapping from empirical entities to numerical entities; but, in concrete terms, an operational process, such as counting, calculating, etc., should be performed to find the value corresponding to an entity attribute. In other words, this part corresponds to the design of the operationalizable method according to which the measurement should be achieved.

If the measurement method involves counting operations, then it describes the rules that should precisely determine:

- how to distinguish the entities to be counted,
- what should be disregarded,
- how to perform the count, etc.

If the measurement is to be performed through calculation from other values, such as other attribute measurement values, then the description of the method involves the rules that determine such a calculation.

If the measurement process is to be carried out with a measuring device, a measurement method influences the kind of measuring instruments that can be considered, but does not necessarily call for a single kind of instrument. In other words, at this level, general requirements as to the kind of measuring device that can be used are involved.

Measurement Method for Temperature

If the attribute to be measured is the temperature of the air, for example, a method can be proposed to measure it through the phenomenon of liquid expansion. This method would be based on the laws of that phenomenon that determine the relationship between the two attributes: the air and the liquid.

Of course, those laws must be provided (that is, in the form of the scale of the relationship between the two attributes).

A family of tools, that is, thermometers, can be designed on the basis of this method.

Measurement of Software

If the measured attribute is the complexity of an algorithm, and the measurement method proposed is to add the number of edges and nodes on the graph representing the algorithm, then the relationship between those two entities (the graph and the algorithm) and their corresponding properties should be described explicitly and analyzed (as would be done in the example of the thermometer, above).

This relationship is neither explicitly described nor analyzed in many software metrics, such as in the Cyclomatic complexity number—see also Chapter 6 in this book.

Such an incomplete description of a measurement method is very frequently seen in the measurement of software, where different measurands (and models of measurands) are used interchangeably (e.g. a requirement document and its corresponding design schema, a piece of code, the flow graph representing the algorithm, etc.), avoiding any explicit analysis of the relationship between those measurands (and models of measurands), thereby avoiding tackling the potential problems underlying such relationships.

5.5. PRODUCTS OF THE MEASUREMENT DESIGN PHASE

The products associated with the design phase are summarized next.

1. ***The measurement principle*** is a precise definition of the entities concerned, and the attribute to be measured.

   According to the representational approach of measurement, the measurement principle involves a description of the empirical world and the numerical world to which the entities are to be mapped.

   a. ***The empirical world*** can be described through conceptual modeling techniques or through mathematical axioms, or both.

   b. ***The numerical world*** can, in the general case, be any mathematical set, along with the operations performed on it.

      It can also be defined through the selection of one scale type (ordinal, interval, or ratio). This also includes the definition of units [VIM 2007], and other permitted composition operations on the mathematical structure.

2. ***The measurement method*** is a description of the mapping that makes it possible to obtain a value for a given entity. It involves some general properties of the mapping (declarative view), along with a collection of assignment rules (operational description).

   a. ***Declarative mapping properties*** can include a description of other mapping properties, in addition to the homomorphism of the mapping. For instance: a unit axiom (the mandatory association of the number 1 with an entity of the empirical set); or, more generally, an adequate selection of a small finite representative set of elements ranked by domain practitioners.

   b. ***The numerical assignment rules*** correspond to an operational description of the mapping, i.e. how to map empirical objects to numerical values, and include: identification rules, aggregation rules, procedural modeling of a measurement instrument family, usage rules, etc.

The products of the design of a measurement method are then used to specify a ***measurement procedure***, which corresponds to: a complete technical description of the *modus operandi* of the measurement method in a particular context (goal, precision, constraints, etc.) and with a particular measuring instrument.

5.6. POST DESIGN ACTIVITY: DETERMINING A MEASUREMENT PROCEDURE

According to the ISO metrology vocabulary of the VIM, a measurement procedure is defined as a detailed description of a measurement according to one or more measurement principles and to a given measurement method:

- This level of description corresponds to a yet more operational and more practical definition of how to map an empirical entity to its corresponding number.
- For practical purposes, a measurement procedure corresponds to a measurement report which gives a precise implementation of a given method for a specific context or set of contexts.
- Moreover, if the measurement process goes through a measuring device, this level involves a precise description of that instrument, its calibration, and the documentation of its metrological properties, such as accuracy (VIM).

Therefore, an important aspect of the definition at this level is to precisely describe the context in which the measurement procedure will take place. The context involves various parameters that are worth investigating. At a minimum, the parameters that should be taken into account are:

- the purpose of the measurement process, and
- the constraints under which the measurement will be performed.

Some constraints are related to a particular application of the measurement method (e.g. existing measuring devices, the possibility of experimentation, available representative sets, etc.).

Other constraints are related to the maturity of our knowledge of the attribute to be measured, e.g. the quality of the models taken as the measurement principle.

As the maturity of software engineering measurement is far from that of the maturity of other disciplines, it can be expected that making such constraints explicit would allow practitioners to accept measurement method designs which can evolve with our knowledge of the domain.

5.7. SUMMARY

The concepts presented in this chapter are aimed at providing practitioners and software measurement researchers with a more complete means:

- to design new software measurement methods,
- to analyze existing ones, and
- to identify the verification criteria needed.

In this chapter, the levels for the design of software measurement methods and the corresponding design activities have been identified and discussed. This included references to:

- practical aspects represented by metrology concepts on the one hand, and
- theoretical aspects represented by the representational theory and related literature on the other.

In conformity with the view of the VIM, the measurement design phase was developed through two successive levels:

- the measurement principle, and
- the measurement method.

Emphasis was placed on the establishment of the measurement principle, on the basis of which the measurement method and the measurement procedure have to be designed.

To define the measurement principle, various modeling techniques were described (mathematical axioms, conceptual models, etc.) and complementary use of these techniques was recommended.

The Advanced Readings 1 section of this chapter lists the verification criteria to be checked throughout the levels of the design of software measurement methods.

Many of the software metrics proposed to industry have not gone through such a design cycle, or through intensive, adequate, and relevant verification at either a high level or at a detailed level.

Indeed, many of them have been based on an intuitive approach and are not based on verifiable foundations. Therefore, a significant number of so-called "software metrics" would not qualify as measurement methods:

- For example, many software metrics do not explicitly specify their model (and meta-model) (entity, entity type, attribute), using terms like "process" and "flows of data" without defining them precisely.
- This lack of exactness explains why the results given by many of these software metrics are context-dependent; i.e., dependent on the way the users of the measures understand the terms.

This is illustrated in Chapters 6 to 9 through the analysis of the designs of four software measures often encountered, and quoted, in the industry (Cyclomatic complexity number, Halstead's equations, Function Points, and Use Case Points).

By contrast, in Chapters 11 and 12, we discuss the design of the COSMIC method, the design process which followed the recommendations of this chapter.

ADVANCED READINGS 1: VERIFICATION CRITERIA FOR SOFTWARE MEASUREMENT METHODS

> **Audience**
>
> This Advanced Reading section is of most interest to practitioners interested in the procedure necessary to verify the design of an existing software measurement method, and to researchers interested in verifying the designs of the new measures they are proposing for software.

The design of software measures should be verified
In the previous sections, we have presented a detailed set of step and sub-step activities for the design of software measurement methods.

From this set of steps, verification criteria can be identified for each output of each step for analyzing the quality of the outcomes at each step.

This does not mean that the design of a measurement method has to be verified every time a measurement method is used, but that the design steps must be verified at least once, documented, and made available to the users of the method.

Measurement method verification requires a good knowledge of the ways in which the various design steps and sub-steps described in this chapter have been successfully completed.

From a verification perspective, it should be possible to provide information about each of these steps and sub-steps for a given measurement method, and, where required, documented evidence of whether or not the specified criterion has been met.

Measurement Design: The verification criteria
This section presents some of the verification activities and associated criteria.

Modeling the empirical world
At this level, it is important to ensure that the characteristics formulated for the empirical world actually represent the concept to be modeled, and that this representation is correct.

The problem is twofold:

- On the one hand, one should be sure that the model built actually corresponds to the consensual representation of the domain practitioners about the attribute to be measured.

    In software engineering, entities are almost always abstract, in the sense that they are often given as documents that model something (e.g. requirements, etc.).

    This being the case, it may be difficult to reach a consensual view of what an entity is all about. Practitioners may appear to be using the same word to mean different things.

Of course, reaching a consensual model for each attribute used in software measurement would represent real progress in software engineering.

For practical purposes, such an objective raises concerns, such as:

- selection of domain experts,
- organization of their debates, and
- cross-verification of their potentially different views of attributes.
- On the other hand, if a mathematical description is given through axioms, some internal properties of the model elaborated (e.g. completeness, consistency) should be verified, as in any formal description.

One should ensure that all the needed characteristics of the attribute are expressed, and that they do not involve contradictions or redundancy.

Of course, the mathematical problem behind such verification is far from trivial.

If the description is given through a graphical modeling language, the model should also respect some internal rules. For example, an attribute model described through UML diagrams should respect rules like connectivity.

Modeling the numerical world

In modeling the numerical world, the selected mathematical structure should preserve the properties of the empirical world.

Mathematically, this means that the numerical structure must be homomorphic with respect to the empirical structure; i.e. the mapping between the empirical structure and the mathematical structure is a homomorphism.

Of course, only properties expressed through mathematics can be checked mathematically.

Moreover, in the literature, various authors [Fenton 1997; Kitchenham 1995; Zuse 1997] have tackled the issue of checking the preservation of general ordering properties, like reflexivity, transitivity, and antisymmetry, which leads us to check whether or not we are using an appropriate scale type.

Such mathematical approaches, though convenient for checking the preservation of general ordering properties, are not sufficient:

- A complete mathematical check would necessitate a complete characterization of the empirical ordering induced by the attribute through axioms that allow mathematical analysis.
- But, in practice, characterizing the ordering relation entirely on an infinite set of entities is a task that is far from straightforward.

Defining the measurement method
A- Verifying the mapping characteristics

According to the theoretical view, a method implements a homomorphic mapping between the empirical world and the numerical world.

- In practice, a method to measure one attribute should produce results that correspond to the knowledge practitioners have about that attribute, that is, the ordering it induces (take, for example, the complexity attribute and the ordering relation "are more complex than": We may ask, what does this mean, and wonder, more complex than what?).
- But, as mentioned above, the mathematical characterization of ordering through axioms is not sufficient, and so verification through experimentation is necessary.

B- Verifying the assignment rules
Verifying the assignment rules (i.e. the operations sequences that describe a measurement method) also involves other activities, depending on the way those rules are expressed.

In all cases, the procedural description (e.g. the counting rules, the operational mode of a particular measuring device, etc.) should be verified to ensure that it embodies the measurement principle.

Some practical verification hints
Verification of the design of a measurement method will be demonstrated mainly while establishing links between the "definition of the concept" and the "definition of the numerical assignment rules" sub-steps.

Verification of the design of a measurement method must, then, take into account information about these two sub-steps.

Hint 1
One approach to complete mathematical reasoning through experimentation is suggested in [Melton 1990] and developed in [Lopez 2003]:

The idea is to complement the characterization of the attribute through a representative set of entities, which should be selected and ordered by domain experts:

- An experimental verification can thus be achieved on that finite set to check whether or not the ranking is indeed preserved by the measurement mapping. Of course, sample selection and ordering should be performed with care, as these activities embody knowledge about the attributes.
- Moreover, such an ordered representative set should, ideally, be a consensual characterization of the attribute under measurement.

Two examples are presented in the boxes: precision and repeatability.

Criterion: Precision

The intended use of the measurement method can impact the precision level to be required from this method.

Thus, a particular degree of precision:

- may be adequate for one measurement method,
- but inadequate for another, depending on the intended uses of the measurement results.

In order to be able to evaluate the adequacy of the degree of precision of a measurement method, the objectives of this measurement method must be known (step 1, "objectives of the measurement method" sub-step).

Criterion: Repeatability

It is said that a measurement method is repeatable if it provides the same result when applied on the same software by people with the *same* skills set.

The repeatability of a measurement method may be tested in a practical way by applying the method to one or several pieces of software, and the results will depend on the way the meta-model and the numerical assignment rules are designed.

Once again, the decision as to whether or not a measurement method is repeatable is made through an analysis of the "characterization of the concept," the "numerical assignment rules," and the "application of the measurement method" steps and sub-steps.

A guide providing the checklist for all operations of each step and sub-step described in the detailed model of a measurement process (in Chapters 2 and 5) would be a valuable contribution in elaborating a comprehensive verification framework for a measurement process.

For example, for the "design of the meta-model" sub-step, some of the points to be checked might be:

- The proposed description of the meta-model is consistent with the software (entity and attribute) to be measured;
- The meta-model states the relationships, if any, between entity types and the attribute;
- The definition of the entity types and the attributes of the meta-models are defined without ambiguities;
- The identification rules for the entity types are not ambiguous; etc.

In order to constitute a complete verification guide, it should also:

- explain how the points on the checklist can be verified;
- establish links between the verification questions (Is the measurement repeatable? What is the error rate of the measurement method?, etc.) and

the various steps of the measurement method model. This could be achieved by describing, for each step and sub-step, what must be checked in order to answer these questions.

Verification of the application of a measurement procedure
In turn, the measurement procedure should be verified to make sure it is a correct implementation of the measurement method.

In programming, this is analogous to checking that a program is a correct implementation of a particular algorithm.

At this level, verification should be achieved with respect to the purpose defined for the context.

A measurement procedure for a specific measurement context must take into account:

- the operator (measurer),
- the measurement method,
- the influence quantity (conditions that could influence the measurement result),
- the measurer's expertise, etc.

ADVANCED READINGS 2: RELATIONAL STRUCTURES IN ASSIGNING A NUMERICAL VALUE

Audience

This Advanced Reading section is of most interest to readers with a mathematical background.

A relational structure is defined mathematically as: a set of distinguishable elements, along with a collection of defined mathematical relations on those elements.

Each relation is a set of tuples (a binary relation is a set of couples).

When the purpose is to formalize measurement, it is useful to distinguish a particular relation which represents a ranking on the entities according to the attribute being measured. Hence, this relation, say $\leq$, should have some ordering characteristics.

An Ordering Relation

An ordering relation should at least represent a weak order, that is, it should be transitive (for any three entities a, b, and c, if $a \leq b$ and $b \leq c$ then $a \leq c$) and connected (for any two entities a and b, either $a \leq b$ or $b \leq a$).

The other relations represent other structuring operations on the entities, such as composition operators, etc.

There are two distinct types of relational structure involved when a numerical value is assigned:

- An empirical relational structure
- A numerical relational structure

It is important to be aware of which type is involved when discussing measurement operations and measurement results.

Some will refer to this as awareness of the definitions related to the mathematical formulation of the representational theory of measurement, according to which measurement is a mapping Φ between an empirical relational structure E and a numerical relational structure N; that is, viewing the measurement as:

$$\text{the triplet:} \quad \langle E, N, \Phi \rangle$$

A- An empirical relational structure

This type of structure refers to the set of empirical entities, that is:

- the population of entities on which the measurement mapping is defined (e.g. software objects, functional user requirements, or Java modules), along with
- the empirical relations between them (e.g. message connections), and
- the operations among them (e.g. combination or concatenation).

At least one of the empirical relations must be an ordering relation, which is a relation representing a ranking of the entities in terms of the attribute considered.

This is the most basic condition of measurement: if it cannot be said that one entity has more of an attribute than another, it cannot be measured in terms of that attribute (except when making a nominal classification).

B- A numerical relational structure

This type of structure refers to:

- the set of target numbers (or more general mathematical symbols), along with
- the relations, and
- the operations on those values.

This corresponds to a classical definition of the relational structure, but it is called a *numerical* structure here to emphasize that target elements are usually numbers (the case of nominal values is a particular one, which will be discussed later).

> **Examples of Mathematical Structures**
> - Natural numbers **N** with "<" as the ranking and "+" as a composition operation.
> - Real numbers **R** with "<" as the ranking and "+" and/or "*" as a composition operation.
> - Positive real numbers R^+.

Specifying the mathematical structures explicitly is of interest, since admissible operations are stated explicitly (e.g. the use of the integer with the + operations, but not with the * operations, the use of a subset of **N** or **R**, etc.)

To remain consistent with the above definitions, we should, in fact, talk about sets of values rather than about sets of numbers, the latter being more general since values are numbers with a reference.

C- A mapping

A mapping from the empirical structure to the numerical structure

- takes each attribute of an entity to a corresponding value, and
- takes empirical relations and operations to corresponding numerical relations and operations.

One of the most basic conditions of the representational theory of measurement is the representational condition itself; the condition that requires the mapping to preserve the structure, that is, the empirical order on two empirical entities should be preserved by their corresponding values.

EXERCISES

1. What do you measure when you measure software: what is the measurand?

2. What do you measure when you measure time: a physical object or a concept about an object? Do you measure time directly?

3. Provide three principles of the measurement of time.

4. Can you trust a software measurement result if you do not understand its design?

5. Of the software measures you know, which have a design that has been thoroughly documented and verified?

6. Take two distinct software measures: what are their measurement principles?

7. When you have to design a software measure, what steps do you have to go through?

8. When there are mathematical operations in the design of a software measure, what must you verify?

9. Do you include the measurement procedure in the design of a software measure?

10. At what stage do you need to identify and document the measurement procedure?

TERM ASSIGNMENTS

1. Take three measures from ISO 9126 and analyze their design.

2. Select a measure of coupling and analyze its design.

3. Select three measures of coupling and compare their designs. Discuss their relative merits.

4. Select three measures of complexity and compare their designs. Discuss their relative merits.

5. Select three measures of functional size and compare their designs. Discuss their relative merits.

6. Develop a template of criteria for the verification of the design of software measurement methods.

7. Use this chapter to investigate some of the issues encountered in object-oriented software measurement, in particular with regard to the measurement of coupling.

8. Explore and document the second step of the measurement life cycle: application of the measurement method. Identify and document the verification criteria related to the application of a measurement method.

9. Explore and document the third step of the measurement life cycle: exploitation of the measurement results. Identify and document the verification criteria related to the exploitation of the measurement results.

PART 2

SOME POPULAR SOFTWARE MEASURES: HOW GOOD ARE THEY?

Most authors proposing new ways of measuring software often document their proposals in terms of an algorithm which they consider as the design of their measurement proposals. However, a number of metrology characteristics, such as measurement units and the admissible mathematical operations by scale types, are not verified in such measurement designs.

Part 1 of this book (Chapters 1 to 5) looked into the key characteristics of measurement from a metrology perspective and discussed on how to design a software measurement method.

Part 2 (Chapters 6 to 10) presents now some analyses of the design of a few of the most popular measures proposed to the industry over the past 30 years, such as the Cyclomatic complexity number, the Halstead's metrics, Function Points and Use Case Points.

Part 2 of this book also illustrates how some weaknesses in the design of a software measure, such as in the Halstead metrics (Chapter 7) are propagated next to subsequent designs such as in the design of Function Points (Chapter 8) and amplified in Use Case points (Chapter 9).

Finally, of the hundreds of software measures proposed to the industry typically by individual researchers or practitioners, a few have been designed collectively, such as the ones proposed in ISO 9126 for the measurement of the quality of software products. Chapter 10 looks into the design of some of the

Software Metrics and Software Metrology, by Alain Abran
Copyright © 2010 IEEE Computer Society

measures proposed in ISO 9126 and identifies some of the metrology issues that must be addressed in future editions of these ISO technical reports on software measurement.

Part 2 of this book does not present an analysis of the OO-related software metrics. It is suggested to researchers to apply the lessons learned in Chapters 6 to 10 to study the designs of the Chidamber & Kemmerer suite of metrics (and of numerous posterior proposed alternatives) to identify their strengths and weaknesses and to propose improvements, including from a metrology perspective.

6

CYCLOMATIC COMPLEXITY NUMBER: ANALYSIS OF ITS DESIGN[1]

This chapter covers:

- The definitions of the cyclomatic number in graph theory
- The transposition of the cyclomatic number to software and related measurement design issues
- Other measurement design issues related in particular to the entity and the attribute being measured

6.1. INTRODUCTION

The software Cyclomatic Complexity number was proposed by [McCabe 1976]. It has since been referred to extensively in academia, as well as in industry, where it is often included in software tools that automatically collect measures from lines of code.

While the rules for calculating the Cyclomatic Complexity number are simple, in that they can be automated, a clear definition (characterization and meta-model) of the complexity attribute has not yet been provided. Without such

---

[1]See also: Alain Abran, Miguel Lopez, and Naji Habra, "An Analysis of the Mc Cabe Cyclomatic Complexity Numberm," 14th International Workshop on Software Measurement—IWSM-MetriKon 2004, Konigs Wusterhausen, Germany, Editor: Shaker-Verlag, pp. 391–405.

Software Metrics and Software Metrology, by Alain Abran
Copyright © 2010 IEEE Computer Society

a definition, the measurement results are difficult to understand, and analyzing McCabe's interpretation of software complexity is a challenge. Not provided either are the properties of the numerical representation derived from the application of the algorithm of the cyclomatic number.

This chapter presents an analysis of the measurement foundations of this number, and highlights some measurement design issues, such as [Abran *et al.* 2004] measurement units and labeling of the cyclomatic number as a complexity concept.

The contents of the chapter correspond to the following topics:

- the cyclomatic number in graph theory
- transposition of the cyclomatic number into software measurement by McCabe
- identification of the measurement units
- identification of the attribute measured
- scale type(s)
- interpretation of McCabe's Cyclomatic Complexity number.

6.2. THE CYCLOMATIC NUMBER IN GRAPH THEORY

McCabe's work is based on his analysis of some measurement concepts in graph theory and on his transposition of these concepts into the domain of software measurement. Understanding the cyclomatic number in graph theory is therefore important to understanding the input to its design.

6.2.1 Definitions and Meta-Model

In graph theory, the **cyclomatic number** is defined in the following way: **the cyclomatic number v(G) of a strongly connected directed graph is equal to the maximum number of linearly independent cycles where:** v(G) is the symbol (with G representing a graph) and the numerical assignment rule is Equation 6.1:

$$v(G) = e - n + p \qquad \text{Equation 6.1}$$

In this equation, there are:

- *e* edges,
- *n* vertices, and
- *p* separate components.

The entity being measured is therefore a "strongly connected directed graph," the meta-model and characteristics of which are described through the following set of definitions.

Simple Graph—a (usually finite) set of vertices V (or nodes) and set of unordered pairs of distinct elements of V, called edges.

A Simple Graph [Berge 2001]

A simple graph, G, could be defined as a pair of sets (V, E), where:

- V is a finite non empty set of vertices, and
- E is a set of pairs of vertices, called edges.

It is often represented by G = (V, E)

Chain—In a simple graph G = (X, A), a chain c is a finite sequence of vertices x0, x1, ..., xm such that, for all i with $0 \leq i \leq m$, xi, xi + 1 is an element of A.

- A chain is represented by c = [x0, x1, ..., xm].
- The length of the path c is the integer m, and it is represented by l = m(c) [Berge 2001].

Connected Graph—A graph G is connected if, for all x and for all y [vertices], there exists a chain connecting x and y [Berge 01]. A graph that is not connected can be divided into connected components.

 Cycle graph—a path that begins and ends with the same vertex.

 Simple Cycle—a cycle that has a length of at least 3, and in which:

- the beginning vertex only appears once more, as the ending vertex, and
- the other vertices appear only once.

Directed Graph—(also called a digraph or quiver) a graph consisting of:

- a set V of vertices,
- a set E of edges, and
- maps E ! V : e !(s(e), t(e)), where:
  - *s(e)* is the source and
  - *t(e)* is the target of the directed edge *e*.

Strongly Connected Graph—a directed graph that has a path from each vertex to every other vertex.

6.2.2 Units of Measurement

A fundamental concept in measurement is the requirement for units of measurement. In looking at the units of measurement in Equation 6.1 of the cyclomatic number, we find the following:

1. On the left-hand side of the equation, the units of v(G) can be derived from the definition itself, that is, a cycle:
   - The characterization of this concept can be derived from the definition itself, that is, "linearly independent cycles in a strongly connected graph."
   - A numerical assignment rule is also given in the definition, that is, the "maximum number" of linearly independent paths.
2. On the right-hand side of the equation:
   - There are three distinct types of units, that is: edges, vertices, and "separate components."
   - A numerical assignment rule is given for these numbers next, in the addition-subtraction format; however:
     - The addition or subtraction of different types of units is explicitly invalid in a numerical sense (for instance, it does not make sense to add apples and oranges).
     - These operations are valid only if the units are transposed into a higher level of abstraction with another type of more generic attribute and with the same corresponding unit—see example.
     - In graph theory, it is considered that cycles are being measured when counting nodes and edges.

Example: Adding Apples & Oranges

Three fruits (of the apple type) can be added to two fruits (of the orange type) to give a total of five pieces of fruit. In this example, the term "pieces of fruit" is a generalization of the apple type and the orange type.

When the unit of the total number is "pieces of fruit," information at the lower level of abstraction is lost; that is, the term "5 pieces of fruit" does not provide information about how many apples and oranges are included in the total.

The way in which units are manipulated in graph theory has not been clearly documented, and this lack of clarity can make it a challenge to transpose these concepts into other fields.

6.3. THE CYCLOMATIC NUMBER FOR SOFTWARE

6.3.1 Transposition into Software

A key contribution of McCabe has been his transposition of the cyclomatic number from graph theory into software. In software, the program is modeled as a *control flow graph*, which is an abstract structure used in compilers; specifically, an abstract representation of a procedure or program, maintained internally by a compiler.

- Each vertex in the graph represents a basic block.
- Directed edges are used to represent jumps in the control flow.

There are two specially designated blocks:

- the entry block, through which control flow enters the flow graph, and
- the exit block, through which all control flow leaves.

Program control flow graphs are not strongly connected, but they become so when a virtual edge is added, connecting the exit node to the entry node [Watson 1995].

Since the control flow graph in the case of software is then transformed into a strongly connected graph, the graph cyclomatic number can be applied to this representation of programs.

So, the cyclomatic number, when applied to software in this transposition, becomes:

$$v(G) = e - n + p + 1 \text{ Virtual edge} \qquad \text{Equation 6.2}$$

Note: one has been added to Equation 6.1 to integrate the supplementary virtual edge.

Furthermore, in this transposition, only individual modules are taken into account, instead of the whole software entity. In the particular situation defined by McCabe, the number of connected components p is always equal to 1. McCabe then defines Equation 6.2 as Equation 6.3:

$$v(G) = e - n + 2 \qquad \text{Equation 6.3}$$

6.3.2   Identification of Measurement Units

When analyzed taking into consideration the units of each related element being added or subtracted, the software Cyclomatic Complexity number in Equation 6.3 is puzzling: the number 2 in Equation 6.3 is derived from the addition of different units; that is, one "connected component," plus one "virtual edge."

Properly rewriting Equation 6.2 taking the units into consideration would lead to Equation 6.4 instead of Equation 6.3, that is:

$$v(G)^{independent\,cycle} = e^{edge} - n^{nodes} + p^{connectedcomponents} + 1^{virtual\,edge} \qquad \text{Equation 6.2}$$

becomes

$$v(G)^{independent\,cycle} = (e+1)^{edge+virtual\,edge} - n^{nodes} + p^{connectedcomponents} \qquad \text{Equation 6.4}$$

Of course, adequate interpretation of the units in Equation 6.4 remains an issue as well.

6.3.3 The Attribute Measured—and Its Association with Complexity

McCabe has suggested that Equation 6.3 is, by association, a measure of "program complexity," which he calls Cyclomatic Complexity and interprets as *the amount of decision logic in a single software module* [Watson 1995].

In other words, it is inferred that a software module is represented by a control flow graph and its *cyclomatic complexity is defined for each module to be e − n + 2, where e and n are the number of edges and nodes in the control flow graph respectively* [Watson 1995].

It must be noted that no definition is provided for the term "complexity," for the attribute itself, or for its direct characterization.

6.3.4 Scale Type(s)?

Typically, a measurement method involves a single scale type. However, Zuse [1997] has identified three concurrent scale types for the software Cyclomatic Complexity number:

- ordinal,
- ratio, and
- absolute!

Zuse [1997] suggests, for example:

- A specified operation of flowgraph concatenation in order to prove that the software Cyclomatic Complexity number is on the *ratio scale*, which is necessary in working with the additive operation.
- Examples of other flowgraph operations *which lead to ordinal or absolute scales*.

As a result, averages and standard deviations on this number must be carefully computed:

- We must ensure that the numerical addition corresponds to the empirical operations proposed by Zuse.
- In other words, does the numerical addition means the same as the proposed empirical operation?

This work of [Zuse 1997] is interesting, since it looks into the mathematical foundations for the analysis of scale types for the Cyclomatic Complexity number. However, such an analysis does not take into account the presence of different measurement units in such equations.

The challenge remains for practitioners to consider the concurrent possibilities of multiple scale types and their correct use in mathematical operations:

- identification,
- interpretation, and
- related uses in practice.

There is also a long-running debate in the software measurement literature on the composition of graphs and corresponding numerical addition of cyclomatic complexity—see Henderson-Sellers & Tegarden [1994a and 1994b].

6.3.5 Interpretation of the Cyclomatic Complexity Number for Software

When only the left-hand side of Equations 6.2 or 6.3 is taken into account, the cyclomatic number is defined in terms of the unit "number of cycles", which clearly qualifies as a "count": this operation produces a numerical number of the *integer* type, the numbers of which are clearly on a *ratio* scale; for instance, 10 independent cycles is clearly five times two independent cycles.

Now, when the term "complexity" is added to label this measure, one would expect users of the number derived from the above equation to interpret it on a ratio scale. They do not, but seem instead to *interpret* this number on some kind unspecified interval scale, which could, for example, be of the *exponential* scale type for testing time.

Interpretation of the Values of the Software Cyclomatic Complexity Number

Given two programs, P_a and P_b, with cyclomatic numbers of 10 and 5 respectively, we are inclined to interpret the testing time P_a as being *"much greater than* twice" the testing time of P_b.

A possible explanation is an intuitive individual perception of the complexity of the graphical representation of the control flow graphs presented in conjunction with the McCabe Cyclomatic Complexity number:

- while the graph of a cyclomatic number of 5 seems easy to represent visually,
- the graph of a cyclomatic number of just double that (10) seems much harder to represent visually, and
- the graph of a cyclomatic number of 20 seems at times spaghetti-like visually!

It appears, therefore, that using both the control flow graphs and the software Cyclomatic Complexity number, practitioners build their own interpretation scale and perhaps do so on a different scale type.

- Of course, this is done implicitly, without clear rules and without measurement-related conventions.
- This might explained partially why this cyclomatic is largely computed.

Cyclomatic Complexity number (ratio-absolute scale?)	Example of an interpretation on an ordinal scale	Questions	Questions
0			
1			
2			
4		Is it twice as complex as $v(G) = 2$?	
5			
10		Is it twice as complex as $v(G) = 5$	Has "twice" the same meaning as "between 2 and 4"?
20		Same question	Same question

6.4. OTHER DESIGN ISSUES: THE ENTITY AND ATTRITUBE MEASURED

6.4.1 The Entity Measured

The entity measured by the Cyclomatic Complexity number is a control flow graph.

Control flow graphs describe the logic structure of software modules. A module corresponds to a single function or subroutine in typical languages [Watson 1995].

The measured entity is the source code of a given module, which corresponds to a function or a subroutine.

So, the meta-model is made up of all the elements present in a graph, i.e. vertices and edges. *The nodes represent computational statements or expressions, and the edges represent transfer of control between nodes* [Watson 1995].

But, do graphs correctly represent the source code entity in order to measure its cyclomatic number? In other words, has the assumption concerning the one-to-one relation of a given module's source code to its corresponding graph been verified?

One module's source code is related to one, and only one, graph. But, the reverse is not necessarily true; that is, one graph can be related to one or many source codes. In [Zuse 1997], this set of source codes is considered as an *equivalence class* of source codes. So, it is not obvious that the final source code corresponds to the measured graph.

In that sense, it could be interesting to test this assumption, which argues that there is a one-to-one relation between a measured graph and a final source code.

Another point discussed in [Watson 1995] is the addition of a "virtual edge" to the control flow graph in order to obtain a strongly connected graph. The rationale of that "work around" is to allow the use of the cyclomatic number of a strongly connected graph.

But, adding a virtual edge does not modify the nature of the entity considered, i.e. the source program. The justification for the addition of a virtual edge is as follows: *This virtual edge is not just a numerical convenience. Intuitively, it represents the control flow through the rest of the programming in which the module is used* [Watson 1995]. So, it can be seen as the connection between the module and the rest of the program.

6.4.2 The Attribute Measured

Referring to the flow graph of a program by its Cyclomatic Complexity number obviates the necessity to explicitly define the complexity of the source code, a definition which remains difficult to formulate and about which there is a lack of agreement in the software community—see the Advanced Readings section for a few of the many definitions of complexity found in the software literature.

By adding the term "complexity" to the term "cyclomatic number," an association was made between this number and a concept of complexity, but such an association was:

- not explicitly described and
- not associated with quantitative numbers for complexity; moreover
- no conditions were described under which it would hold for particular values of complexity.

In the software measurement literature, researchers have often not been precise enough when discussing the use of measurement results in various evaluation models by failing to use the appropriate specialized terminology; for example, they still use the immature metrics terminology when discussing the use of their *measurement result*, rather than the terminology of theoretical hypothesis and of experiments to explore:

- whether or not there is a relationship across multiple variables,
- the strengths of such relationships, and
- how much these relationships vary (or not) under various conditions.

This lack of recourse to a terminology appropriate for the statement of a hypothetical theory, and the required experimental work, has led to ambiguous statements being made by some authors and to insufficiently well supported claims.

This lack of clarity has led practitioners, and researchers alike to make associations with few proven quantitative properties, such as: *Complexity can be used directly to allocate testing effort by leveraging the connection between complexity and error to concentrate testing effort on the most error-prone software* [Watson and McCabe 1996].

This assertion has led to generalizations like: "The higher the Cyclomatic Complexity number, the greater the error." Of course, "the higher the error rate" and "the most error prone" clearly do not belong on a ratio scale, but on an ordinal scale at best.

[The] cyclomatic complexity measure correlates with errors in software modules [Watson and McCabe 1996]. Again this statement has led users of this Cyclomatic Complexity number to associate low numbers of errors with a low cyclomatic number.

However, a coefficient of correlation (r) between two given variables X and Y does not measure any causality relation between those variables: A coefficient close to one does not mean that one variable implies the other, but simply expresses the fact that the two variables vary in the same direction.

Maintainers can keep maintenance changes from degrading the maintainability of software by limiting the cyclomatic complexity number during a modification [Watson and McCabe 1996]. The same comments as above apply.

While the calculation rules for the Cyclomatic Complexity number are simple, and can therefore be automated, a clear definition (characterization and meta-model) of the complexity attribute has not been provided. This does not facilitate an understanding of this measure and makes it challenging to analyze McCabe's interpretation of software complexity.

Similarly, while defining a numerical assignment rule, the properties of the numerical representation derived from the application of the algorithm are not provided.

Lopez and Habra [2005] have also noted the challenge of using the cyclomatic complexity number in Object Oriented, and in particular the relevance of the cyclomatic complexity threshold for the java programming language.

In summary, this chapter has presented an analysis of the measurement foundations of the cyclomatic number and highlighted several measurement design issues, such as:

- measurement units
- the artificial labeling of the cyclomatic number as a complexity concept.

See the Advanced Readings section on the lack of consensus on the definition of software complexity.

ADVANCED READINGS: LACK OF CONSENSUS ON COMPLEXITY IN SOFTWARE

> **Audience**
>
> This Advanced Reading section is of most interest to the researchers investigating the measurement of complexity, and to the practitioners looking for a single number about complexity.

In software engineering, many authors have investigated the generic concept of complexity and provided a variety of definitions of that concept [Whitmire 1997]. A few of the numerous views of software complexity are presented here.

IEEE Standard Computer Dictionary
In [IEEE 1990], complexity is defined as *the degree to which a system or component has a design or implementation that is difficult to understand and verify*. So,

- on the one hand, the definition argues that complexity is a property of the design implementation, i.e. source code or design;
- while on the other, the definition embodies a relationship to the effort needed to understand and verify the design implementation.

This means that two different entity types are involved in the definition:

- process (effort), and
- product (design or source code).

This, of course, can lead to a number of interpretations.

Evans and Marciniak [1987]
In Evans and Marciniak [1987], complexity is defined as *the degree of complication of a system or system component, determined by such factors as:*

- *the number and intricacy of interfaces,*
- *the number and intricacy of conditional branches,*
- *the degree of nesting, and*
- *the types of data structures.*

This definition refers to the structure of the system (entity type = *product)* and defines some of its characteristics and some elements of its meta-model. Such a view focuses on a single concept to be measured, and, therefore, facilitates its understanding.

Whitmire [1997]

In Whitmire [1997], the characterization and meta-model of complexity has broader scope and includes a topology for the complexity concept, including computational, psychological, and representational complexity:

- *Computational complexity* is based on the notion proposed by [Henderson-Sellers 1996, Whitmire 1997], and is defined in terms of the hardware resources (processors cycles, memory, disk space) required to execute the software.
- *Psychological complexity*, proposed by [Henderson-Sellers 1996; Whitmire 1997], refers to the complexity problem solved by the software, structural complexity, which includes characteristics of the software (size, cohesion, coupling, etc.) and programmer complexity, which includes the programmer's knowledge and experience of the problem and solution domain.

Although this list is far from exhaustive, it illustrates the lack of consensus on:

- the definition of software complexity, and
- the design of a measurement method for this software attribute.

This lack of consensus on the concept of software complexity (and the related entity attribute and its characterization) makes any attempt to design measures of software complexity quite challenging for researchers. For every view of complexity, a related measurement design can be relevant.

It is important, then, to clearly define the attribute to be measured and the entity to which it is related in order to correctly design a measurement method.

EXERCISES

1. What is the measurement unit of the software cyclomatic complexity number?

2. What is the scale type of the cyclomatic complexity number?

3. What is the attribute measured by the cyclomatic complexity number?

4. What is the numerical difference between a cyclomatic complexity number of 4 and one of 7?

5. How do you interpret this difference between 4 and 7 for a cyclomatic complexity number?

6. What is the "standard etalon" to verify the accuracy of the cyclomatic complexity number for the software you just measured?

7. What institutional support is there for references for the cyclomatic complexity number?

TERM ASSIGNMENTS

1. Refer to a specific implementation of the cyclomatic complexity number in a software tool: define a procedure to verify that the automated tool provides the correct answer. Test the procedure with the automated tool and discuss the test results.

2. Explain the transformation of scale types from the ratio scale in the cyclomatic complexity number to the ordinal scale on a look-alike log scale in the evaluation models of association, with testing for error-prone modules, for instance.

3. Illustrate the relationship between the numbers obtained with equation (3) and the perception of complexity of the flow graph which is not on a ratio scale.

4. Refer to a specific implementation in a software tool of the McCabe cyclomatic complexity number:
   - Identify the scale type
   - Provide a description of the treatment of measurement units.
     - Explain the transformation of scale types from the ratio scale in the "cyclomatic number" to the "ordinal" scale on a look-alike log scale in the evaluation models of associations with "testing" for "error-prone" modules, for instance.
     - Illustrates the relationship between the numbers obtained with equation (3) and the perception of complexity of the flow graph which is not on a ratio scale.

7

HALSTEAD'S METRICS: ANALYSIS OF THEIR DESIGNS[1]

This chapter covers:

- The definitions of Halstead's metrics
- An analysis of the design and definitions of five of Halstead's metrics, including entities and attributes measured, scale types and measurement units
- A discussion on the findings
- Advanced Readings: An analysis of the other Halstead's metrics

7.1. INTRODUCTION

What we refer to here as Halstead's *metrics*—commonly known collectively as "software science" [Halstead 1977]—are often quoted:

- Researchers have used them to evaluate student programs and query languages to measure software written for a real-time switching system, to measure functional programs, to incorporate software measurements into

---

[1] See also: Rafa Al Qutaish and Alain Abran, "An Analysis of the Designs and Definitions of Halstead Metrics," 15th International Workshop on Software Measurement—IWSM 2005, Montréal, Canada, Sept. 12–14, 2005, Editor: Shaker-Verlag, pp. 337–352.

---

a compiler, and more recently to measure open source software [Samoladas *et al.* 2004].

• Some are included in commercial tools that count software lines of code.
• A number of authors have adopted their structure as the basis for their own proposed measures, such as Albrecht for the initial design of his Function Points method, which he based on the Halstead's "volume" metrics. Of course, measures based on Halstead's metrics have also inherited the design weaknesses of those measures, as discussed later in this chapter.

In this chapter, we explore the various elements of the design of Halstead's metrics, including their definitions, objectives, scale types, measurement units, and measurement method [Al Qutaish and Abran 2005].

The term *metrics* is used in this chapter, rather than more precise terms like measurement method and measurement procedure from the metrology domain; readers will readily understand why we have done so in this chapter.

This chapter is organized as follows:

• Section 7.2 presents the definitions of Halstead's metrics.
• Section 7.3 presents an analysis of 5 of Halstead's metrics.
• Section 7.4 presents a discussion on the findings.
• The Advanced Readings section presents an analysis of the other five of the Halstead's metrics.

7.2. HALSTEAD'S METRICS: DEFINITIONS

According to Halstead, a computer program is an implementation of an algorithm considered to be a collection of tokens which can be classified as either operators or operands. In other words, a program can be thought of as a sequence of operators and their associated operands.

All Halstead's metrics are functions of the counts of these tokens. By counting the tokens and determining which are operators and which are operands, the following base measures can be collected:

n_1: Number of distinct operators.
n_2: Number of distinct operands.
N_1: Total number of occurrences of operators.
N_2: Total number of occurrences of operands.

In addition to the above, Halstead defines the following:

n_1^*: Number of potential operators.
n_2^*: Number of potential operands.

Halstead refers to n_1^* and n_2^* as the minimum possible number of operators and operands for a module and a program respectively.

This minimum number would be embodied in the programming language itself, in which the required operation would already exist (for example, in C language, any program must contain at least the definition of the function *main()*), possibly as a function or as a procedure; in such a case,

- $n_1^* = 2$, since at least two operators must appear for any function or procedure, one for the name of the function and one to serve as an assignment or grouping symbol.
- n_2^* represents the number of parameters, without repetition, which would need to be passed on to the function or the procedure [Menzies *et al.* 2002].

Halstead's metrics are all defined based on the above set of base quantities (n_1, n_2, N_1, N_2, n_1^* and n_2^*).

Halstead defines his first three metrics as follows:

- The **length (N)** of a program P is:

$$N = N_1 + N_2. \qquad (1)$$

- The **vocabulary (n)** of a program P is:

$$n = n_1 + n_2. \qquad (2)$$

- The **volume (V)** of a program P is defined as:
  a) a suitable measure for the size of any implementation of any algorithm;[2]
  b) a count of the number of mental comparisons required to generate a program.[3]

V can be computed using the following equation:

$$V = N * \log_2 n. \qquad (3)$$

The next five of Halstead metrics are listed in the side-box (details of the definitions and of their analysis are presented in the Advanced Readings section).

---

[2][Halstead 1977, p. 19].
[3][Halstead 1977, p. 47].

Box 1: Five of the Halstead Metrics

Program potential (minimal) volume (V*):

$$V^* = \left(2 + n_2^*\right) \log_2 \left(2 + n_2^*\right).$$ (4)

Program level (L)

$$L = \frac{V^*}{V}.$$ (5)

Program difficulty (D)

$$D = \frac{1}{L}.$$ (6)

The program level estimator (L̂) of L

$$\hat{L} = \frac{2}{n_1} * \frac{n_2}{N_2}.$$ (7)

The intelligent content (I) of a program

$$P : I = \hat{L} * V.$$ (8)

See the corresponding analysis in the Advanced Readings section

---

Finally, the last two of Halstead's metrics are presented in detail in Equations 9 and 10.

Programming effort (E) is defined as a measurement of the mental activity required to reduce a preconceived algorithm to a program P. **E** is defined as the total number of elementary mental discriminations required to generate a program:

$$E = \frac{V}{L} = \frac{n_1 N_2 N \log_2 n}{2 n_2}.$$ (9)

In the definition of **E**, the unit of measurement of **E** is claimed by Halstead to be an *elementary mental discrimination*.

The required **programming time (T)** for a program P of effort E is defined as:

$$T = \frac{E}{S} = \frac{n_1 N_2 N \log_2 n}{2 n_2 S}.$$ (10)

where **S** is the Stroud number[4], defined as the number of elementary discriminations performed by the human brain per second.

- The S value for software scientists is set to 18 [Hamer and Frewin 1982].
- The unit of measurement of T is the second.

7.3. ANALYSIS OF THE DESIGN OF HALSTEAD'S METRICS

7.3.1 The Measurement Objectives

The objectives of most of Halstead's metrics are to measure the following *attributes of a program*:

- length,
- vocabulary,
- volume (or potential volume),
- level, difficulty, level estimator, and
- intelligence content.

In addition, two of Halstead's metrics aim to measure something quite different, that is:

- *programming effort,* and
- *required programming time.*

These last two metrics refer to the measurement of *entities of the development process*, rather than to attributes of the source code.

7.3.2 The Measurand: The Entities and the Attributes Measured

Entities: the entities to which Halstead's metrics can be applied are the source code itself and the algorithm of that source code.

Attributes: All of Halstead metrics are based on identifying and counting only two types of attributes of the program to be measured:

- the number of operators, and
- the number of operands.

The empirical worlds of these two types of attributes can be easily mapped to a corresponding mathematical structure by respectively counting and adding the

---

[4]In 1967, psychologist John M. Stroud suggested that the human mind is capable of making a limited number of mental discrimination per second (Stroud Number), in the range of 5 to 20.

number of operators and operands in the source code (or the equivalent algorithm).

In the metrology sense, the number of operators and the number of operands correspond to "base quantities" in metrology.

However, to obtain a value for each of the ten Halstead metrics, equations have to be computed (see section 7.2).

Note that all the equations associated with the ten metrics (Equations 1 to 10) correspond to a "derived attribute" (or to a "derived quantity", as defined by the *international vocabulary of basic and general terms in metrology* (VIM)—see box 2 on metrology terms and definitions).

Box 2: Metrology Terms & Definitions

Attribute: the property of an entity that can be determined quantitatively, that is, for which a magnitude can be assigned. In the metrology vocabulary, this is called a *measurable quantity*, or *quantity* for short.

Attributes of same type: attributes which can be placed in order of magnitude relative to one another.

Base attribute: a simple property defined by convention, with no reference to other attributes, and possibly used in a system of attributes to define other attributes; in this case, we talk about a *base attribute*. In the metrology vocabulary, this is called a *base quantity*.

Derived attribute: a property defined in a system of attributes as a function of base attributes. In the metrology vocabulary, it is called a *derived quantity*.

See also Appendix B: Measurement Definitions.

7.3.3   Analysis of the Numerical World: Scale Types and Units

Issues in scale types

While Halstead's ten equations do not appear overly complex, identification of their corresponding scale type is highly challenging.

For instance, it has been noted by Fenton and Pfleeger [1997] that:

- Equation 3 on program Volume is of the ratio scale type, while
- Equation 5 on program Level is of the ordinal scale type.

By contrast, Zuse [1997] maintains that:

- Equation 1 is of the ratio scale type, and
- Equations 2, 3, 6, and 9 are of the ordinal scale type.

Moreover, it is not clear to which scale type Equations 4, 7, 8, and 10 belong.

This challenge in identifying the scale types in Halstead's metrics immediately points to major design issues, and, consequently, to practical issues:

- for practitioners, when using and attempting to interpret the outcome of these metrics, as well as
- for all other measures, the design of which has been derived totally (or partially) from Halstead's metrics such as in:
  - the initial design of Function Points and
  - subsequent measures based on the design of Function Points, such as Use Case Points, Object Points, etc.

Issues in measurement units

The above statements on the scale types of Halstead's metrics also need to be revisited when the units of measurement in Halstead's equations are taken into consideration.

For instance: in Equation 1, the program *length* (N) is calculated by adding the total number of occurrences of operators to the total number of occurrences of operands. However, since their units are different, operators and operands cannot be directly added unless the concept common to them (and its related unit) is taken into consideration, that is, "occurrences of tokens" then, the right-hand side of Equation 1 would give "occurrences of tokens" as a measurement unit on the ratio scale:

$$N^{\text{occurrences of tokens}} = N_1^{\text{occurrences of operators}} + N_2^{\text{occurrences of operands}}.$$

In Equation 2, the program *vocabulary* (n) is calculated by adding the number of distinct operators to the number of distinct operands:

$$n^{\text{distinct tokens}} = n_1^{\text{distinct operators}} + n_2^{\text{distinct operands}}.$$

Again, since their units are different, distinct operators and distinct operands cannot be directly added, unless the concept common to them (and its related unit) is taken into consideration, that is, "distinct tokens." This measurement unit must then also be assigned to the left-hand side of this equation, labeled "vocabulary", and associated with the related concepts.

It can be noted that, while the concept of length is associated with a number to represent program size, the concept of vocabulary is not.

- Indeed, the program *vocabulary* (n) reflects a different view of program size, being a measure of "the repertoire of elements that a programmer must deal with to implement the program" (that is, the set of distinct tokens——n_1 and n_2).
- Most probably, an expression such as "size of a vocabulary" would have been more appropriate.

In Equation 3, program **volume** (V) has been interpreted with two different units of measurement: "the number of bits required to code the program" [Hamer and Frewin 1982] and "the number of mental comparisons needed to write the program" [Menzies *et al.* 2002] on the left-hand side of the equation:

$$V^{\text{bits or mental comparisons}} = N^{\text{occurrences of tokens}} * \log_2 n^{\text{distinct tokens}}.$$

Thus, there is no relationship between:

- the measurement unit on the left-hand side, and
- the measurement units on the right-hand side of this equation.

Furthermore, on the right-hand side, the true meaning of the multiplication of "occurrences of tokens" and "distinct tokens" is not clear. Such a multiplication would normally produce a number without a measurement unit—see box 3.

Box 3: The Measurement Unit Produced by log₂

In general, in engineering applications, we do not take the logarithm of a dimensioned number, only that of a dimensionless quantity. For instance, in calculating decibels, we take the logarithm of a ratio of two quantities. A ratio of quantities with the same dimensions is itself dimensionless. We can write

$$log(a/b) = log(a) - log(b)$$

making it appear that we are taking the *logs* of dimensioned quantities (*a*) and (*b*), but the dimensions "come out in the wash": by the time we have finished (subtracting one *log* from the other), we have effectively taken the log of a dimensionless quantity (*a/b*).

We can regard units as factors in an expression, for instance:

$$8 \ meters = 8 * [1 \ meter]$$
$$800 \ cm = 800 * [1 \ cm]$$
$$= 800 * 0.01 * [1 \ meter]$$

In these terms, we have:

$$(8m) * log_2(8m) = 8 * [1m] * log_2(8 * [1m])$$
$$= 8 * [1m] * (log_2(8) + log_2[1m])$$
$$= (8 * log_2(8) + 8 * log_2[1m]) * [1m]$$

The inconvenient term $8*log_2[1m]$ is an additive term that depends on the units being used. If it is part of a valid engineering calculation, it will be canceled out somewhere in the process. It may be, for instance, that when we take the *log* of 8 *meters*, we are actually taking the *log* of a ratio of 8 *meters* to a *one-meter* standard length.

Equation 9 is used by Halstead to compute the **effort** (E) required to generate a program:

$$
E^{\text{discriminations}}_{\text{mental}} = \frac{n_1^{\text{operators}} \; N_2^{\text{occurrences of operands}} \; N^{\text{occurrences of tokens}} \; \log_2 n^{\text{distinct tokens}}}{2^{\text{potential operators}} \; n_2^{\text{distinct operands}}}.
$$

The measurement unit on the left-hand side of this equation, referred to as "effort", would be expected to be "hours" or "days." Halstead, however, referred to "the number of elementary mental discriminations" as the unit of measurement for the left-hand side.

Next, in the sense that the "distinct operators," the "distinct operands," and the "occurrences of operands" are, in a generic sense, "tokens", then it can be concluded the measurement unit on the right hand-side of this equation is a combination of these measurement units. Therefore, there is no relationship between the units of measurement on the left-hand and right-hand sides of Equation 9.

Finally, Equation 10 is used to compute the required **programming time** (T) for the program:

$$
T^{\text{seconds}} = \frac{n_1^{\text{distinct operators}} \; N_2^{\text{occurrences of operands}} \; N^{\text{occurrences of tokens}} \; \log_2 n^{\text{distinct tokens}}}{2^{\text{potential operators}} \; 18^{\text{psychological moments per second}} \; n_2^{\text{distinct operands}}}.
$$

Again, the measurement unit on the left-hand side, that is, seconds, does not in any way relate to the measurement unit on the right-hand side, which is, in fact, a combination of many different measurement units. In the right-hand side of equation (10), Halstead refers to the "moments" in this equation as "the time required by the human brain to perform the most elementary discrimination"[5], but no specific time measurement unit is specified.

7.3.4   The Measurement Method

All ten of Halstead's metrics are based on the results of n_1, n_2, N_1, N_2, n_1^*, and n_2^*, which themselves must be based on a counting strategy to classify the program tokens as operators or operands.

Unfortunately, there is a problem here in distinguishing between operators and operands. This problem occurs because Halstead has provided an example[6]

[5][Halstead 1977, p. 48]
[6][Halstead 1977, pp. 6–8].

with specific illustrations of operators and operands, but without generic definitions applicable to any program context. That is, Halstead:

- has not explicitly described the generic measurable concepts of operators
  and operands,
- and has asserted only that—in the example he provides—their description
  is intuitively obvious and requires no further explanation. In practice, for
  measurement purposes, intuition is an insufficient means for obtaining
  accurate, repeatable, and reproducible measurement results.

Through his example, Halstead has not illustrated a "measurement method," but
merely a "measurement procedure"—see side box 4 for further terms in
metrology.

Therefore, in the specific context of Halstead's metrics, we use the less
precise expression "counting strategy" in this section, which, of course, may vary
from one measurer to another.

Box 4: Further Terms in Metrology

Measurement method: a logical sequence of operations, described generically, used
in the performance of measurements.

Measurement procedure: a set of operations, described specifically, used in the performance of particular measurements according to a given method.

See also Appendix B: Measurement Definitions.

It is important, therefore, that the term "measurement method" be clearly
defined and consistently used, since all Halstead's software science depends on
counts of operators and operands [Lister 1982].

However, more than 30 years later, there is still no general agreement among
researchers on the most meaningful way to classify and count these tokens:

- Individual researchers (and practitioners as well) must state their own
  interpretation or, alternatively, use one of the available counting strategies
  proposed by other researchers, such as in [Szentes 1986; Conte *et al.* 1986;
  Abd Ghani and Hunter 1996].
- More recently, rule have been proposed for identifying operators and operands in the object-oriented programming (OOP) languages [Li *et al.* 2004].

Of course, it is to be expected that different counting strategies will produce different values of n_1, n_2, N_1, and N_2, and, consequently, different values for the
above ten equations.

Furthermore, applying Halstead's metrics to either the source code or
directly to the algorithm of the source code might produce different values for
the same base quantities—see side box 5.

> **Box 5: The Entity Measured: the Source Code or the Algorithm?**
>
> In Java language, the number of operators in the source code is different from the number of operators in the equivalent algorithm for that source code, since—as an example—in Java source code, each statement must end with a semicolon (;), which is an operator.

7.4. DISCUSSION ON THE FINDINGS

In this chapter, Halstead's well-known set of metrics was analyzed by focusing on their design and, in particular, on their measurement units. The following comments can be made about them:

- Based on the ISO International vocabulary of basic and general terms in metrology (VIM), Halstead's metrics consist of ten derived quantities—Equations 1 to 10—which use any of six base quantities (n_1, n_2, N_1, N_2, n_1^*, and n_2^*).
- Halstead has not explicitly provided a clear and complete counting strategy to distinguish between the operators and the operands in a given program or algorithm. This has led researchers to come up with different counting strategies and, correspondingly, with different measurement results for the same derived measures and for the same program or algorithm.
- There is ambiguity and uncertainty about the scale types in Halstead's metrics.
- There are major problems with the units of measurement for both the left-hand and the right-hand sides of most of Halstead's equations.
- Implementation of the measurement functions of Halstead's metrics has been interpreted in different ways than according to the goals specified by Halstead in their design. For example, the program length (N) has been interpreted as a measure of program complexity, which is a different characteristic of a program [Fenton 1994].

In summary:

- Most of Halstead's metrics, which were designed almost thirty years ago, do not meet key design criteria of measurement methods in engineering and the physical sciences.
- Measures designed subsequently based on concepts from Halstead's metrics have inherited many of the same design flaws.

Further research is required to address the weaknesses identified in the design of Halstead's metrics in order to transform them into *bona fide* measurement methods.

As a follow-up to these observations above, Zuse [2005] has investigated some of these issues and explored them from the perspective of the extensive structure of measurement theory.

- In doing so, he made a number of assumptions, and the conclusions he reached depend on those assumptions being valid, such as the non relevance of the topic of units.
- However, when such assumptions are removed, the conclusions could differ, and this requires further investigation.

ADVANCED READINGS: OTHER HALSTEAD'S METRICS

> **Audience**
>
> This Advanced Reading section is of most interest to the readers with a mathematical background interested in the more complex of the Halstead's metrics.

This section presents an analysis of the five Halstead's metrics listed in Box 1.

Definitions

- Program *potential (minimal) volume* (V*): the volume of the minimal size implementation of a program P, which is defined as[7]:

$$V^* = \left(2 + n_2^*\right)\log_2\left(2 + n_2^*\right). \tag{4}$$

- The *level* (L) of a program P with volume V is:

$$L = \frac{V^*}{V}. \tag{5}$$

The program *level* emphasizes that growth in volume leads to a lower level of the program, and conversely.

- The largest value for L is 1.
- In addition, this value is interpreted as referring to the most ideally written program and as measuring how well written a program is.
- Thus, programs with L values close to 1 are considered to be well written; in general L < 1 [Chuan *et al.* 1994].

---

[7]No objective evidence documented in [Halstead 1977] that this is indeed a minimal implementation.

- Program *difficulty* (D) is defined as the inverse of program level L:

$$D = \frac{1}{L}. \tag{6}$$

- The program *level estimator* ($\hat{L}$) of L is defined as:

$$\hat{L} = \frac{2}{n_1} * \frac{n_2}{N_2}. \tag{7}$$

and interpreted by [Menzies *et al.* 2002] and by [Fenton and Pfleeger 1997] as:

$$\hat{L} = \frac{1}{D} = \frac{2}{n_1} * \frac{n_2}{N_2}. \tag{7.1}$$

- The *intelligent content* (I) of a program P is a measure of the information content of program P, and is defined as:

$$I = \hat{L} * V. \tag{8}$$

Analysis

Equation 4 gives the definition of the program *potential volume* (V*), which is a prediction of the program volume of the minimal size implementation of a program P:

$$V* = \left(2^{\text{potential}}_{\text{operators}} + n_2^{*\,\text{potential}}_{\,\text{operands}} \right) \log_2 \left(2^{\text{potential}}_{\text{operators}} + n_2^{*\,\text{potential}}_{\,\text{operands}} \right).$$

In this equation, the value 2 has been assigned to n_1^*. The measurement unit of the left-hand side is the same as in Equation 3, while there is no recognizable measurement unit for the right-hand side. As in Equation 3, such a multiplication would also normally produce a number without a measurement unit—see Box 3.

The program *level* (L) can be calculated using Equation 5, in which there is no measurement unit for the left hand-side, either provided by Halstead himself or by other researchers. To the extent that this is the correct structure for a ratio with the same unit in both numerator and denominator, the end result is a percentage:

$$L = \frac{V^{*\,\text{bits}}}{V^{\text{bits}}} = \frac{V^{*\,\text{mental comparisons}}}{V^{\text{mental comparisons}}}.$$

For Equation 6, the *difficulty* (D) is a measure of "ease of reading", and can be seen as a measure of "ease of writing" as well [Christensen *et al.* 1981]. The right-hand side is also a percentage. What the right-hand side of Equation 6 means is a riddle, as is its associated label on the left-hand side.

In Equation 7, for the program *level estimator* ($\hat{L}$), there is no measurement unit for the left-hand side, while the right-hand side consists of a combination of four distinct measurement units. The exact meaning is again a riddle.

$$\hat{L} = \frac{2^{\substack{\text{potential} \\ \text{operators}}}}{n_1^{\substack{\text{distinct} \\ \text{operators}}}} * \frac{n_2^{\substack{\text{distinct} \\ \text{operands}}}}{N_2^{\substack{\text{occurrences} \\ \text{of operands}}}}.$$

In Equation 8, referred to as the *intelligent content* of the program (I), there is no measurement unit on the left-hand side. For the right-hand side of this equation, the measurement unit of $\hat{L}$—which is not known since it is a combination of units—is multiplied by the measurement unit of V:

$$I = \hat{L} * V^{\text{bits}} = \hat{L} * V^{\text{mental comparisons}}.$$

As for Equations 6 and 7, the exact meaning of the left-hand side of Equation 8 is a riddle if we attempt to interpret this "I" number with measurement units.

Discussion
Equations 6 and 7.1, using basic mathematical concepts, leads to $\hat{L}$ being identical to L, a point which can be clarified as follows:

$$\hat{L} = \frac{1}{D} \quad (6), \quad D = \frac{1}{L} \quad (7.1),$$

$$\hat{L} = \frac{1}{\frac{1}{L}}, \tag{11}$$

$$\hat{L} = L.$$

Therefore, using Fenton's description of $\hat{L}$[8], the program level estimator is identical to the program level.

Using the previous observation (that is, L = $\hat{L}$), and from Equations 5 and 8, it can be concluded that I = V*. The clarification of this point is as follows:

---

[8][Fenton and Pfleeger 1997], p. 251.

$$I = \hat{L} * V \quad (8), \quad L = \frac{V^*}{V} \quad (5), \quad L = \hat{L} \quad (11),$$

$$I = L * V,$$

$$I = \frac{V^*}{V} \times V,$$

Bits

$I = V^* = $ size unit

Mental

which means that we can ask the following questions:

- How can the same value be used to measure both I and V*, which are two different attributes of a program or algorithm?
- Also, how can different units of measurement be given to the same value?

EXERCISES

1. What is the measurement unit of Halstead's volume (v)?

2. What is the typical dimension in the measurement of a volume?

3. What is the measurement unit of Halstead's Programming Effort (E)?

4. What are the base measures in all of Halstead metrics?

5. In the Halstead Programming Effort metrics, position the corresponding elements with respect to the ISO 15939 Measurement Information Model.

6. Where is the measurement method for each of Halstead's metrics documented?

7. What are the standard etalons for verifying the accuracy of each of Halstead's metrics?

TERM ASSIGNMENTS

1. Propose improvements to the designs of two of Halstead's metrics.

2. Explain how you can implement Halstead's metrics in Object-Oriented analysis and OO programming.

3. Are there other software measures based on the design of some of Halstead's metrics? Were the design deficiencies in Halstead's metrics corrected or repeated? Illustrate with examples.

8

FUNCTION POINTS: ANALYSIS OF THEIR DESIGN

This chapter presents an analysis of the design of Function Points:

- The origin of Functional Size Measurement
- The global design of Function Points—FP
- Analysis of the design of Unadjusted Function Points
- Analysis of the design of the Value Adjustment Factor
- What is a Function Point?
- What if the Function Points weights were dropped?
- Advanced Readings: Evolution of Functional Size Measurement

8.1. INTRODUCTION

A very large number of software measures have been proposed in past decades, but most are not yet close to international standardization. By contrast, the measurement of the functional size of software has a unique status in software engineering: it is the first, and only, type of software measurement with international standards adopted by the ISO.

However, just because a measurement method is recognized as an international standard does not guarantee that its design is perfect. In this chapter, we

Software Metrics and Software Metrology, by Alain Abran
Copyright © 2010 IEEE Computer Society

assess one of the functional size measurement (FSM) methods, Function Points (FP), pointing out some of its weaknesses.

It is particularly important to conduct this assessment, since the basic design of Function Points has subsequently been reused in the design of a number of variants of the method.

- In general, the weaknesses inherited by these variants, e.g. Use Case Points, were not corrected—see chapter 9 for a discussion on the design of Use Case Points.
- Fortunately, some of the weaknesses that we identify were corrected in the design of COSMIC Function Points—see chapters 11 and 12.

The analysis method we use here for the Function Points design can also be used for other measurement methods, including in particular "weights" or "points" in their designs.

8.2. THE ORIGIN OF SOFTWARE FUNCTIONAL SIZE MEASUREMENT

With the advent of large scale software development in the mid-sixties, the software engineering community recognized the need to better control the economic aspects of software production and maintenance. One key aspect of this endeavor was to figure out a way to quantify software as the output of a complex process, in order to be able to better understand and manage the multiple facets of its production.

The size of software is typically used to build cost estimation models, productivity models, and cost-benefit models. There are typically two kinds of software size:

- technical size, and
- functional size.

The *technical size* of software is used to measure software products from a *developer's perspective*: number of lines of code, number of components, number of modules, number of sub-systems, etc. It is typically based on the counts of some entities, and can be used in efficiency analysis to improve, for example, design performance.

The *functional size* of software is used to measure software products from a *user's perspective*. It must be independent of technical development and implementation decisions, and, as such it can be used to compare the productivity of different techniques and technologies.

Alan Albrecht was the first to propose, in 1979, a new way of quantifying software size, based on the user's view of software. Albrecht, in his landmark 1979 communication at the IBM GUIDE Users Conference [Albrecht 1979], described the results of an initiative started in the mid-seventies in one IBM business unit to measure the productivity of software development, as viewed from an economic perspective. The functional size of software was proposed as a generic measure of the output of the development process, which allows for projects in which software was developed using different programming languages to be compared.

The lasting merit of Albrecht's proposal was to offer a new approach to quantifying the size of software.

Box 1: Albrecht Key Contribution

At a time when software size meant "lines of code" for the majority of software engineers, many of whom wrestled with problems where lines of code meant different things, depending on the programming language, Albrecht proposed a method of sizing software which was independent of the programming language used.

In 1984, the International Function Point Users Group (IFPUG) was formed to foster and promote the evolution of the Function Points method. Much work went into the subsequent releases of the method to include rules allowing an interpretation of functionality which was increasingly independent of the physical implementation of the software.

- The major contribution of IFPUG to the FSM field has been to document measurement rules aimed at improving the level of uniformity in the application of this measurement method.
- The base structure of Function Points, though, has remained unchanged from what was proposed by Albrecht.

8.3. THE DESIGN OF FUNCTION POINTS—FP

8.3.1 Global Design

In the IFPUG Counting Practices Manual, Function Points—FP—are described in terms of:

- definitions,
- rules,
- decisions tables,
- an interpretation guide, and
- examples.

For a better understanding of the measurement concepts embedded within the Function Points design, we have elected to present here the Function Points concepts through a set of models.

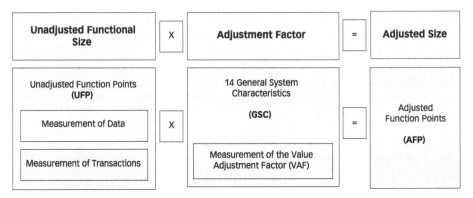

Figure 8.1. Global model of Function Points—Albrecht-IFPUG

TABLE 8.1. Data Measurement Steps

ID	Step Description
F1	The input in this step is the available information about the functions of the software (from the software documentation or from the software itself). From this information, the measurer identifies the logical data files.
F2	The same available information is examined to determine the boundaries between the application (or the project) being measured and the other external applications, in order to classify the logical files as *internal logical files* (e.g. files created or modified within the software being measured) or as external interface files (e.g. files that are read by the software being measured, but not modified by this software).
F3	The files identified in F2 are used as input by the measurer to identify and count, for each of these files, the number of data element types (DET) in each file, as well as the number of record element types (RET) for the internal logical files and the file types referenced (FTR) (e.g. accessed) by each of the external interface files.
F4	The measurer applies the Function Points data algorithm using five types of input: • the lists of internal logical files and external interface files, • the count of their record elements (RET), • the count of their data element types (DET), • the complexity model for data (i.e. the structure of the complexity table with its two dimensional axes), and • the weights within the tables (i.e. the points) for the files (internal and external) which correspond to the step-function.
F5	The points from each file are added together, leading to the number of *UFP* for the data (that is, for all the internal logical files and all the external interface files).

At the highest level of abstraction, there are three main parts to the measurement process of Function Points (Figure 8.1): the unadjusted functional size (UFP), the Value Adjustment Factor (VAF), and their combination.

- The *unadjusted functional size* is calculated from the counts of all the *individual functions* of the software application being measured. This first measurement result represents the addition of the parts of the whole, and is referred to the *Unadjusted Function Points (UFP)*. The process of measuring the UFP is broken down into two distinct steps:
  - The measurement process for the Data (i.e. logical data files),
  - The measurement process for the Transactions.
- The *value adjustment factor (VAF)* is calculated by adding the values attributed to the 14 General System Characteristics (GSC) of the software application *as a whole*.
- The final *adjusted functional size* is then obtained by multiplying the two figures together, that is, UFP times VAF—referred to as the *Adjusted Function Points (AFP)*.

The measurement process for the **data** consists of five steps, referred to as *Fi* in Table 8.1 and Figure 8.2. In Figure 8.2, the inputs of each step are shown in the left-hand column, and the outputs are shown in the right-hand column. If an output of step Fi is reused as an input to step F(i + 1), this is indicated by an arrow towards the following step F(i + 1).

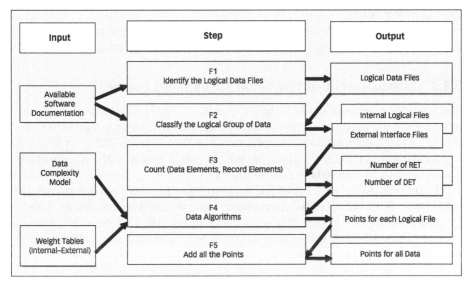

Figure 8.2. Data Measurement Model

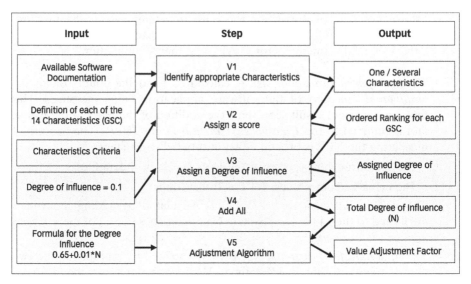

Figure 8.3. Model of the Value Adjustment Factor

This measurement process for the data (logical files) calls upon several implicit models[1], such as models of functional specifications, boundaries between applications, and structures, as well as complexity and weights for the logical files.

It must be noted that none of the relations of these models is based on any experimentally justified theories in any precise framework, either in Albrecht's original paper or in the IFPUG documentation; they are still only described in a set of rules established by the normative committee of IFPUG, the Counting Practices Committee.

The corresponding analysis of the design of the measurement of the transactions in Function Points is documented in Abran and Robillard [1994].

8.3.3   Measurement of the Value Adjustment Factor

The adjustment process of the Function Points measurement method is intended to adjust the unadjusted functional size by multiplying it by an adjustment factor that reflects the complexity of the processing of the software and of its development environment. Figure 8.3 and Table 8.2 shows a model of the measurement process that determines the value of this factor.

Figure 8.3 shows a model of the measurement process that determines the VAF, while Table 8.2 presents the corresponding detailed measurement steps.

Using Albrecht's design, this adjustment factor will vary from a minimum of 0.65 (when all 14 characteristics have all been assigned a so-called "degree

---

[1]An implicit model is a set of intuitive relations between different objects or concepts.

TABLE 8.2. Value Adjustment Factor: Measurement Steps

ID.	Step Description
V1	The available information about the software, as well as the definitions of each of the 14 GSC of the application, are taken as inputs to identify which of these 14 characteristics are present for this software.
V2	Each of the characteristics present in the software being measured is analyzed using its corresponding category criteria to classify it into an ordered ranking from 0 to 5, each step representing 5 distinct irregular intervals.
V3	Each of the numbered intervals assigned for any characteristic is multiplied by a value of 0.1, which gives a degree of influence to each: the range of the derived quantities is then between 0.0 and 0.5.
V4	The degrees of influence assigned to each characteristic are added together to obtain a *total number* of degrees of influence (say, N) – min = 0.00 and max = 0.70.
V5	The following linear transformation is used to obtain the total number of degrees of influence for the whole software being measured: $VAF = 0.65 + 0.01 * N$

of influence" of 0) and a maximum of 1.35 (when all 14 characteristics have been assigned the maximum degree of influence of 5). This linear transformation therefore provides a maximum adjustment of +/– 35 % to the functional size.

8.4. WEAKNESSES OF THE FUNCTION POINTS MEASUREMENT DESIGN

To better understand the design of Function Points as a measurement method, the focus here is on the design of Function Points itself and on the mathematical significance of the various steps and sub-steps of its embedded measurement processes.

School students learn the rules that govern the manipulation of quantities very early on. These rules are referred to as the admissible mathematical operations and are dependent on scale types. For example:

- on a **ratio** scale, quantities can be **added** and **multiplied**,
- on an **ordinal** scale, quantities **can only be ordered**.

Section 8.4.1 reviews these measurement scale types and related admissible mathematical operations, while subsequent sections look at them within the measurement processes of Function Points.

8.4.1   Properties of Measurement Scales

There are five scale types: nominal, ordinal, interval, ratio, and absolute—see Table 8.3. This section shows the mathematical operations (i.e. equality, addition, multiplication, division) permitted for each type of scale—see Table 8.4.

8.4.2   Analysis of the Measurement Design for Data

This section identifies the measurement scale types within the measurement design for the data (Figure 8.2) and analyzes the corresponding mathematical operations.

In the presentation of the FP rules, the numerical assignment of size points is described in three steps:

- a logical file is first classified as simple, medium, or complex,
- a weight (in points) is assigned depending on its position in a reference table, and, finally,
- the points are added together.

TABLE 8.3. Properties of Scale Types

Scale type	Description (See also section 5.3.5, Chapter 5)
Nominal	This scale type is used to name objects or events. It is used only in identifying requirements, and the only quantitative notion associated with it is that of equality. Only non-parametric statistics can be used.
Ordinal	This scale type is used to put objects in order, based on a criterion that may be subjective, but it is preferably objective. Ranking order statistics can be used, as well as those that apply to the nominal scale.
Interval	This scale type (also called the cardinal scale) is used to determine the difference between ranks. It is a continuum between two points which are not necessarily fixed. With this scale, objects can be distinguished and ranked; moreover, the differences between the ranks can be measured. The mathematical average can be used, as well as all the statistical methods that apply to the ordinal scale.
Ratio	In this scale type, it is significant to multiply a measurement by a non-negative value. It is then possible to say that an item X has n times the value of item Y with respect to a given attribute. It follows from this that the value zero has a special significance for that attribute. This allows us to distinguish a ratio scale from an interval scale. The calculation of percentages is allowed, as well as all the statistical methods that apply to the interval scale.
Absolute	The absolute scale type possesses a unique origin from which to start the measurement process. This allows us to count entities, and there is only one way to do this [Fenton, 1991]. Here, only the *identity* transformation ($f(x) = x$) is admissible. All the statistical methods for the previous types of scale apply.

TABLE 8.4. Measurement Scale Types and Admissible Transformations

Scale type	Admissible Transformation	Operations	Examples	
Nominal	(R,=)	f unique	Name, distinguish	Colors, shapes
Ordinal	(R,>=)	f strictly increasing monotonic function	Rank, Order	Preference, hardness
Interval	(R,>=,+)	$f(x) = ax + b, a > 0$	Add	Calendar time, temperature (degrees Celsius)
Ratio	(R,>=,+)	$f(x) = ax, a > 0$	Add, multiply, divide	Mass, distance, absolute temperature (degrees Kelvin)
Absolute	(R,>=,+)	$f(x) = x$	Add, multiply, divide	Entity count

---

Box 2: Example of the Measurement of Data in IFPUG Function Points

A software application has three internal logical files as follows:

- file 1 has 1 RET and 5 DET,
- file 2 has 3 RET and 21 DET,
- file 3 has 6 RET and 26 DET.

Using the table of weights for the Internal Logical Files:

- file 1 is classified as simple with a weight of 7,
- file 2 is classified as medium with a weight of 10,
- file 3 is classified as complex with a weight of 15.

Adding their weights yields a total of 32 FP for these three files.

In the measurement of the internal and external files, three different types of attributes are taken into account in the measurement design:

1. the data element types (DET),
2. the record element types (RET), and
3. the file types referenced (FTR).

It is to be noted that these three types of attributes are not independent, but organized in a hierarchical structure:

- a record consists of 1 or more data element types (DET), and
- a logical file (FTR) consists of 1 or more record types (RET).

These represent different levels of abstraction of the data in software:

- the RET represents a structure of DET, and
- the FTR, a structure of RET.

To identify the types of scale and to analyze their use in this measurement design, the numerical assignment rules are decomposed for the internal logical files as follows:

1) A file is analyzed, and then each of its DET and RET or FTR is identified and counted; this corresponds to the addition of numbers in an *absolute scale type*.
2) Each of these DET and RET counts is compared to the three DET and RET intervals within the three ranks listed in Table 8.5.

In Function Points, the intervals within these ranks are not equal, and, of course, the results of a mapping into one of them cannot be added. This classification within one of these ranks leads to an *ordinal scale type*.

> From this point on, it is only possible to say that an observation in rank 2 is greater than an observation in rank 1, but not that it contains twice or three times as many elements.
> There is, therefore, a significant loss of flexibility in the mathematical operations allowed.

For the sake of clarity, the various ranks (for data elements and record elements) are identified below by the notation used in Table 8.6, that is, ranks D1 to D3 and ranks R1 to R3.

TABLE 8.5. Ranges and Ranks for the Internal Logical Files

Attributes		Rank 1	Rank 2	Rank 3
Data element types (DET)	**Intervals**	1 to 19	20 to 50	51+
Record element types (RET)		1	2 to 5	6+

TABLE 8.6. Ranks Labels

Attribute	Rank 1:	Rank 2:	Rank 3:
Data element types (DET)	D1	D2	D3
Record element types (RET)	R1	R2	R3

TABLE 8.7. 2-Dimensional Matrix of Ranks

Data Elements			
Record Elements	Range D1	Range D2	Range D3
Range R1	D1,R1	D2,R1	D3,R1
Range R2	D1,R2	D2,R2	D3,R2
Range R3	D1,R3	D2,R3	D3,R3

3) The ranks are taken as parameters in a function. This step is more complex from the point of view of a measurement design, as it can be represented in mathematical notation as a function of two arguments, $f(D_i, R_j)$, and is illustrated with a 2-dimensional matrix—see Table 8.7.

However, while the parameters in such a function are typically on an absolute or ratio scale type, here the parameters are on an ordinal scale type. Therefore, the positioning of a specific file on the basis of its ranks of DET and RET does not produce a result of an ordinal type:

> Even though the contents of cell (D1,R1) can be perceived intuitively as being smaller than the contents of cell (D3,R3), it is not possible to deduce whether the contents of a cell (D1,R3) are equal to, smaller than, or greater than the contents of a cell (D3,R1).

Therefore, this step corresponds strictly to:

- the positioning in the matrix on a *nominal scale type*, with
- a loss of measurement information, as compared to the ordinal scale of measurement for the individual parameters of this function.

4) The cells in Table 8.7 are next segregated into one of three categories, according to their position in the matrix:

1. Above the inverted diagonal
2. On the inverted diagonal
3. Below the inverted diagonal

> The inverted diagonal in Table 7 does not correspond to the usual mathematical notation for a matrix. It does not express a symmetry between the two axes, but rather a simultaneous increase in rank on the intervals.

The objective seems to be to express the equivalence of these cells when they are combined on 2 axes. This corresponds to a *nominal scale type*.

TABLE 8.8. Assignment of Ordered Labels

Record Elements	Data Elements		
	Rank D1	Rank D2	Rank D3
Rank R1	Simple	Simple	Medium
Rank R2	Simple	Medium	Complex
Rank R3	Medium	Complex	Complex

TABLE 8.9. Weights for the Data in Function Points

File type	Range 1: Simple	Range 2: Medium	Range 3: Complex
Internal	7	10	15
External	5	7	10

Example

The smallest range on one axis combined with the highest range on the other axis yields a category similar to that of the inverse:

$$(D1, R3) = (D3, R1)$$

5) These 'nominal' categories are assigned the following labels, *the semantics of which are of the ordinal scale type*—see Table 8.8:

- Above the inverted diagonal = **simple**
- On the inverted diagonal = **medium**
- Below the inverted diagonal = **complex**

This move from a nominal to an ordinal scale type is not, of course, an admissible mathematical transformation.

6) Weights (or points) are assigned to these ordered labels (simple, medium, complex), as shown in Table 8.9: these weights for the files are numbers varying from 5 to 15, according to the type of file (Internal or External).

The intent of this step is clear: to obtain numbers which will be *interpreted/perceived as being of a ratio scale type*: a complex External File is assigned a weight of 10, that is, twice the weight of a simple one.

This set of weights is the 'trick' used in Function Points to add different functions (Data or Transaction) together (otherwise, the additions would not be allowed, either on the ordinal elements of step 4 or on the nominal elements of step 3).

7) Finally, the weights (or points) assigned to the files are added together. Under the hypothesis that the numbers obtained previously are on a ratio scale type, the result of the addition will also be a point on a ratio scale type.

Of course, such a hypothesis is obviously not supported. This assignation has an incorrect foundation for a ratio scale type. It uses:

- ranges of irregular intervals for two distinct axes of the matrices,
- as well as nominal identification within these matrices to which ordinal labels are assigned that are not strictly ordinal values.

In conclusion, the mathematical operations used in this set of measurement steps are not all admissible. A number on a nominal scale type (see the steps above) cannot be transformed mathematically into a number on interval or ratio scale type.

A summary of this analysis of the types of scale in the measurement of the data is presented in Table 8.10.

The measurement process for the logical files calls upon several implicit models, such as those of functional specifications, boundaries between applications, structures, complexity, and weights.

- It must be noted that none of the relations of these models is based on any experimentally justified theory in any precise framework, either in Albrecht's original paper or in the IFPUG documentation.
- They are only described in a set of rules established by the normative committee of IFPUG, the Counting Practices Committee.

8.4.3   Analysis of the Measurement Design for Transactions

All the comments in section 3.2 also apply to the measurement design for the Transactions.

To be noted here again is that the transaction measurement processes rely on several implicit models, such as those of documentation, the subdivision of elementary processes and functions, the weights of the transactions, and the selection of weights for the inquiry transactions.

It is worth pointing out again that none of the relations of these models is based on any experimentally justified theory in any identifiable framework, either in Albrecht's original paper or in the IFPUG documentation,.

8.4.4   Addition of All the Function Types

In the final step of calculating the total number of UFP, all the points for the five function types (i.e. the five different types of entities: internal logical files, external interface files, input, outputs, and inquiries) are added together.

To add such number requires that they be of a ratio scale type:

- This would be possible if the assignment of weights to the various types of entities had transformed these five different types of entities into a single

TABLE 8.10. The Types of Scale in the Measurement of the Data in FP

Step	Object	Operation	Scale Type (from)	Scale Type (to)	Mathematical validity	Transformation
1	Data elements	Addition	Absolute	Absolute	Yes	No
	Record elements	Addition	Absolute	Absolute	Yes	No
2	Data elements	Interval identification	Absolute	Ordinal	Yes	Yes and with loss of information
	Record elements	Interval identification	Absolute	Ordinal	Yes	Yes and with loss of information
3	Interval function (data, record)	Position in the matrix	Ordinal	Nominal	Yes	Yes and with loss of information
4	Function of position in the matrix	Name and rank	Nominal	Ordinal	No	Yes and with extra information
5	Function of perceived value	Assign weights	Ordinal	Ratio	No	Yes and with extra information
6	Weights for internal files	Addition	Ratio	Ratio	Yes	No
	Weights for external files	Addition	Ratio	Ratio	Yes	No
7	Internal and external weights	Addition	Ratio	Ratio	Yes	No

type of entities, different from the five original components of these entities.

• Unfortunately, none of this is explained in the Function Points measurement method.

While the end results (i.e. the Function Points totals) are considered by the users of Function Points to be numbers on a ratio scale type, they are not derived from the set of mathematical operations embedded within the measurement design of this measurement method.

Summary of the Analysis

The final results, UFP, are extremely difficult to interpret.

There are so many implicit dimensions and there is so much use of different types of measurement scale types that what seemed simple and intuitively reasonable is a pot-pourri of measurement scale types and of entities which cannot have any mathematical significance, unless the validity of each of the transformations is demonstrated either theoretically or empirically (and this has obviously not yet been done).

Even though the users of Function Points take for granted that FP are on a ratio scale, the nature of these points is unknown:

- What is a Function Point (i.e. What is the measurement unit)?
- What is the intrinsic scale type of Function Points?

8.4.5 Analysis of the Measurement Design for the Value Adjustment Factor (VAF)

The Value Adjustment Factor (VAF) transforms the Unadjusted FP (UFP) into Adjusted FP (AFP), using the 14 General System Characteristics (GSC) of the software application and a linear transformation—Figure 8.4.

Within the design of the VAF, there are also serious methodological weaknesses in the use of quantities with distinct scale types:

1. The IFPUG Counting Practices Manual provides rules for classifying the software being measured into one of the five classifications for each of the 14 GSC.

When a GSC is not present at all: the characteristic of this software is assigned a classification of 0

When a GSC is at its maximum, the characteristic is assigned a classification of 5.

Various other criteria are provided to assign the intermediate classifications of 1, 2, 3, and 4.

This classification from 0 to 5 represents an *ordered set*, where each value from 0 to 5 is considered greater than the previous one for that characteristic; however, the intervals for the classification are typically:

- irregular within each characteristic, and
- different across all 14 characteristics.

Therefore, the values of 0, 1, 2, 3, 4, and 5 for a characteristic do not represent numbers on a ratio scale, but rather *ordered labels, that is, labels with an ordering scale type.*

2. In the next measurement step for calculating the VAF, the classification in the previous step of a GSC is multiplied by a degree of influence of 0.1. The design of this measurement step contains a number of incorrect and inadmissible operations:

   a. A multiplication typically requires that the numbers being multiplied be at least on a ratio scale type. This is obviously not the case here: the values of 0 to 5 of the previous steps are not on a ratio scale, but are merely ordered degrees of influence which have no precise quantitative meaning to allow them to be either added or multiplied.

   b. Furthermore, the same degree of influence value of 0.1 is assigned to each of the irregular ordered intervals within one GSC.

      • Such an equality (i.e. impact = 0.1 for each interval) across irregular intervals has no theoretically verified justification and is not based on empirical evidence.

   c. Finally, while all 14 GSC obviously have different definitions and distinct interval ranges, it could be reasonably argued that they could each have distinct *sets of* degrees of influence, rather than exactly the same set.

3. In this final step, all the numbers obtained in the previous step for each of the 14 GSC are added together and included in a linear transformation of the VAF to allow an impact of +/–35% to the unadjusted functional size.

Here again, it can be noted that the measurement design for the VAF calls on several implicit models, such as those of:

- the set of 14 GSC selected;
- the five interval structures of each of the 14 GSC;
- the criteria for each interval for each GSC;
- the equivalence tables for the degrees of influence (that is, 0.1 for each interval);
- the addition of the various degrees of influence.

Again, and as mentioned for the data measurement design, not one of the measurement design of each GSC is based on a theory which has been experimentally verified in a well-defined context.

8.4.6 Summary of Weaknesses in the Measurement Designs

The various measurement designs within Function Points have been analyzed, and it has been shown that:

- Several different scale types are used in the various steps.
- On a strictly mathematical basis, the results of many of the steps and sub-steps of the measurement designs are based on inappropriate use of mathematical properties of corresponding scale types.

The consequences are as follows:

- There is a loss of information and of mathematical flexibility when moving to a lower type of measurement scale (in terms of mathematical properties for the scale type).
- From a strictly mathematical standpoint, there is an inappropriate use of mathematical properties in the results of many of these measurement steps.
- There are a large number of unsupported semantical transformations to higher scale types.

This, of course, leads to serious challenges in the interpretation of the end results:

- What is a Function Point exactly?
- Can Function Points really be treated on a ratio scale, such as is being done by both practitioners and researchers?

Is Function Points a Base Quantity or a Derived Quantity?

The structure of Function Points combines a number of steps and a number of base quantities, such as DET, RET, and FTR.
    Does this make Function Points a *derived measure*?
    Not really:

- The aim of Function Points is to measure a single concept, that is, functional size.
- The end measurement result in Function Points is not a combination of units, but a single unit, that is, the Function Point, even though such a unit is not formally defined.

Function Points, representing a single concept and having a single unit (i.e. the Function Point), could therefore be considered a base quantity.

8.5. OTHER WEAKNESSES

8.5.1 Mix of Semantics: Functional Size, Technical Size, and Complexity

The ISO requires that FSM methods quantify only the functional size of software, without taking into account its technical and quality characteristics [ISO 14143-1].

On the one hand, the 14 GSC of Function Points definitively take into account a number of the technical characteristics of software, such as performance, response-time, reuse, etc. Therefore, the ISO does not recognize any of these as meeting the ISO requirements, and only the unadjusted part of Function Points has been adopted as an ISO standard.

On the other hand, within the Function Points design, it is explicitly stated that the data (and transactions) are being classified on a *complexity scale* embedded within its tables of weights. Since complexity can be considered as part of the quality of software, it can be easily argued that the Function Points design includes a quality characteristic of the software. This was not addressed when Function Points was submitted to the ISO with the claim that it met all the mandatory requirements of ISO 14143-1.

8.5.2. Implicit Relational System

The design of Function Points was based on expert judgments, and it is described in terms of rules, rather than in terms of models and measurement principles.

Some of the implicit models of Function Points are listed below (this list is by no means exhaustive):

- a model of the user's perspective
- a model of five types of functions
- a model of the logical file type (internal and external)
- a model of the transaction function type
- a sub model of transactions (add, modify, delete)
- a model of elementary components
- a model of the structure of the decision tables
- a model of the weights in the above structures

It is therefore necessary to clarify the domain of the relations or the measurement space of Function Points [Fenton and Kitchenham 1991], and the domain of the measured relations must be explicitly defined if we want to use it in an appropriate manner and possibly to modify it in order to extend its domain of application.

Since there are no explicit models, it is not easy to examine the fundamental principles of the structure of Function Point Analysis (FPA), and its credibility as a *bona fide* measurement method has suffered as a result.

This absence of explicit models has made it next to impossible, in practice, to foster an evolution over the past 30 years of the numerical assignment rules and of the structure of the official version of Function Points.

8.6. WHAT IS A FUNCTION POINT?

8.6.1 The Original Definition of Function Points

Albrecht's initial intention was to measure productivity, and to do this he had to define and measure an output (i.e. the software product developed) and an input (i.e. the effort). He defined this software output as "*function value delivered*" and his objective was "*to develop a relative measure of function value delivered to the user that was independent of the particular technology or approach used*" [Albrecht, 1979].

The result of that methodology in terms of his objective had given him, in his words, a "*dimensionless number defined in function point(s)*" [Albrecht, 1979].

There is, however, a certain contradiction in expressing the size of an application in terms of a dimensionless number, since every measurement system necessarily depends on a reference system which allows us to interpret the measurements [Fenton and Kitchenham 1991].

It must be remembered that a measurement is not a number in itself, but the assignment of a number: it is the establishment of a relation between the entities and the characteristic under observation.

Every time a characteristic is measured, it must be in terms of a specific set of relations.

It seems that, because Albrecht stated that Function Points did not have any dimension, this assertion has not been challenged, either by researchers or by practitioners.

In this context, there is room to revisit the significance of FP as a measurement concept and to examine what Function Points mean from the point of view of measurement.

8.6.2 Revisiting the Original Definition

The existence and true description of the system of relations cannot be deduced just from Albrecht's incomplete definition; it must be deduced from the reference context and the selection criteria of the experiment he used to design FP.

Therefore, it becomes essential to clarify the interpretation of FP in relation to traditional metrology and in relation to its initial application in Albrecht's empirical model.

The analysis of Albrecht's intentions (i.e. his implicit measurement model) and of the reference system he used to specify the structure and the parameters of FP must therefore serve as a basis for an interpretation of his initial definition, from the perspective of a measurement system in the metrology sense.

It is important to properly understand the reference context in which a function type is developed. If the composition of the reference context is known, it is then possible:

- to analyze it, and
- to define new contexts in terms of the reference context.

This is what allows a reference function type to be moved from one context to another.

8.6.3 Function Points Relational System

To identify and analyze the domain of the relations in FP, it is necessary to go back to its original sources.

> The empirical model of FP, including the procedures and weights, can be traced back to Albrecht's development environment and to his criteria for selecting the projects to be measured, as described in his initial 1979 paper.

Albrecht's 1979 paper describes:

- his global context of measurement (Table 8.11), as well as
- the criteria for selecting projects to be measured—Table 8.12.

TABLE 8.11. Albrecht 1979—Description of the Initial Reference Context

- The organization includes 450 people who develop applications.
- Development is under contract to clients of IBM.
- The developers and the clients are dispersed throughout the US.
- At any time, between 150 and 170 contracts are open.
- An average contract involves two or three people.
- Each contract is made in the context of a specific development framework.
- The majority of the contracts are limited to certain phases of the methodology.
- Based on their experience, the design phase accounts for 20% of the work hours, the implementation for 80%.
- It is necessary to measure the whole process, including the design and the costs incurred during the design.
- The projects were completed between mid-1974 and the start of 1979.
- The size of the projects varies from 500 to 105,000 hours of work.
- Of about 1500 contracts for the period, only 22 met the selection criteria.

TABLE 8.12. Albrecht 1979—Selection Criteria for Admissible Projects

1	The project must have passed through all phases of the methodology (from definition of requirements to implementation) and must have been delivered to the client.
2	The whole project must have been properly managed with consistent definitions of the tasks and the processes of management.
3	All the hours of work put in by IBM and by the client must be known and must have been carefully measured.
4	The functional factors must be known.

This paper therefore documented, and defined, the reference context in which, and for which, FP had been built.

The analysis of this initial reference context allows us to clarify the domain of the mapping of the initial empirical model which formed the starting point for the rules and procedures: Albrecht derived his measurement space (i.e. model of relationships) using the criteria enumerated in Tables 8.11 and 8.12.

It is also important to note that this set of criteria defined a stable and relatively homogeneous set of development conditions (i.e. his experimental design), thus explicitly limiting the number of outside influences on the development process as much as on the software products analyzed.

Now, if we examine this system of relations in which FP was defined, it becomes obvious that the notion of effort (or productivity) has been present from the beginning with the introduction of weights, which were set by "debate and trial."

Albrecht defined:

- an initial *reference context* as part of the process that led to his selecting 22 observations to measure from among the 1,500 observations available to him during this period—Table 8.11;
- *selection criteria* based on how much information was available to describe the effort required for the complete development cycle for the selected projects—Table 8.12.

We may observe, therefore, that his selection of projects depended (for the selection of weights) on a productivity model based on knowledge of

- a complete and homogeneous development process—Table 8.11, and
- all the efforts required to complete a full development cycle—Table 8.12.

The quality of this system of relations can be deduced from the analytical methodology used by Albrecht [1979 and 1983] to study the relation between effort and Function Points in his own reference context (i.e. his empirical design).

TABLE 8.13. Empirical Relation between FP and Effort in Albrecht's Dataset

Dependent Variable	Independent variable	Comment	R^2
Effort	Adjusted FP	All 22 projects in the 1979 paper (* 24 projects in the 1983 paper)	0.869
Effort	Adjusted FP	Excluding the 3 largest projects [Knaff and Sacks 1986]	0.42

Albrecht used the statistical technique of linear regression to build his productivity model, quantifying the relationship between the dependent variable (effort) and the independent variable (functional size in Function Points). He obtained a linear model with a fairly high coefficient of determination of R^2 of 0.869 (the maximum of an R^2 being 1.0).

Influence of Outliers in Regression Models

[Knaff and Sacks 1986] and [MacDonell 1991] have pointed out that Albrecht's dataset contained three projects which were much larger than the others, and that these three projects served as anchor points in the statistical regression (these three points should then be considered as outliers and excluded from further analysis).

When these three outlier projects are excluded from the building of the regression model, the value of the coefficient of determination (R^2) falls to 0.42 for the other nineteen projects in Albrecht's sample.

8.6.4 An Interpretation of a Function Point

To gain insight into the initial FP structure, it is necessary to distinguish between various concepts, such as the measurement of size, the measurement of effort, and the measurement of the general relation between them, expressed in the form of implicit or explicit productivity models.

In terms of the analysis of the initial reference context described in the previous section and the implicit system of relations, if the context is to be changed, the transformation must be a linear one. It is therefore desirable to revise the initial definition of a Function Point and make it more precise, using the following interpretation:

Interpretation of a Function Point

Function Points constitute a system of relations between:

- **the measurement of a "reference function type", and**
- **the measurement of the effort in the initial reference context established by Albrecht.**

Unfortunately, the term "reference function type" is not explicit in Albrecht's work. It is implicit only, and it has to be inferred from:

- the rules for identifying functions, and
- the rules for identifying and counting the elementary components of these functions.

The implicit system of relations between the measured value of a reference function type and the measured value of the effort is based on weights, as well as on Albrecht's algorithm for assigning them, i.e. the system of implicit relations that would justify—should such justification be properly documented—the scale-type transformations included in the algorithm and the weights.

ISO 14143-1 requires that functional size in an ISO-recognized measurement method not be related to effort.

The above interpretation of a Function Point challenges the assumption that FP meets this mandatory requirement of ISO 14143-1.

8.7. OTHER RESEARCH FINDINGS

8.7.1   What if the FP Weights were Dropped?

We have seen in the previous sections the numerous problems underlying the introduction of weights into FP. It leads, in particular, to a potpourri of scale types with inadmissible mathematical transformations.

What would happen, then, if these weights were dropped from this measurement design? Would it still be possible to obtain a reasonably good productivity (and estimation) model using only the base components of the Function Points measurement method?

This specific issue was explored with an industrial dataset in Abran & Robillard [1996]. Various subsidiary questions were also addressed, for example:

- Is the conventional FP model (i.e. its five types of functions, all combined) better than the sub-models, where the functions are taken individually or combined in a different way?
- How relevant and useful are the weights?
- How relevant and useful are the algorithms?
- Do any of the steps lower the quality of the relation between size and effort?

The key findings from the empirical research with this industrial dataset can be summarized as follows: productivity models built using only the base components (i.e. DET, RET, FTR, and various combinations of these components) are as good as models built with the full FP design (with weights and algorithms).

The corollary of this key finding is: the weights and algorithms do not contribute much to the quality of the productivity models built with this dataset.

Said differently, these weights and algorithms could be considered as "feel good" artifices. The fact that they are included within a measurement method leads the practitioners to *believe* that many details have been duly and adequately taken into account in the analysis of the effort relationship.

- However, since the mathematical structure that handles these artifices is improper, none of these weights and algorithms brings a significant contribution to the effort relationship.
- Therefore, these artifices give practitioners a false sense of security, even though they "feel good" about them.

These Findings on Weights are also Important to Researchers

Attempting to improve the *set of weights or the algorithms* does not address the fundamental issues of the design of measurement methods based on a design including such exogenous factors and weights.

8.7.2 What if the Value Adjustment Factor is Dropped?

We have seen, in section 8.4.5, the numerous mathematical issues hampering the correct treatment of the 14 GSC of Function Points. What happens when these 14 GSC of Function Points are dropped in the construction of productivity models?

A number of researchers have investigated this issue by building estimation models with both AFP and UFP:

- Findings from these empirical studies lead to the conclusion that models built *without* the 14 GSC of Function Points *are as good as those taking them into account.*
- Said differently, the VAF built from the 14 GSC are "feel good" artifices that lead practitioners to *believe* that many cost factors have been taken into account in the analysis of effort relationships. Since the mathematical structure that handles these artifices is improper, none of these brings a significant contribution to those relationships.

In summary, the GSC artifices give practitioners a false sense of security that so many factors have indeed been taken into account.

> **These Findings on GSC are also Important to Researchers**
>
> Attempting to improve the set of 14 GSC of Function Points is not addressing the fundamental issues associated with measurement methods in which such exogenous factors are used in their design.

ADVANCED READINGS: EVOLUTION OF FUNCTIONAL SIZE MEASUREMENT

> **Audience**
>
> This Advanced Reading section is of most interest to the readers interested in learning how industry tackled a context with a large number of variants of measures of functional size and how industry managed to develop a consensus on the necessary criteria and the recognition as international standards for the FSM methods that met such criteria.

Evolution Channels

The size of the software to be developed is well recognized as the key independent variable in software productivity and estimation models.

The origin of the measurement of the functional size of software is credited to Allan Albrecht, who, in 1979, proposed Function Points—the first software measurement method not bound to take into account the technology incorporated in the software; it is based only on what the users of a software application can see from the outside [Albrecht 1979].

Since then, the FP measurement method has evolved through two main channels:

- Within IFPUG, which set up its own Counting Practices Manual to document the measurement rules and to provide examples.
- Outside the IFPUG organization, through:
  - Various *individual* practitioners and researchers who published their findings and improvements to FP in the form of variants at conferences and in academic journals, and
  - *Groups* of experts in FSM who jointly developed and supported complementary adaptations of the FP measurement method (such as in the UK and The Netherlands).

ISO Strategy for the Standardization of Functional Size Measurement

In the mid-90s, FP was proposed for international standardization. What happened?

The national representatives at the ISO (supported by their respective FSM experts):

- agreed on the expected benefits of FSM—and standardization at the ISO level.
- did not agree that FP was the only solution.
- agreed on the setting up of criteria for controlling the quality of FSM methods.
- agreed to recognize multiple measurements methods, providing that they met ISO criteria.

Through these actions, they facilitated:

- the progressive recognition as ISO standards of those measurement methods with sufficient documented strengths.
- the emergence, and official recognition, of a second generation of an FSM method (COSMIC—ISO 19761—see Chapters 11 and 12).
- the integration of FSM into the software engineering standards infrastructure (assessment models and frameworks, plus individual standards related to management and measurement) to ensure that the technology fit did materialize (for example, through ISO 9001 and ISO 90003).

This should result in increasing awareness of functional size standards not only on the part of software people, but also by all levels of management in software-intensive organizations.

ISO Meta-Standard on Functional Size Measurement

The software engineering community worked through the ISO process to establish generic guidelines, both for FSM and for approving specific methods. The ISO suite of documents on this topic is referred to as the 14143 Series, and it includes six documents [ISO 14143].

The aim of the ISO 14143 Series is to provide an internationally accepted set of meta-standards to describe the concept and practices of FSM methods. It is important to stress that this first set of standards does not define a specific FSM method, but rather the characteristics that any method must have before it can be properly referred to as an ISO-recognized FSM method.

ISO 14143-1 defines the *functional size* of software as the size "*derived by quantifying the functional user requirements.*" Also specified in this ISO standard is the fact that the "*functional user requirements*" (FUR) represent:

- "user practices and procedures that the software must perform to fulfil the user's needs.
- exclude quality requirements and any technical requirements."

FSM methods based on FUR can be used at any phase of the software life cycle. At the end of the development phase, for example, functional sizes can be used to derive productivity ratios and to develop estimation models.

When used at the beginning of the life cycle phase, at the requirements phase, for example, the measurement results can be used in estimation models to forecast software project effort. The software size information can then provide valuable information for requirements control, project estimation, and project productivity analyses.

ISO Standards on Specific Functional Size Measurement Methods
Even though a large number of variants of the FPA method have been proposed over the years to tackle various weaknesses in the design of the original FP method, only five have achieved recognition as ISO measurement standards:.

- ISO 19761: COSMIC—Common Software Measurement International Consortium
- ISO 20926: Function Point Analysis (e.g. IFPUG 4.1, UFP only);
- ISO 20968: Mk II.
- ISO 24570: NESMA (A Dutch interpretation of FPA v. 4.1 which produces similar results).
- ISO 29881: FISMA (Finnish Software Measurement Association)

Four methods (IFPUG, originating in the US, the MkII FPA method from the UK, the NESMA method from The Netherlands, and the FISMA method from Finland) have been approved by the ISO.

These four first-generation FSM were all designed 15 to 25 years ago to work for business application software. They are used in that domain for performance measurement, estimating, and benchmarking, as well as in outsourced software contracts to control scope and price/performance.

Developers of other types of software have had to use counts of Source Lines of Code (SLOC) as their size measure. But, as this size is only known accurately after the software is complete, it is difficult to use it for estimation. Moreover, being technology-dependent, SLOC counts are difficult to use for performance comparisons, especially across multiple technologies.

To meet these challenges, the second generation of the COSMIC method was designed from the outset to measure the functional size of real-time, multi-layered software, such as used in telecommunications, process control, and operating systems, as well as business application software, all on the same measurement scale.

The COSMIC method has been extensively tested and its use is increasing, especially in the real-time and telecommunications worlds. Having been developed in the last few years, the COSMIC method is compatible with modern specification methods such as UML, and with OO techniques.

This newer COSMIC method of sizing the functional requirements of software was approved as an International Standard [ISO/IEC 19761] in 2003.

The ISO/IEC 19761:2003 standard for COSMIC-FFP can be purchased directly online from the ISO at www.iso.ch. The COSMIC group's "Measurement Manual for the Implementation Guide for ISO 19761" can be downloaded free of charge from: www.cosmicon.com/portal/dl.asp

The evolution of FSM is outlined in Figure 8.4.

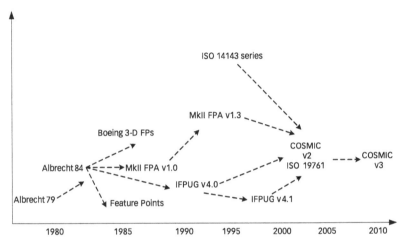

Figure 8.4. Evolution of FSM Measurement Methods from 1980 to 2000

EXERCISES

1. The design of Function Points is similar in some ways to that of other software measures. Which ones? What are the similarities? What are the differences?

2. The design of Function Points has influenced the design of subsequent software measures. Identify some of these and discuss their relative merits.

3. Is Function Points a base or a derived measure? Explain your answer.

4. What was innovative in the initial design of Function Points?

5. What are the scale types used in the steps required for assigning a number to the data files in Function Points?

6. What are the scale types used in the steps required for assigning a number to the 14 Value Adjustment Factors in Function Points?

7. What is the measurement unit in Function Points?

8. What does the term "Function Point" mean?

9. Design a measurement procedure to obtain 1 Function Point.

10. How is complexity defined in Function Points? Does Function Points really measure complexity?

11. What single attribute is measured by this one measurement method?

12. If Function Points measure more that one attribute, what is the contribution of each to the measurement result? Can you identify such a contribution of each attribute?

13. Was Function Points designed without reference to effort?

14. What is the impact of including the 14 General System Characteristics in productivity and estimation models?

15. What institutional support is there for the Function Points measurement method?

16. In the Function Points measurement method, there is a claim that it can measure all types of software. Discuss this claim.

TERM ASSIGNMENTS

1. Identify and document the functional specifications for the automation of the measurement of Function Points.

2. Can you extract Function Points from lines of code? Illustrate your answer with a specific programming language.

3. Take the same software implemented in a specific environment, and, with three of your classmates, independently measure the Function Points of this software. Next, compute the differences in measurement results across measurers at the total Function Points level and at the detailed level for each function measured. Discuss findings and compare the error rates. Explain the differences. Is the difference at the total level meaningful?

4. There are now five ISO standards on functional size measurement. Why is this so? Discuss.

5. What are the key differences across the five ISO standards for the measurement of the functional size of software?

6. A number of weaknesses in Function Points have been documented in the literature. Identify and document your findings.

7. Take two of the weaknesses of Function Points identified in your literature survey and discuss why the solutions proposed by the researchers have not been implemented in the later official version of Function Points.

9

USE CASE POINTS: ANALYSIS OF THEIR DESIGN[1]

This chapter covers:

- An overview of the Use Case Points (UCP) method: its origins and initial design.
- An analysis of the design of the UCP, including the entities and attributes measured, the scale types and measurement units.
- Related work on the UCP relationships with development effort.

9.1. INTRODUCTION

With the increase in the popularity of development methodologies based on use cases (e.g. UML, Agile, RUP) has come a concomitant interest in effort estimation based on Use Case Points (UCP). The UCP sizing method was initially designed by Gustav Karner [1993] of the company Objectory AB in 1993. UCP is an adaptation of FP for measuring the size of projects, the functional requirements specifications of which are described by a use-case model.

[1]See also: Joost Ouwerkerk and Alain Abran, "Evaluation of the Design of Use Case Points (UCP)," MENSURA2006, Cadiz, Spain, Nov. 4–5, 2006, Editor: University of Cádiz Press www.uca.es/publicaciones, pp. 83–97.

To evaluate the usefulness and validity of UCP sizing, this chapter presents an analysis of the design of the UCP measurement method, looking into [Ouwerkerk and Abran 2006]:

- the explicit and implicit principles of the UCP method,
- the correspondence between its measurements and empirical reality, and
- the consistency of its system of points and weights.

This chapter is organized as follows:

- Section 9.2 presents a description of the Use Case Points (UCP) method.
- Section 9.3 presents an analysis of the UCP design.
- Section 9.4 presents a survey of the relationships of UCP with project effort.

9.2. USE CASE POINTS DESCRIPTION

9.2.1 Origins

The use-case approach was developed by Ivar Jacobson [1987] while at Ericsson in the 1960s. A use case is a simple but flexible technique for capturing the requirements of a software system. Each use case is composed of a number of *scenarios*, written in an informal manner in the language of the business domain to describe the interactions between the actors and a system.

In 1993, Gustav Karner proposed the UCP measurement method, an adaptation of Function Points, to measure the size of software developed with the use-case approach. This method was aimed at measuring software functional size as early as possible in the development cycle [Karner 1993].

9.2.2 Initial Design of UCP

The initial design of UCP takes three aspects of a software project into account:

1) Use cases,
2) Technical qualities, and
3) Development resources.

9.2.2.1 *Unadjusted Use Case Points—UUCP.* Use Cases are represented by a number of *Unadjusted* Use Case Points (UUCP). Each actor and each use case is classified at a complexity level (simple, average, or complex) and assigned a corresponding weight (from one to three points for the actors, and from 5 to 15 for the use cases).

9.2.2.2 *Technical Qualities.* The technical qualities of UCP are represented by a Technical Complexity Factor (TCF), which consists of 13 technical qualities, each with a specific weight, combined into a single factor. To calculate the TCF, an expert must assess the relevance to the project of each technical quality, evaluated on a scale from zero to five (where zero is "not applicable" and five is "essential").

The weights are *balanced* in such a way that a relevant factor of three for each quality will produce a TCF equal to one.

The TCF is thus the sum of all the relevant factors (one for each technical quality) multiplied by their corresponding weights plus two constants, C2 (0.1) and C1 (0.6):

Karner based his design for these weights on the constants and weights of the 1979 FP Value Adjustment Factors [Albrecht 1979].

9.2.2.3 *Development Resources.* The development resources for UCP are represented by the Environment Factors (EF), also referred to as experience factors [Carroll 2005]. The UCP model identifies eight such factors contributing to the effectiveness of the development team.

- To calculate the EF, an expert must assess the importance of each factor and classify it on a scale from zero to five (zero meaning "very weak;" five meaning "very strong").
- The selection of the weights is balanced such that a value of 3 for each factor will produce an EF of one.

The EF is the sum of all the factors multiplied by their weights and two constants, C2 (0.03) and C1 (1.4).

9.2.2.4 *Total UCP Size.* The final size in terms of the number of UCP is the product of these three components:

$$\text{Total UCP size} = \text{UUCP} \times \text{TCTP} \times \text{EF}.$$

For estimation purposes, the number of UCP is combined with a productivity constant (referred to as Mean Resources—MR) representing the ratio of man-hours per UCP.

Karner proposed that each organization require its own productivity constant. The MR constant for the Objectory projects described in Karner's paper was approximately 20.

9.3. ANALYSIS OF THE UCP DESIGN

9.3.1 The Measurand: The Entities and the Attributes Measured

UCP is aimed at measuring the functional size of a software system described by a functional requirement specification written in use-case form.

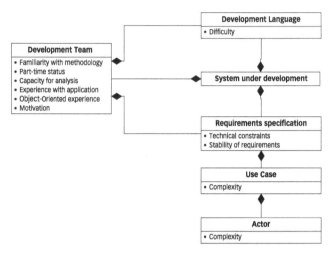

Figure 9.1. The five types of entities and eleven types of attributes measured in UCP

However, the UCP design includes a measurement of five distinct types of entities:

- Actor
- Use case
- Specification of requirements (functional and non functional)
- Development team (a project-related entity)
- Programming language (a project-related entity)

For this set of entities, eleven different types of attributes are taken into account and measured by the UCP method described in [Carroll 2005]—see Figure 9.1 and Table 9.1.

9.3.2 Analysis of the Numerical World: Scale Type and Units

9.3.2.1 Issues in Scale Types. These eleven types of attributes are quantified using a variety of scale types, and then they are combined. This section analyzes some of these scale-type manipulations and identifies corresponding measurement issues.

The "complexity" attribute, assigned to actors and use cases, is at the core of UCP (collectively defined as the UUCP factor). This complexity is categorized as being of the *ordinal scale type* using a scale of three values: simple, average, and complex:

- Thus an actor categorized by the measurer as "simple" is considered less complex than an "average" actor, and an average actor less complex than a "complex" actor.

TABLE 9.1. Entities, Attributes, and Measurement Rules

Entity	Attribute	Measurement Rule
Actor	Complexity (of actor)	The type of complexity (simple, average, or complex) of the interaction between the actor and the system
Use case	Complexity (of use case)	The type of complexity (simple, average, or complex) measured in the number of transactions
Specification of requirements	Relevance of the technical quality requirements	The level of relevance (from 0 to 5) of each of the 13 known non-functional qualities
	Stability of the requirements	The level of stability (from 0 to 5) of the functional and non-functional requirements
Development team	Familiarity with the methodology	The level (from 0 to 5) of skills and knowledge of the development methodology in use for the project
	Part-time status	The level (from 0 to 5) of part-time staff on the team
	Analysis capability	The level (from 0 to 5) of analysis capabilities of the development team with respect to project needs
	Application experience	The level (from 0 to 5) of team experience with the application domain of the system
	Object-oriented experience	The level (from 0 to 5) of team experience with object-oriented design
	Motivation	The level (from 0 to 5) of team motivation
Programming language	Difficulty	The level (from 0 to 5) of programming difficulty

- The scale is similar for use cases: the same category labels are used (simple, average, and complex),
- However, it cannot be assumed that the categories and the categorization process are similar, since different entity types are involved.

The technical and resource factors are also all evaluated through a categorization process with integers from 0 to 5 (0, 1, 2, 3, 4, or 5):

It must be noted that these numbers do not represent numerical values on a ratio scale, but merely a category on *an ordinal scale type*, that is, **they are merely ordered labels and not numbers**.

Measurement of a Programming Language

A programming language assigned a difficulty level of 1:

- is considered to be less difficult for the development team than a programming language of difficulty level 2,
- but cannot be considered to be exactly one unit less difficult than one categorized as having a difficulty level of 2, because these levels are being measured on an ordinal scale.

In fact, there is no justification provided in the description of the UCP model to support a ratio scale. For example, there is nothing in the UCP design that allows room to consider that a programming language of factor 4 is twice as difficult as a programming language of factor 2.

Levels in the Quantification of the Attribute

In the UCP design, each label for a level—see Table 9.1—might represent a different interval, and each interval may not be, and does not need to be, regular within an attribute being measured.

See, for instance, the measurement rules for the Value Adjustment Factor of Function Points in Chapter 8, Section 8.4.5.

It should be noted that Karner had indicated that the EF constants and weights were preliminary and estimated. That said, more recent sources, like [Carroll 2005], have not revisited this issue and have integrated the same values without modification into their own measurement models of UCP variants.

9.3.2.2 *Issues in Measurement Units.*
In measurement, each distinct type of attribute should have its corresponding measurement unit. This is not the case with UCP, where each type of attribute is assigned some "points" of an unspecified nature and for which the measurement unit is not described.

The UCP measurement process clearly includes a mix of several entities (actors, use cases, requirements, team, programming language) for which distinct attributes are quantified and then combined:

- It is obvious that the end-result cannot be expressed solely in terms of use cases.

• The resulting units of measurement (i.e. UCP points) are of an unknown and unspecified nature, despite the UCP label.

9.3.3   Issues in the Measurement Method

Without a detailed measurement method for identifying the entities and attributes to be measured, the UCP measurement process lacks strict repeatability, or even reproducibility. One measurer (beginner or expert) can easily evaluate a factor differently from another measurer.

9.3.3.1 Use Cases. For instance, the fairly flexible definition of a use case poses an important problem for the measurement of UCP [Smith 1999]. The way in which a use case is written is not standardized: a use case can be identified and documented at any level of granularity.

• The UCP method does not take this into account and does not describe any means to ensure the consistency of granularity from one use case to another.
• The impact is the following: quantities as the outcome of UCP are not necessarily comparable, and a poor basis for benchmarking and estimation.

This raise a number of consistency questions with respect to the inputs to the measurement process, such as:

• What is an elementary use case?
• How can the level of granularity of a particular use case even be characterized?
• Are use cases being characterized in a consistent manner by one or more analysts working on the same project, and across projects?

Improved measurement using the UCP method will therefore directly and strongly depend on a degree of uniformity in the writing of use cases from one project to another.

9.3.3.2 Technical and Resource Factors. Both the technical factors and the resources are evaluated qualitatively by a measurer.

9.3.3.3 Technical Qualities. The UCP model does not propose any criteria for measuring the attribute values of technical qualities. The result is a subjective interpretation by a measurer. To address the same kind of arbitrary assignment of values in the "technical adjustment factors" of the FP model, the IFPUG organization worked out detailed evaluation criteria for each of the non functional characteristics of the system and documented these in its Counting Practices Manual.

9.3.3.4 Resource Factors. The UCP model does not propose any criteria for measuring resource factors. Once again, this measurement is a subjective interpretation by a measurer.

The UCP method does not prescribe any rule for assigning a value to, for example, the level of familiarity with a methodology.

9.3.4 Relations between the Empirical and Numerical Worlds

The principle of homomorphism requires that the integrity of attribute ratios and relationships be maintained when translating from the empirical model to the numerical model.

9.3.4.1 Actor Complexity. The measurement procedure for assigning a value to the complexity attributes of actors and use cases is based on categorization rules.

Quantifying an Actor

If an actor acted on the system by means of a graphical user interface, then the value assigned to it is labeled "complex"; as explained in the previous section, this value is on an ordinal scale.

If we accept that an application programming interface (API) represents less functionality than a command-line interface, which in turn represents less functionality than a graphical user interface, then it can be said that the categorization of the actors by their type of interface constitutes a valid correspondence.

But if, after assigning a weight of 1, 2, or 3 to the actor types, the model then uses these ordered values in sums and products, it is effectively making a translation from an ordinal scale (complexity categories) to a ratio scale (UCP weights) without justification, which is not a mathematically valid operation.

Furthermore, there are no documented data to demonstrate that a graphical user interface represents three times more "functionality" than an application programming interface.

9.3.4.2 Use-Case Complexity. For use-case entities, the measurement process for assigning a value comes:

- first, from counting the number of transactions or the number of analysis classes,
- and then looking up the correspondence rules in a two-dimensional table (transactions and analysis classes) to assign a corresponding ordered label of an ordinal-type scale.

Thus, if a use case contains four (4) transactions, it is assigned the category label "simple."

The UCP model transforms the measurements of use-case complexity from a ratio-type scale (the number of transactions or classes of analysis) into an ordinal-type scale (complexity categories), and then moves it up to a ratio-type scale (UCP weights).

The arbitrary assignment of the weights (5 for simple, 10 for average, and 15 for complex) could have been avoided if the number of transactions or classes of analysis had been kept as numbers on a ratio-type scale (rather than losing this quantitative precision by mapping them to only three ordered categories with arbitrarily assigned values of 5, 10, and 15).

Both the constants and weights of UCP's technical quality calculation (TCF) are derived directly from the Albrecht's FP model—See Chapter 8 for a discussion on the related weaknesses in Function Points.

9.3.5   Inadmissible Numerical Operations

The formula to calculate the number of UCP is as follows:

$$\textbf{UCP} = \textbf{UUCP} * \textbf{TCF} * \textbf{EF}$$

More specifically, for UCP, the final UUCP value is calculated by multiplying the number of use cases and actors of each type of complexity by their weights.

- In doing so, the ordinal-scale values (categories of complexity) are transformed into interval-scale values.
- These values on an interval-scale type are next multiplied, resulting in a value on a ratio scale, another algebraically inadmissible mathematical operation.

This analysis applies equally to TCF and EF factor calculations, which, in addition to the transformations of ordinal-type scale into interval-type scale (confounding numerical values with the ordering of categories by numerical label), also introduce multiplications with ratio-scale constants. The same error in the FP measurement method was described in chapter 8, the origin of the EF and TCF calculations.

It was further pointed out in chapter 8 that the interaction between the technical factors would have been better accounted for by multiplying the factors together, rather than adding them. This analysis also applies for the EF factors.

In summary, TCF has inherited most of the defects of FP, and in some cases has compounded them by adding more inadmissible mathematical operations.

The UCP measurement method assigns numbers to several entities (actors, use cases, requirements, etc.) and attributes (complexity, difficulty, etc.). Combining many concepts at once, as this method does, makes it a challenge to figure out what the end-result is from a measurement perspective.

- The impact of this is that the end-result is of an unknown and unspecified entity type; that is, what has been measured is not known.
- The UCP measurement method is based on the constants and weights of Albrecht's FP Value Adjustment Factors without supporting justification.
- The evaluation of attributes is performed by a measurer without criteria or a guide to interpretation—a five for one measurer could be a two for another. This could result in very poor repeatability and reproducibility.
- UCP method calculations are based on several algebraically inadmissible scale type transformations. It is unfortunate that this has not yet been challenged, either by UCP users or the designers of subsequent UCP variants.

The measurement of functional size using use cases (therefore, very early in the development life cycle) constitutes an interesting opportunity for an industry which is increasingly using RUP and Agile use-case-oriented methodologies. Unfortunately, the UCP method suggested by Karner appears fundamentally defective: by adopting the basic structure of FP, UCP has—from a measurement perspective—inherited most of its structural defects.

9.4. THE MODELING OF RELATIONSHIPS OF UCP WITH PROJECT EFFORT

The adoption of Use Case Points for estimation purposes has been discussed in a number of publications. This section reports on three studies on the use of variants of UCP to analyze the relationship between UCP and project effort.

9.4.1 Nageswaran [2001]

On the basis of a single case study, [Nageswaran 2001] reports that the UCP method can be more reliable than an estimation model with Function Points to predict testing effort.

The approach described in [Nageswaran 2001] is a variant of Karner's, proposing:

- nine technical qualities (instead of thirteen) associated with testing activities (for example, test tools and test environment), and
- ignoring the development resource factors (EF).

For the single project studied, the effort estimated by the UCP method was reported to be only 6% lower than the actual effort.

The author himself stresses that this "*estimation technique is not claimed to be rigorous.*" Of course, this single case study lacks generalization power.

9.4.2 Mohagheghi [2005]

The adapted UCP method described in [Mohagheghi 2005] suggests that iterative projects need special rules to account for the ongoing re-estimation of changing requirements during the course of a project.

Realizing that an organization's resources are more or less constant, the adapted method replaces the resource factor (EF) by a simple increase in the productivity constant (MR).

In this variant of the UCP method, another dimension, the overhead factor, is introduced: the overhead factor (OF) represents the effort of project management and other activities not directly related to functionality.

For the two projects presented in [Mohagheghi 2005], the efforts estimated by UCP were 21% and 17% lower than the actual effort. Again, this study refers to only two projects and lacks generalization power.

9.4.3 Carroll [2005]

The method used in [Carroll 2005] is, in essence, the same as Karner's, but with the addition of a new "risk coefficient", specific to each project, to account for risk factors not already covered by the basic model (for instance, "reuse effort").

The risk coefficient is a simple percentage of effort added according to the opinion of an estimation expert.

The method described in the [Carroll 2005] study was reportedly used with over 200 projects over a 5-year period, and produced an average deviation of less than 9% between estimated effort (using the UCP method) and recorded effort.

However, no information is provided about:

- the dispersion across this average,
- the statistical technique used to build the estimation model, or
- the classical quality criteria of estimation models such as the coefficient of determination (R^2) and Mean Relative Error.

In brief, no documented details are given to support the claim about the accuracy of the estimates.

9.5. SUMMARY

The UCP measurement method itself was modified in the three studies surveyed.

- Care must be exercised when comparing data from these three method variants, since no information about convertibility back to the original UCP is provided.

- The empirical information given in these three studies cannot be generalized to a larger context due to either the very small sample (one or two case studies) or lack of supporting evidence.

There have been claims for the relevance of UCP for estimation purposes, but with very limited empirical support. Even when empirical support is claimed, it is based either on UCP variants and anecdotal support or on undocumented evidence.

The idea of measuring size and estimating effort with use cases remains attractive, and Karner's method is a first step towards that objective. That said, the lessons learned through this investigation of the UCP design clearly indicate that:

- On the one hand, significant improvements to UCP design are required to build a stronger foundation for valuable measurement;
- On the other hand, much more robust and documented empirical evidence is required to demonstrate the usefulness of UCP for estimation purposes.

EXERCISES

1. What is the measurand in Use Case Points?

2. What is the attribute measured in Use Case Points?

3. Is Use Case Points a base or a derived measure?

4. What is the measurement unit of a Use Case Point?

5. How is a single Use Case Point defined?

6. How do you ensure accuracy, repeatability, and reproducibility in the measurement of Use Cases?

7. How is complexity defined in Use Case Points?

8. What is the contribution of "complexity" to the numerical rules for Use Case Points?

9. With respect to conventional Function Points, what has been correctly improved in the design of Use Case Points?

10. In Use Case Points, what is the real impact of all the other "entities" and "attributes" added to conventional Function Points?

11. What is the documented and independently verified evidence that the use of Use Case Points contributes to better estimation models?

TERM ASSIGNMENTS

1. A number of fairly recent papers have proposed improvements to design of Use Case Points. Identify some of these from the literature and discuss the empirical evidence supporting the proposed improvements.

2. A number of fairly recent papers on the usefulness of estimation models built with Use Case Points have been published. Identify and discuss the quality of the empirical evidence supporting the proposed improvements to estimation models built with Use Case Points.

3. Can Use Case Points be approved as an ISO functional size measurement standard? Discuss.

10

ISO 9126[1]: ANALYSIS OF QUALITY MODELS AND MEASURES

This chapter covers an analysis of ISO 9126 from multiple perspectives:

- The analysis models in ISO 9126 as standard reference models.
- The metrology related part of ISO 9126: the base and derived measures.
- Analysis of the designs of the measurement of Effectiveness in ISO 9126.
- The missing links from Metrology to the Analysis Models.
- Advanced Readings 1: Analysis of the design of the Productivity measure in ISO 9126.
- Advanced Readings 2: Measurement issues associated with the attributes and related base measures in ISO 9126.

10.1. INTRODUCTION TO ISO 9126

In 1991, the ISO published its first international consensus on the terminology for the quality characteristics for software product evaluation: ISO 9126—*Software Product Evaluation—Quality Characteristics and Guidelines for their Use.* From

---

[1]See also: Alain Abran, Rafa A1 Qutaish, and Juan Cuadrado-Gallego, "Investigation of the Metrology Concepts within ISO 9126 on Software Product Quality Evaluation," 10th WSEAS International Conference on Computers, Athens, Greece, July 13–15, 2006, pp. 864–872.

Software Metrics and Software Metrology, by Alain Abran
Copyright © 2010 IEEE Computer Society

2001 to 2004, the ISO published an expanded four-part version, containing both the ISO quality models and inventories of proposed measures for these models.

These ISO 9126 quality models provide by far the most comprehensive coverage in software engineering on software quality:

- Both national and international standards experts have invested a great deal of energy over the past two decades to improve them, and are still working to improve them further.
- These ISO quality models are considerably more detailed than the quality models proposed since the 1980s by individual authors.

The current version of the ISO 9126 series consists of:

- one International Standard (ISO 9126 Part 1) which documents the structure of the ISO quality models for software products, and
- three Technical Reports (ISO TR 9126 Parts 2 to 4):
  - Part **2** proposes a list of derived measures of **external** software quality.
  - Part **3** proposes a list of derived measures of **internal** software quality.
  - Part **4** proposes a list of derived measures for the **quality in use** model.

This is complemented by a set of guides in the ISO 14598 series:

- Developers Guide
- Evaluators Guide
- Evaluation Modules, etc.

The ISO 9126 quality models are also gradually penetrating software organizations in a number of countries. That said, practitioners and researchers alike still encounter major difficulties in the use and exploitation of these quality models, and the ISO itself is putting a great deal of effort into further improvements.

- For instance, within the next two to three years, the ISO expects to issue a major update of this series, which will be relabeled the ISO 25000 series on software product quality.

The analyses presented in this chapter can be useful to both practitioners and researchers:

- For analyzing the foundations of the measures proposed to them.
- For designing the measures themselves, when required, but avoiding the pitfalls inherent in a number of them, including the ISO models.

This chapter is organized as follows:

- Section 10.2 presents the analysis models of ISO 9126.
- Section 10.3 presents the metrology part: base and derived measures.
- Section 10.4 present an analysis of some of the design of the measurement of "Effectiveness" in ISO 9126-4.
- Section 10.5 identifies some of the missing links between the measures and the quality models.
- Section 10.6 identifies an improvement strategy.
- The Advanced Readings 1 section presents an analysis of the design of the Productivity measure in ISO 9126-4.
- The Advanced Readings 2 section presents an illustration of measurement design issues identified in the analysis of the attributes and base measures in ISO 9126.

10.2. ANALYSIS MODELS OF ISO 9126: THE (QUANTITATIVE) MODELS

10.2.1 The Standard Reference Model

The first document in the ISO 9126 series—*Software Product Quality Model*—contains what can be considered as the **ISO Standard Reference Model** for the quality of software products (see also Chapter 4, section 5 and Figures 4.2 and 4.4 for the concept of "standard reference model").

This reference model includes three views of the quality of a software product at the highest level—see Figure 10.1:

- Internal quality of the software
- External quality of the software
- Quality in use of the software

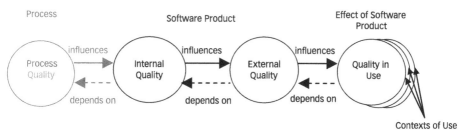

Figure 10.1. Quality in the software lifecycle—ISO 9126-1. This figure was adopted from Figure 2 (p.3) of ISO/IEC 9126-1:2001(E). This figure is not to be considered an official ISO figure nor was it authorized by ISO. Copies of ISO/IEC 9126-1:2001(E) can be purchased from ANSI at http://webstore.ansi.org.

Next, ISO 9126-1 presents two structures of quality models for software product quality:

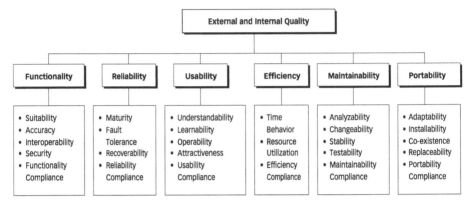

Figure 10.2. Quality model for External and Internal Quality: characteristics and sub-characteristics—ISO 9126-1. This figure was adopted from Figure 4 (p.7) of ISO/IEC 9126-1:2001(E). This figure is not to be considered an official ISO figure nor was it authorized by ISO. Copies of ISO/IEC 9126-1:2001(E) can be purchased from ANSI at http://webstore.ansi.org.

- a 1st structure for both the internal and external quality models—see Figure 10.2, and
- a 2nd structure for the quality in use model.
- The 1st structure (Figure 10.2) includes six characteristics, subdivided into 27 sub characteristics for internal and external quality.
- The 2nd structure includes four "quality in use" characteristics: effectiveness, productivity, safety, and satisfaction.

It must be noticed that ISO 9126 does not provide any reference values for any of its quality characteristics and sub-characteristics.

10.2.2 An Organizational Reference Context Model: Interpretation of ISO 9126 for Evaluation & Decision Making

For the application of the ISO quality models to specific software within an organization, an Organizational Reference Context would typically be set up and used. How to do this is described in the ISO 14598 series, from various perspectives (developers, third party, etc.).

The application of this analysis model (which corresponds to evaluation and decision making on the basis of decision criteria in ISO 9126) is usually performed as a four-step quantification process:

1. Identification of quality-related requirements, that is, the selection of the parts of the ISO quality models that are relevant to a particular context of quality evaluation.

2. Identification of the context of interpretation, that is:
   - the selection of reference values, such values being either generic or specific threshold values, or
   - the determination of targets specified for a particular context.

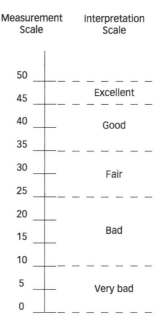

Figure 10.3. Reference values with a measurement scale and an interpretation scale

3. Use of the derived measures from the data preparation phase to fill out the instantiated quality model determined in Step 1.
4. Comparison of the results of Step 3 with either the set of reference values or the targets determined in Step 2 to take a decision based on both the information provided and whatever relevant information is available to the decision maker.

This is illustrated in Figure 10.3, with:

- reference values for the decision criteria (or evaluation criteria) for this **organizational context**
- target values (or an evaluation scale) **for the specific software to be measured**

For the set of relationships over the set of objects of interest for the Information Needs (see ISO 15939 and Chapter 4), the Analysis Model would typically either:

1. quantify a relationship which is well understood, well described over time, and for which there is a large consensus, or
2. attempt to "quantify" a relationship (i.e. a concept) for which it is not yet well known how to capture it within a single measurement dimension and

a single (base or derived) measure (with its corresponding single measurement unit, or set of such units).

While the ISO 9126 quality models are described at a very high level, the relationships across the models, the quality characteristics and sub-characteristics are definitively not well understood and not well described.

Therefore, to use in practice any one of such relationships described textually in ISO 9126 represents an "attempt to quantify" without a prescribed standard or organizational reference context nor empirically verified foundation [Abran *et al.* 2005a, 2005b]. Some of the related issues are described next.

Also, neither of ISO 9126 and ISO 14598 (and the upcoming ISO 25000 series) proposes specific "reference models of analysis" nor an inventory of "organizational reference contexts" with reference values and decision criteria. Each organization has to define its own, thereby limiting possibilities of comparisons industry-specific wide or industry-wide.

10.3. THE METROLOGY-RELATED PART OF ISO 9126: BASE AND DERIVED MEASURES

The implementation of analysis models, including the ones from ISO 9126, has to be based on the data collection of base measures (and derived ones, where relevant).

The measures available for the data collection for the ISO 9126 quality models are proposed and described in the three technical reports in the ISO 9126 series. These reports propose:

- an inventory of +250 derived measures for each quality characteristic or sub characteristic,
- 80 base measures (and corresponding 80 attributes) which are used to build the above +250 derived measures,
- explanations of how to apply and use them, and
- some examples of how to apply them during the software product life cycle.

A key question, then, is: what is the quality, from a measurement perspective, of this extensive list of 250+ proposed measures? Put differently, should practitioners trust and use these proposed measures?

Derived Measures in ISO 9126—2001+

Each of the over 250 derived measures proposed in ISO 9126 is typically defined as a formula composed of base measures.
   An example from ISO 9126 Part 4: Quality in use:

- Base Measure 1 (B1): Number of detected failures.
- Base Measure 2 (B1): Number of test cases performed.
- Derived Measure: B1 / B2 with the following measurement units:

$$\frac{B1}{B2} = \frac{\text{Number of detected failures}}{\text{Number of test cases performed}}$$

In this example from ISO 9126, the derived measure (with the corresponding measurement units above) is assigned the following name: "**Failure density against test cases.**"

However, while the numerical assignment rules (that is, the formula for the derived measures) for each derived measure are described as mathematical operations (here, a division), neither B1 nor B2 for these operations is described with sufficient clarity to ensure the quality (accuracy, repeatability, and reproducibility) of the measurement results of:

- these base measures, and, of course,
- the derived measures built upon them.

In general, this is a fairly weak foundation from a measurement perspective, and both practitioners and researchers should be very careful in the implementation, use, and interpretation of the numbers that result from the use of these ISO quantitative models.

Notwithstanding the above comments, these ISO documents remain at the forefront of the state of the art on software measurement, and efforts are under way to improve them.

A review from the metrology perspective of the designs of a derived measure in ISO 9126 is presented next and illustrates some of their weaknesses as measurement methods from a metrology perspective.

10.4. ANALYSIS OF DERIVED MEASURES

10.4.1 Analysis of the Derived Measures in ISO 9126-4: Quality in Use

The ISO 9126-4 technical report on the measures proposed for the ISO **Quality in use** model is used to illustrate some of the metrology-related issues that were outstanding in the ISO 9126 series in the late 2000s. Many of the measurement issues raised with respect to ISO Part 4 would also apply to Parts 2 and 3.

In ISO 9126-4, 15 derived measures are proposed for the 4 quality characteristics of the ISO Quality in use model—see Table 10.1.

The objective of the analysis is to enable us to identify the measurement concepts that were not tackled in the ISO 9126 series of documents, that is, their gaps in their measurement designs.

TABLE 10.1. Derived Measures in ISO 9124-4: Quality in Use

Quality Characteristic	Derived Measures
Effectiveness	— task effectiveness
	— task completion
	— error frequency
Productivity	— task time
	— task efficiency
	— economic productivity
	— productive proportion
	— relative user efficiency
Safety	— user health and safety
	— safety of people affected by use of the system
	— economic damage
	— software damage
Satisfaction	— satisfaction scale
	— satisfaction questionnaire
	— discretionary usage

- Each of these gaps in the design of the derived measures represents an opportunity to improve the measures in the upcoming ISO update, which is the ISO 25000 series.
- This analysis provides an illustration of the improvements that are needed to many of the software measures proposed to the industry.

10.4.2   Analysis of the Measurement of Effectiveness in ISO 9126

In ISO 9126-**4**, it is claimed that the proposed three measures for the **Effectiveness** characteristic—see Table 10.1—assess whether or not the task carried out by users achieved the specific goals with accuracy and completeness in a specific context of use.

This sub-section identifies a number of issues with:

1. the base measures proposed,
2. the derived measures,
3. the measurement units,
4. the measurement units of the derived quantities, and
5. the value of a quantity for Effectiveness.

10.4.2.1   *Identification of the* Base Measure *of Effectiveness.* The 3 Effectiveness-derived measures (task effectiveness, task completion, and error frequency) come from a computation of four base measures, which are themselves collected/measured directly, namely:

- task time,
- number of tasks,
- number of errors made by the user, and
- proportional value of each missing or incorrect component.

The first three base measures above refer to terms in common use (i.e. task time, number of tasks, and number of errors made by the user), but this leaves much to interpretation on what constitutes, for example, a task.

Currently, ISO 9124 does not provide a detailed measurement-related definition for any of them:

- In summary, it does not provide assurance that the measurement results are repeatable and reproducible across measurers or across groups measuring the same software, or across organizations either, where a task might be interpreted differently and with different levels of granularity.
- This leeway in the interpretation of these base measures makes a rather weak basis for both internal and external benchmarking.

The third base measure, number of errors made by the user, is defined in Appendix F of ISO TR 9126-4 as an "instance where test participants did not complete the task successfully, or had to attempt portions of the task more than once."

This definition diverges significantly from the one in the IEEE Standard Glossary of Software Engineering Terminology, where the term "error" has been defined as "the difference between a computed, observed, or measured value or condition and the true, specified, or theoretically correct value or condition. For example: a difference of 30 meters between a computed result and the correct result.

The fourth base measure, referred to as the "proportional value of each missing or incorrect component" in the task output is based, in turn, on another definition, whereas each "potential missing or incorrect component" is given a weighted value A_i based on the extent to which it detracts from the value of the output to the business or user.

This embedded definition itself contains a number of subjective assessments for which no repeatable procedure is provided:

- the value of the output to the business or user,
- the extent to which it detracts from that value,
- the components of a task, and
- potential missing or incorrect components.

10.4.2.2 *The* Derived Measures *of Effectiveness.* The proposed three derived measures for the Effectiveness characteristic, which are defined as a prescribed combination of the base measures mentioned above, inherit the weaknesses of the base measures of which they are composed. In summary, there is no assurance that the measurement results of the derived measures are repeatable and reproducible across measurers, across groups measuring the same software, or across organizations either, where a task might be interpreted differently and with different levels of granularity.

10.4.2.3 The Measurement Units of the Base Measures. Of the four base measures, a single one, i.e. task time, has:

- an internationally recognized standard measurement unit: the second, or a multiple of this unit;
- a universally recognized corresponding symbol: "s" for the second as a measure of time.

The next two base measures (tasks and errors) do not refer to any international standard of measurement and must be locally defined. This means that:

- They are not reliably comparable across organizations.
- They are also not reliably comparable within a single organization when measured by different people, unless local measurement protocols (i.e. measurement procedure) have been clearly documented and rigorously implemented.

The fourth base measure (proportional value of each missing or incorrect component) is puzzling:

- it is based on a given weighted value (number), and
- it has no measurement unit.

10.4.2.4 Measurement Units of the Derived Measures. *Task effectiveness:* In ISO 9126-4, this derived measure leads to a derived unit that depends on a given weight:

$$\text{Task effectiveness} = 1 - (\text{a given weight})$$

Therefore, its derived unit of measurement is unclear and undefined.

Task completion: The derived measure is computed by dividing one base measure by the other (task/task) with the same unit of measurement. The measurement results is a percentage.

Error frequency: The definition of the computation of this derived measure provides two distinct alternatives for the elements of this computation. This can lead to two distinct interpretations:

- errors/task, or
- errors/second.

Of course,

- this, in turn, leads to two distinct derived measures as a result of implementing two different measurement functions (formulae) for this same derived measure;
- and leaves open the possibility of misinterpretation and misuse of measurement results when combined with other units. For example: measures in centimeters and measures in inches cannot be directly added or multiplied.

> In software measurement, who cares about this mixing of units?
>   Should you care as a software manager?
>   Should you care as a software engineer?

10.4.2.5 *Value of a Quantity for Effectiveness.* The five types of metrology values of a quantity are[2]:

- Numerical quantity value
- Quantity-value scale
- Ordinal quantity-value scale
- Conventional reference scale
- Ordinal value

In the measurement of Effectiveness with ISO 9126-4, for each *base measure* numerical values are obtained on the basis of the defined data collection procedure:

For each *derived measure*, numerical values are obtained by applying their respective measurement function. For instance, the derived measures task effectiveness and task completion are expressed as percentages, and are interpreted as the effectiveness and completion of a specific task respectively.

- For task effectiveness in particular, it would be difficult to figure out both a true value and a conventional true value.
- For task completion and error frequency, the true values would depend on locally defined and rigorously applied measurement procedures, but without reference to universally recognized conventional true values (as they are locally defined).

Finally, in terms of the metrological values:

- Only task time refers to a conventional reference scale, that is, the international standard (etalon) for time, from which the second is derived.

[2]See Table 3.1 in chapter 3 on metrology.

- None of the other base measures in these derived measures of effectiveness refers to a conventional reference scale, or to a locally defined one.

See the Advanced Readings section for an additional example.

10.5. THE MISSING LINKS: FROM METROLOGY TO QUANTITATIVE ANALYSIS

10.5.1 Overview

In ISO 9126, there is an *implicit* claim that the proposed (base or derived) measures capture the intended concept to be quantified. However, there is no *explicit* claim about how much each of the proposed measure quantitatively captures the concept intended to be quantified.

At best, each proposed measure in ISO 9126 is considered as an unspecified contributor to such a quantification for evaluation and decision-making. Put differently, they are:

- not considered as a contributor to concept measurement in terms of a specific scale and a standard etalon,
- but only as a contributor (in some proportion) to its quantification (without an agreed-upon and widely recognized reference scale and a standard etalon).

In other words, in the ISO 9126 analysis models, the practical solution (when a decision criterion cannot be measured directly) is to quantify through an association or mapping (direct or indirect), with, it is hoped, better understood concepts that have been quantified.

An example is presented next with some of the ISO 9126 base measures combined into derived measures which are associated with other concepts (i.e. the quality characteristics and sub-characteristics within the ISO model of software product quality).

This section illustrates the missing links between the quantitative models proposed in ISO 9126 and the detailed measures proposed as the contributors to this quantification. The example selected is that of the **Maturity** sub-characteristic and of the 7 derived measures proposed for this sub-characteristic.

For the **Maturity** sub-characteristic as an example:

- The relationships between the attribute being measured by the derived measure "failure density against test cases" and the "maturity" sub-characteristic and the "reliability" characteristic are not identified, neither described.
- No model of such relationships is proposed either.

10.5.2   Analysis of the Measurement of "Maturity"

The model proposed by ISO to quantify the external quality of a software product contains—as previously seen in Figure 10.2—six quality characteristics and 27 sub-characteristics:

- One of the 6 quality characteristics is "**Reliability**" which is itself composed of 4 sub-characteristics.
- One of these 4 sub-characteristics is "**Maturity**" which is chosen here as an example.

To quantify this single **Maturity** sub-characteristic, ISO 9126-3 proposes a list of seven distinct derived measures:

1. Failure density against test cases
2. Estimated latent fault density
3. Fault Density
4. Fault removal
5. Mean time between failures (MTBF)
6. Test coverage
7. Test maturity

Related ISO 9126 Definitions

Reliability:
The capability of the software product to maintain a specified level of performance when used under specified conditions

Maturity:
The capability of the software product to avoid failure as a result of faults in the software.

10.5.2.1   Metrology Perspective. Each of these seven derived measures is presented only at a fairly abstract level as formulae composed from a set of base measures, themselves lacking detailed descriptions, including the attributes they are attempting to measure.

This leaves each of them highly susceptible to individual interpretation: neither the base measures for these operations, nor the corresponding attributes, have been described with sufficient clarity to ensure the quality of the measurement results.

They are not documented at a detailed enough level to provide sufficient guidance to ensure the accuracy, repeatability, and repetitiveness of measurement results, in the event that the same software is measured by different measurers, which in turn leads to potentially significantly different values.

TABLE 10.2. A Derived Measure Proposed for Quantifying Maturity in ISO 9126-2: Failure Density Against Test Cases

Step (ISO 15939)	Description
Data Collection:	• Base Measure 1 (B1): Number of detected failures. • Base Measure 2 (B1): Number of test cases performed.
Data Preparation	• Algorithm of Derived Measure: B1 / B2 • Name of Derived Measure: Failure density against test cases.
Analysis	The derived measure, Failure density against test cases, is associated * with (mapped to): • The quality sub-characteristic: Maturity • Within the quality characteristic: Reliability • Within the quality sub-model: External Quality—ISO 9126-2
	* Associated: there is not an explicit description in ISO 9126 of how much of the proposed measure quantitatively captures the concept intended to be quantified.

Each one of the seven proposed derived measures are described individually as illustrated in the side box and Table 10.2 with the "Failure density against test cases" as an example.

Example: "Failure Density Against Test Cases"

Purpose of this derived measure in ISO 9126: how many failures were detected during defined trial period?

Method of application for this derived measure: count the number of detected failures and performed test cases.

However, none of the embedded base measures are defined precisely in ISO 9126, including failure and test cases.

10.5.2.2 Perspective of the Analysis Model in ISO 9126. There is no ISO defined context or values for such context. Each group within each organization has to build its own set of values for analysis within a specific context.

• What is the specific contribution of any one of the above seven derived measures to the Maturity sub-characteristic?
• Are there some overlaps across the relationships of any of these seven derived measures, and if so, to what extent?
• If not all seven derived measures are mandatory-necessary, which one or which ones are the most representative of the Maturity sub-characteristic, and if so, to which extent?

We now ask how well the derived measure, "Failure density against test cases," fully describes (i.e. quantifies) the above hierarchy of concepts of the ISO 9126 model of software product quality:

How much of the Maturity sub-characteristic is captured by it?

- In practice, the derived measure, Failure density against test cases, is only a contributor, that is, an indicator—see definition of "indicator" in side box in Section 4.5.1 of Chapter 4—within that piece of the hierarchy of quality-related concepts.
- How can we quantify this contribution? The answer is not documented in ISO 9126-4, or even identified as an issue.

10.5.2.3   Missing Links. None of the expected links between this (weak) metrology basis for the measurement of the base and derived attributes and the quantification of the quality sub-characteristic (e.g. Maturity) and characteristic (e.g. Reliability) is described in ISO 9126.

Hopefully, such links will be described but it will take years of research and development to gain insights into this problem and to develop analysis models based on solid empirical evidence.

10.6. OUTSTANDING MEASUREMENT DESIGN ISSUES: IMPROVEMENT STRATEGY

As has been illustrated throughout this chapter, the base measures and their current lack of adherence to metrology principles and characteristics constitute one of the major impediments to the overall applicability and deployment of ISO 9126.

It is also recognized that, to properly analyze, verify, and correct the design of all 80 base measures will require considerable time and work on the part of a single, isolated research team.

To tackle this challenge, a larger, multi-group research team has to be set up, its members to work concurrently on this issue, including research groups at universities across the world, all of whom in coordination with the work in progress of ISO/IEC JTC1/SC7 Working Group 6. Organizing the work in this way should facilitate the transition of the research results to the ISO normative level and, consequently, enable quicker integration of adequately structured base measures into the ISO 25000 series of standards for the measurement of the quality of software products.

In particular, improvement work should focus on five of the 80 attributes in ISO 9126 which appear in more than 10 derived measures; that is, function (38 occurrences), duration (26), task (18), case (16), and failure (11)—See the Adanced Readings 2 section.

- Work on the detailed design of the base measures and on the definitions of the attributes should leverage relevant measurement definitions from other international standards wherever possible.

- Even definitions from existing standards still need further refinement to facilitate their use in operational procedures from a measurement viewpoint.
- Finally, the ISO 9126 standard also includes a number of qualifiers of the base measures which will require further clarification from a measurement viewpoint.

In conclusion, much work remains to be done:

- To define the base measures in detail, even those identified as requiring priority attention.
- To identify the links across the quality models and their corresponding base and derived measures proposed in ISO 9126.

ADVANCED READINGS 1: ANALYSIS OF THE DESIGN OF THE PRODUCTIVITY MEASURE IN ISO 9126

Audience

This Advanced Reading section is of most interest to those interested in additional examples of difficulties currently found in many of the measurements proposals to industry.

This includes measures proposed in some ISO documents that are not yet approved as International Standard, but only on an interim basis as ISO Technical Reports such as ISO 9126 Technical Reports 2 to 4.

In ISO 9126-4, a claim is made that the five derived measures of the **Productivity** characteristic—see Table 10.1—assess the resources that users consume in relation to the effectiveness achieved in a specific context of use. The time required to complete a task is considered to be the main resource to take into account in the measurement of the Productivity characteristic of quality in use.

Of the five proposed measures of **productivity** in ISO 9126-4, one is a base measure: task time. The other four are derived measures:

- task efficiency,
- economic productivity,
- productive portion, and
- relative user efficiency.

It is to be noted that task efficiency refers explicitly to another derived measure, task effectiveness, which was analyzed in a previous section.

It is also to be noted that these four *derived measures* are themselves based on five *base measures*:

- task time,
- cost of the task,
- help time,
- error time, and
- search time.

Measurement Units of the derived measures

The measurement unit for *task efficiency* is not completely clear, since it depends on an ill-defined "given weight:"

$$\text{"task efficiency" unit} = \frac{\text{"task effectiveness" unit}}{\text{second}}.$$

$$= \frac{1 - \text{"a given weight" unit}}{\text{second}} = \frac{?}{\text{second}}. \tag{1}$$

Similarly, the measurement unit of *economic productivity* depends on the measurement unit of task effectiveness, a derived measure, which is unknown:

$$\text{"economic productivity" unit} = \frac{\text{"task effectiveness" unit}}{\text{currency unit}}$$

$$= \frac{1 - \text{"a given weight" unit}}{\text{currency unit}}$$

$$= \frac{?}{\text{currency unit}}. \tag{2}$$

The *productive proportion* is expressed as a percentage and, as such, has no measurement unit (it has the same measurement unit in both the numerator and the denominator):

$$\text{"productive proportion" unit} = \frac{\text{second}}{\text{second}}. \tag{3}$$

Finally, *relative user efficiency* has no measurement unit either, since the measurement units in both the numerator and the denominator are the same here as well (the task efficiency measurement unit), and therefore the result of this derived measure is also expressed as a percentage:

$$\text{"relative user efficiency" unit} = \frac{\text{"task efficiency" unit}}{\text{"task efficiency" unit}}$$

$$= \frac{\dfrac{\text{"task effectiveness" unit}}{\text{second}}}{\dfrac{\text{"task effectiveness" unit}}{\text{second}}}$$

$$= \frac{\dfrac{1-\text{"a given weight" unit}}{\text{second}}}{\dfrac{1-\text{"a given weight" unit}}{\text{second}}}$$

$$= \frac{\dfrac{?}{\text{second}}}{\dfrac{?}{\text{second}}}. \qquad (4)$$

ADVANCED READINGS 2: ATTRIBUTES AND RELATED BASE MEASURES WITHIN ISO 9126

> **Audience**
>
> This Advanced Reading section is of most interest to researchers and industry practitioners interested in improving measurement standards such as those of the ISO 9126 and upcoming ISO 25000 series, and in figuring out priorities in the selection of the base measures to be improved.

Introduction

An inventory of the base measures in ISO 9126 has identified 80 distinct base measures [Desharnais *et al.* 2009]: Have the attributes to be measured in ISO 9126 by these 80 base measures been described with sufficient clarity to ensure the quality of the measurement results?

Improving the design of these 80 base measures is essential for the use of the ISO models in industry. To do so is a daunting task, considering the number of steps and iterations typically necessary to design software measures adequately, as illustrated in Part 1 of this book (Chapters 2 to 5):

- This design task is even more challenging when, in addition to the view of the person designing a measure, a consensus must be developed progressively at an international level, such as within an ISO committee composed of domain experts from a number of countries.
- Similarly, to determine which of these base measures must be improved in the timeliest fashion is a challenge.

A framework to define base measures

In terms of improving the measurement foundation of ISO 9126, the main interest is in the first phase, the design of the measurement method, which includes the following activities:

1. Defining the measurement principle where this activity gives the precise description of what is going to be measured.
2. Defining a measurement method on the basis of that principle, an activity which gives a general description of how to measure.
3. Determining an operational measurement procedure; that is, an implementation of the method in a particular context, an activity which gives a detailed description of how to measure.

It can be observed that, for most of its *base measures*, the ISO 9126 standard:

- does not provide a precise definition of the attribute being measured, i.e. the "what,"
- does not provide a generic description of how to measure that attribute, and
- does not provide operational measurement procedures.

For the upcoming version of ISO 9126 in 2010+ (i.e. ISO 25021), the "what" and the "how" should be spelled out by going through the above three steps to improve the design of the base measures.

- In the late 2000s, only a very small number of software base measures in the whole set of software engineering standards, such as those for the measurement of software functional size, have already gone through all these steps.
- Most in ISO 9126 do not even have a normalized definition of their attributes, and therefore no precise description of what must be measured.

Defining the full set of 80 attributes and necessary base measures is not considered a task which will be feasible to perform within the next two to three years, even by a large organization such as the ISO, which has access to a large international network of domain experts.

- Which of these 80 base measures and corresponding attributes should be addressed first, and which ones will have the most impact initially?
- Which of these 80 base measures are used most in the ISO 9126 series?

Table 10.3 presents a summary of the distribution of occurrences of the 80 base measures (and corresponding single attribute) within the full set of 250 derived measures in the three Parts of ISO 9126:

TABLE 10.3. Occurrences of Base Measures within the Derived Measures of ISO 9126

Occurrences of the Base Measure (Single Attribute) in Derived Measures	Number of Base Measures (Attributes)	Percentage
More than 10	5	6%
From 3 to 10	15	19%
2	13	16%
1	47	59%
TOTAL	**80**	**100%**

- 5 of the 80 base measures (and corresponding single attribute) appear in more than 10 derived measures,
- 15 base measures occur from 3 to 10 times,
- 13 base measures occur twice, and
- 47 base measures have a single occurrence (or 59% of the 80 distinct base measures).

Defining the attributes with more than 10 occurrences
The five base measures (and corresponding distinct attribute) with more than 10 occurrences:

- function (38),
- duration (26),
- task (18),
- case (16), and
- failure (11).

These five base measures appear between 11 and 38 times.

1. The attribute **function** is consistently used with "number of …" in ISO 9126—Parts 2 to 4.
   However, nowhere is this attribute defined precisely. Therefore, its interpretation in practice can vary considerably across individuals, technology, functional domains, etc.
   Nevertheless, the industry has developed various consensuses over the years on the measurement of the functional size of software. This has led to the adoption of the following international standards for functional size measurement:
   - COSMIC-FFP v2.1 [ISO 19761],
   - IFPUG FPA v4.1 Unadjusted [ISO 20926],
   - Mk-II FPA v1.3.1 [ISO20968],

- NESMA FPA v2.1 [ISO 24570]
- FISMA FPA v1.1 [ISO 29881].

Since these standards have already been recognized by the ISO and are extensively used in practice for productivity and benchmarking studies, they could also be used as normalization factors in quality measurement, such as in the measurement of defect density (that is, the number of defects in software normalized by the functional size of that software, allowing a meaningful comparison of defect density in two distinct pieces of software of different sizes).

2. The other attribute, **case** (with 16 occurrences) is not defined in the ISO 9126 standard. But a "case" is defined as follows in ISO 24765: *"a single-entry, single-exit multiple-way branch that defines a control expression, specifies the processing to be performed for each value of the control expression, and returns control in all instances to the statement immediately following the overall construct."*

3. The attribute **duration** is a length of time in seconds, minutes, hours, etc. The "second" as a unit of measurement is already well defined and is a part of the set of international standards for units of measurement.

4. The attribute **task** has multiple definitions within the ISO standards:
   - a sequence of instructions treated as a basic unit of work by the supervisory program of an operating system, in ISO 24765;
   - in software design, a software component which can operate in parallel with other software components, in ISO 24765;
   - the activities required to achieve a goal, in 4.3 of ISO TR 9126-4;
   - a concurrent object with its own thread of control, in ISO 24765;
   - a term for work, the meaning of which and placement within a structured plan for project work varies by the application area, industry, and brand of project management software, in the PMBOK;
   - required, recommended, or permissible action, intended to contribute to the achievement of one or more outcomes of a process, in section 4.5 of ISO 12207 and in section 4.34 of ISO 15288.

   Therefore, for the task attribute, it is necessary to revise each usage of task for each attribute in each quality characteristic and sub-characteristic.

5. The attribute **failure** is quite challenging, since it has multiple definitions:
   - termination of the ability of a product to perform a required function or its inability to perform within previously specified limits—see 4.2 in ISO 25000;
   - the inability of a system or component to perform its required functions within specified performance requirements—ISO 24765;

- an event in which a system or system component does not perform a required function within specified limits—IEEE 982.1;
- the termination of the ability of a functional unit to perform its required function—IEEE 982.1.

NOTE: A failure may be produced when a fault is encountered.

The first definition of the failure attribute could be suggested, but should be revised in the context of each attribute in each quality characteristic and sub-characteristic.

It should be noted that, even though a number of definitions may exist in the standards (or in the literature) for the attributes mentioned above, this does not necessarily mean that they should be used without further scrutiny:

- the definitions might not have been tested operationally,
- a definition might not be useful in a particular measurement context, or
- there may be multiple definitions of an attribute.

Attribute qualifiers

In addition to the 80 different base measures and over 250 derived measures, ISO 9126—Parts 2, 3, and 4 include a number of qualifiers which characterize some aspects of the base measures (and corresponding distinct attribute). For example, the base measure, number of failures, may refer at times to the number of **resolved** failures or at others to the number of failures **actually detected**. The terms "resolved" and "actually detected" are referred to here as qualifiers of the term "failures" for this base measure; that is, they qualify a subset of the same attribute.

Sometimes the qualification of the base measure uses a broader qualifier. For example, the number of *critical and serious* failure *occurrences avoided*.

Most of the time, the qualifiers in the ISO 9126 quality model are added to measures using a sentence, not just a word.

A solution would be to suggest, whenever possible, a reference in the set of ISO standards.

Example: Type of Maintenance

Type of maintenance could be aligned, along with its corresponding concepts, with the ISO standard on software maintenance—ISO 14764.

Another possibility, when there is no reference to a standard for specific qualifiers, would be to modify them when relevant. To define the important attributes for the ISO 9126 quality model would represent an important improvement.

After completing the priorities in this first iteration of improvements, further effort will be necessary to define the qualifiers.

EXERCISES

1. Describe and explain the link between the Analysis Models and the derived measures in the ISO 9126 models of software quality.

2. There are 80 base measures in ISO 9126. Name a few that are specific to software.

3. How many of these base measures are related to international standards of measurement?

4. Name a base measure specific to software in ISO 9126 that is supported by a well-documented measurement method?

5. What is the measurement unit of the "task efficiency" derived measure?

6. What is the measurement unit of the "productive production" derived measure?

7. Describe the relation and contribution of the "task efficiency" derived measure to the "productivity" characteristic in ISO 9126-4?

TERM ASSIGNMENTS

1. Use the four derived measures proposed by ISO 9126-4 for the "productivity" characteristic. Compare the measurement results obtained with each of these distinct measures and discuss differences (and similarities) in measurement results. What is the contribution of each to the "productivity" characteristic?

2. Design an analysis model using the above 4 derived measures for the "productivity" characteristic that could be used to evaluate "productivity" and take a decision based on the numerical results.

3. Select one of the base measures from ISO 9126-2 and improve its design.

4. Select one of the base measures from ISO 9126-3 and improve its design.

5. Identify and document a process to progressively develop a much larger consensus on the proposed improved design of one the base measures from ISO 9126.

6. Take any one of "metrics" proposed in Parts 2 to 4 of ISO 9126 and propose a design of a *base* measure.

7. Take the *base* measure designed by one of your classmates and analyze the quality of this design. Also, suggest some improvements to your classmate's design.

8. Take any of the base measures from ISO 9126 designed by one of your classmates (see assignments 6 and 7 above) and build a measurement

procedure to ensure that such a base measure produces measurement results that are accurate, reproducible, and capable of replication.

9. Take any one of the "metrics" proposed in Parts 2 to 4 of ISO 9126 and propose a design for a *derived* measure.

10. Take the *derived* measure designed by one of your classmates and analyze the quality of the design. Also, suggest some improvements to your classmate's design.

11. Take any of the quality sub characteristics in ISO 9126 and discuss the methodology you would use to describe the linkages between the sub characteristic selected and one of the metrics actually described in ISO 9126.

12. Take any of the derived measures from ISO 9126 and identify sources of uncertainty in their measurement process.

13. Propose an ISO 9126 quality model for Web software in your organization and provide:
    - the rationale for the quality characteristics and sub characteristics selected;
    - the rationale for the determination of the evaluation scales for each;
    - the rationale for the determination of the target values for each.

14. Assess the maintainability of a piece of software by using a software source code assessment tool (for example, Checkstyle, Logiscope, etc.). Identify which of the ISO9126 maintainability measures can be assessed.

PART 3

THE DESIGN OF COSMIC – ISO 19761

Part 1 (Chapters 1 to 5) looked into the key characteristics of measurement from a metrology perspective, and discussed how to design a software measurement method.

Part 2 (Chapters 6 to 10) presented analyses of the design of a few of the most popular measures proposed to the industry, such as the Cyclomatic complexity number, Halstead's metrics, Function Points (FP), Use Case Points and ISO 9126.

Generally, authors introducing new ways of measuring software will document their proposals in terms of an algorithm which they consider to be the design of their measurement method. Most of the time, such a proposal represents the design of either a single researcher or practitioner or a single research team (to the exception of ISO 9126 and).

Of the hundreds of individual software measures proposed over the past 30 years, only a handful have been picked up collectively by organized groups of practitioners and have attracted a consensus large enough to become international measurement standards (i.e. the five functional size measurement methods recognized by ISO) .

Part 3 of this book describes how the key characteristics of measurement, and of metrology in particular, were put to work in the design of the COSMIC (COmmon Software Measurement International Consortium) approach to the measurement of the functional size of software.

Software Metrics and Software Metrology, by Alain Abran
Copyright © 2010 IEEE Computer Society

Chapters 11 and 12 present the design process of the software measurement method that became ISO 19761: the COSMIC functional size measurement method. Chapters 11 and 12 illustrate:

- how to design a software measurement method, and
- how to introduce metrological strengths into the design of software measurement methods in order to bring them to market.

Specifically, chapters 11 and 12 present an overview of the design process of the COSMIC Function Points measurement method, from its initial prototype developed in a research center at the request of industrial sponsors (chapter 11) to its scaling up by a user group which took it through the ISO process to achieve its status as an international standard—ISO 19761 (chapter 12).

Lessons learned from the design process of this measurement method can then be put to work to tackle standardization for the measurement of a number of software attributes, such as software complexity and software quality, and many others of interest to practitioners and to the software industry in general.

11

COSMIC: DESIGN OF AN INITIAL PROTOTYPE

This chapter covers:

- The industry's need for a functional size measure for real-time software
- Research project planning
- Design of the initial prototype
- Field tests in industry
- First-year feedback from industry

11.1. INTRODUCTION

11.1.1 Why Improve Function Points?

In the mid-1990s, a number of practitioners and organizations in various software domains, including the real-time domain, had come to the conclusion that the first generation of functional size measures, based on the design of FP (which had itself inherited many of the weaknesses of Halstead's metrics[1]), did not provide an adequate measure of the functionality of real-time and embedded software:

---

[1]See chapters 7 and 8.

Software Metrics and Software Metrology, by Alain Abran
Copyright © 2010 IEEE Computer Society

Given software to be measured and a method to measure it, a measurement method will produce a "number," however:

- This number has limited practical meaning unless it is certain that it provides a meaningful quantification of the attributes being measured.
- Said differently, applying FP rules to software of types other than MIS will produce such a number, but does that number represent an adequate quantification of the functional size of that software?

11.1.2   Industry-Led Initiative

In the late 1990s, a number of organizations in the USA, Canada and Japan recognized that a good solution would not be found by luck alone, and they decided to get together to put up the financial resources required to set up a research project with dedicated staff and a project schedule, including tests in industry.

These organizations commissioned a research project to be conducted by the research group headed by Dr. A. Abran, in collaboration with the following researchers and industry participants: J.-M. Desharnais, M. Maya and D. St-Pierre [Abran 1997].

Later on, other organizations in Europe and Australia provided more funding to finance a second round of tests in industrial settings.

11.2. IMPROVEMENT PROJECT

11.2.1   Industry Focus and Objectives

The expression "real-time software" is a generic one, which often means different things to different people. There is not yet a consensus on a single definition of "real time" in industry or among software researchers.

For the purposes of the research project set up to tackle this issue, the following two definitions of real time were adopted as representing a minimal consensus:

- "A system in which computation is performed during the actual time that an external process occurs, in order that the computation results can be used to control, monitor or respond in a timely manner to the external process" [IEEE 610 1990].
- "Any system in which the time at which the output is produced is significant. This is usually because the input corresponds to some movement in the physical world, and the output has to relate to that same movement. The lag from input time to output time must be sufficiently small for acceptable timeliness." [Illingworth 1991].

The focus was therefore on software that reacts to an external process or event subject to very tight time constraints.

The prototype for the design of the new measurement method had to retain the key quality characteristics of FP from a measurement perspective, such as:

- Relevance: The measurement technique is perceived by practitioners (within a functional domain) as adequately measuring the functional size of the applications in their domain.
- Measurement instrumentation: Instrumentation is an essential factor in achieving one of the quality attributes of a good measurement method: repetitiveness.
- This means that different individuals, in different contexts, at different times, and following the same measurement procedures will obtain measurement results with the following quality criteria:
  - They are relatively similar.
  - They have been obtained with minimal judgment.
  - They are auditable.
- The measurement instrumentation is in the form of a measurement standard which documents and clarifies the measurement objectives and perspective, and defines the measurement procedures adopted by a user group.
- The measurement method is in the public domain.
- The measurement method is practical:
  - The measurement method is based on current software development practices and on the content of the software documentation.

11.2.2   Project Plan

The following five major steps were followed to develop an initial prototype:

Step 1—Literature review. This step consisted of conducting a literature review on three aspects:

- Reported usage of FP to measure real-time software,
- Identification of extensions proposed to adapt FP to this type of software, and
- Analysis of these proposals to identify their strengths and weaknesses.

Step 2—Proposal for an extension to FP for real-time software. This proposal was based on the lessons learned from the analysis of previous attempts to extend FP, and to improve or develop a new approach to adapting FP for the measurement of real-time software.

Step 3—Field tests of the design of the prototype. This step consisted of measuring some real-time software applications in industry. Since this project was supported and financed by three large USA and Canadian organizations (from the power supply and telecommunications areas) and a Japanese organization (automotive), one or more real-time applications from each partner were measured.

Step 4—Analysis of the measurement results. This step of the project consisted of carrying out an analysis of the measurement results and of the measurement process against criteria such as:

- Perception of the application specialists participating in the measurement sessions with respect to the coherence between the measurement results and the size of the applications measured.
- Time required to identify and measure the function types.
- Difficulty in learning and applying the basic concepts, as well as the measurement procedures and rules of the proposed prototype.
- Comparison between the measurement procedures and results obtained with the prototype and the standard version of FP (IFPUG, version 4.0 at that time).

Step 5—Public release. The last step consisted of preparing a public release of the proposed measurement method, including:

- a description of the extension proposed,
- the measurement procedures and rules,
- an overview of the field tests, and
- comments on the measurement results from a measurement instrumentation perspective.

Figure 11.1 illustrates the project steps, their inputs, and their deliverables.

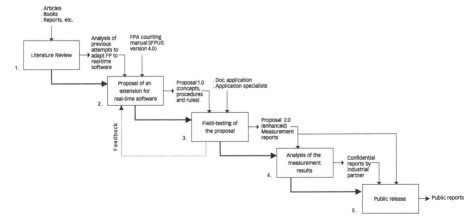

Figure 11.1. Project Phases for the Initial Prototype

It is important to note that steps 2 and 3 are strongly related and interactive:

- That is, as the field tests were progressing, the initial prototype was improved based on the feedback obtained from the industry participants in the measurement sessions.

These five steps are presented in greater detail in the following sections.

11.3. LITERATURE REVIEW

11.3.1 Findings and Lessons Learned

Most of the publications on FP up to the time of that literature review in 1997 did not deal with its application to real-time software, and the datasets used in most publications originated from MIS software applications (this is still the situation in the late 2000s).

Furthermore, several authors [Jones 1991; Reifer 1990; Whitmire 1992, 1995; Galea 1995] agreed that the FP structure was not adequate for measuring processor-intensive software with a high number of control functions and internal calculations.

Five attempts to adapt FP to real-time software were identified at that time:

1. Status quo: IFPUG Case Study 4 on real time [IFPUG 1997].
2. Application Features [Mukhopadhyay and Kerke, 1992].
3. Feature Points [Jones 1988].
4. Asset-R [Reifer 1990].
5. 3D Function Points [Whitmire 1992, 1995].

However, none of these approaches had succeeded by the late 1990s in gaining any significant market acceptance in the real-time software market.

11.3.1.1 Status Quo: IFPUG. The status quo approach assumes that Albrecht's FP method is applicable as is to non MIS software.

- It is the approach that was adopted by IFPUG.
- However, many practitioners and researchers have indicated that the status quo method applied as is to non MIS software does not adequately capture the functional size of this software.

11.3.1.2 Application Features. "Application Features" were proposed as a measurement technique by [Mukhopadhyay & Kerke 1992]. These researchers were not directly interested in redefining FP as a measurement method, but were rather looking for a way to estimate functional size, in FP, earlier in the development life cycle.

Their goal was to apply this measurement technique to process control software in the manufacturing domain (a category of real-time software). This is interesting, because it identifies specific characteristics of a certain category of real-time software which contribute to functional size and which are known very early in the development life cycle.

However, these characteristics (physical positioning and movement) were specific to a specialized application domain and could not be generalized across all types of real-time software. Detailed procedures and rules, to ensure accuracy and repeatability over time in the measurement of the three application features identified, were not provided. The authors focused on the presentation and analysis of an estimation model. The measurement process itself was not covered.

11.3.1.3 Feature Points. Feature Points were developed by [Jones 1988].

- According to Jones, real-time software is high in algorithmic complexity, but sparse in inputs and outputs, and, when the FP method is applied to such software, the results generated appear to be misleading.
- However, it was pointed out by [Whitmire 1992] that the definition of algorithms and the rules proposed were not sufficient for measurement purposes: "*No guidance is provided to identify algorithms at the desired level of abstraction.*"

11.3.1.4 Asset-R. "Asset-R" was proposed by [Reifer, 1990]. According to [Reifer, 1990], Albrecht's method failed to successfully handle four important characteristics associated with real-time and scientific software: parallelism, synchronization, concurrency, and intensive mathematical calculation.

- New function types were therefore introduced, according to the type of software measured, while the weighting factors and the adjustment factors proposed in Albrecht's method were eliminated.
- However, there was a lack of detailed definitions, measurement rules, and examples for the new function types (modes, stimulus/response relationships, rendezvous), and it was not clear how to measure them.

11.3.1.5 3D Function Points. "3D Function Points" were developed by [Whitmire 1992, 1995] as a result of a study investigating the use of FP in the measurement of scientific and real-time software.

According to this study, FP does not accurately measure this type of software because it does not factor in all the characteristics that contribute to the size of the software.

- His criticism is based on the premise that all software has three dimensions: data (stored data and user interfaces), functions (internal processing), and control (dynamic behavior).

- According to this scheme, FP measures only one dimension: the data dimension. Whitmire therefore proposed a set of function types for each of the dimensions identified and a mechanism to combine the points assigned into a single "3D FP index".

11.3.2 Pre-Tests

Of the five candidates identified in the literature review, the 3D Function Points method looked to be the most relevant at that time. The method was therefore selected for a pre-test on some industrial applications in order to obtain empirical observations, and, perhaps, for use as the starting point for the project.

Two different software applications from two different domains (power supply and telecommunications) were measured.

The following key problems were encountered: The concepts in [Whitmire 1992, 1995] and the procedures and rules in [Galea 1995] were not detailed enough to allow the identification, without ambiguity, of the new function types proposed (Transformations, States, and Transitions).

For the identification of the proposed States and Transitions function types, documentation for the finite state machines (FSM) was a prerequisite:

- However, at the industrial sites where this proposal was tested, this type of documentation was not in use.
- Furthermore, feedback from many real-time designers in other organizations also indicated that, even though most practitioners knew about this type of notation system, they did not document functional requirements using state diagrams.

The feedback from these pre-tests in industry and from other contacts in industry gave an indication that industry might be very reluctant to endorse a measurement method based on such a state diagram-type of notation of requirements when they were not using it even for the design of their own software.

11.4. DESIGN OF THE INITIAL PROTOTYPE

11.4.1   The Mismatch between the Perceived Size of Functionality in Real-Time Software and Its Size in FP

The transactional function types in FP (External Inputs, External Outputs, and External Inquiries) are based on the concept of the elementary process.

- An elementary process was defined in IFPUG, 1994: "The smallest unit of activity that is meaningful to the end user of the business."
- This elementary process must be self-contained and leave the business of counting the application in a consistent state.

However, the number and nature of the steps or *sub processes* required to execute the elementary process are not taken into account.

- Based on empirical observations, MIS processes of the same type have a relatively stable number of sub processes.
- However, in real time software processes, by contrast, the number of sub processes varies substantially—see the control process in Examples 1 and 2.

Example 1—An Engine Temperature Control Process

Main purpose of the process: to turn on the engine's cooling system when necessary.

- A sensor enters the temperature into the application (sub process 1).
- The temperature is compared to the overheating threshold temperature (sub process 2).
- A Turn On message can be sent to the cooling system if needed (sub process 3).

The application is not in a consistent state until all the sub processes of the temperature control process are completed.

The temperature control process has, therefore, *3 sub processes*.

According to standard FP rules, only one transactional function would be identified, because there is only *1 elementary process*.

Example 2—An Engine Diagnostic Process

Main purpose of the process: to turn on an engine alarm when necessary.

- 15 engine sensors (all different) send data to the diagnostic process (15 sub processes, 1 unique sub process for each kind of sensor).
- For each sensor, the set of external data received is compared to threshold values read from an internal file, 1 unique file for each kind of sensor (15 more sub processes, 1 unique sub process for each kind of sensor).
- Depending on a number of conditions, an alarm on the dashboard may be turned on (1 sub process).

In this example, the engine diagnostic process consists of *31 sub-processes*.

The application is not in a consistent state until all the sub processes of the diagnostic process are completed.

According to standard FP rules, only 1 transactional function would be identified, because there is only *1 elementary process*.

Therefore, when the IFPUG rules are used,

- Example 1 with 3 sub-processes and Example 2 with 31 sub-processes would have approximately the same number of points related to transactions,
- even though the real-time community would vigorously disagree that these two functional processes have the same functional size.

There is a strong case to be made that an adequate functional measure of real-time software should take into account the fact that some processes have only a few sub processes, while others have a large number of sub processes.

11.4.2 The Initial Solution: A Real-Time Extension to FP

To measure these functional characteristics of real-time software adequately (i.e. to avoid this mismatch between the numbers obtained and the practitioners' perception of corresponding functional sizes), it is necessary to consider the sub processes executed by a control process.

The extension to FP proposed in 1997, referred to as Full FP (FFP), introduced new transactional function types to measure these characteristics:

- External Control Entry—ECE,
- External Control Exit—ECX,
- Internal Control Read—ICR, and
- Internal Control Write—ICW

In this extension, the new function types were only used to measure real-time control data and processes. See the Advances Readings section for a discussion on the key differences between FP and the extension proposed.

11.5. FIELD TESTS OF THE PROTOTYPE

11.5.1 Field Test Planning

The objective of the field tests was to measure some real-time software applications to verify in an empirical way the applicability of the concepts proposed, answering the following questions:

- Do the users of the measurement technique agree that the proposed measure has met its stated objective of measuring the functional size of real-time software?
- Is the proposed measure "good enough" from the users' own perspective, in the sense that it is achieving the right balance of multiple simultaneous goals, even though any one goal might not have been achieved optimally [Bach, 1997]?

- Do the users agree that the extension proposal has been designed objectively, precisely, and in an auditable manner, and that someone else with the same set of rules would come up with the same results (relatively), and again, results that are "good enough"?
- Do the users agree that the proposed measurement procedures are based on current practices of what is effectively documented at the present time?

To answer these questions, it was mandatory that an application specialist be present at the measurement sessions.

- Due to the typical industrial constraints, such as the availability of application specialists, site measurement sessions were restricted to two days. This meant that the industrial partners had to select small applications or a self-contained portion of a medium-sized or large application.
- The software applications were measured with the extension proposed, as well as with IFPUG version 4.0, so that comparisons could be made.
- Three field tests were conducted over a 4-month period. For the measurement of these applications, at least three people participated in each measurement session: at least one application specialist, and two certified FP specialists who were members of the FFP design team.

11.5.2   Analysis of the Field Test Results

Table 11.1 presents the FP and FFP measurement results for the transactional function types. It can be observed that, in the presence of multiple sub processes of a single process, FP produced fewer points than FFP.

Indeed, FP has been criticized for generating small FP sizes in a real-time environment [Jones 1991; Galea 1995] which seem unrelated to the perceived larger functional size of the software measured [Galea 1995].

Since the FFP design takes into account the sub processes integrated within a single control process by identifying the different groups of data received, sent, read, and written, FFP will generate more points than the standard FP method—see examples above.

The real-time specialists consulted strongly concurred that a measure not taking into account user requested sub processes, like FP, could not be a "good enough" functional size measure of their applications.

Therefore, FFP results represented for them a more relevant measure of the functional size of their applications; that is, it had a greater ability to discriminate software functional size in accordance with their own intuitive perception of differences in functional size.

The results of the field tests also confirmed that, in those tests, the number of sub processes in a real-time process varies substantially. For example, there were processes with only 3 sub processes, while others had over 50 sub processes.

TABLE 11.1. FFP and FP Measurement Results for Transactional Function Types

Function Type	Application A		Application B		Application C	
	Occurrences	Points (Size)	Occurrences	Points (Size)	Occurrence	Points (Size)
FP (IFPUG 4.0)						
—External Input (EI)	40	202	6	21	15	50
—External Output (EO)	2	14	2	11	17	73
—External Inquiry (EQ)	12	40	1	6	0	0
Total Size	**54**	**256 FP**	**13**	**69 FP**	**32**	**123 FP**
Full FP (FFP)						
—External Control **Entry** (ECE)	123	123	10	10	67	69
—External Control **Exit** (ECX)	93	97	8	10	136	139
—Internal Control **Read** (ICR)	395	403	14	18	100	103
—Internal Control **Write** (ICW)	142	154	8	8	165	168
Total Size	**753**	**777 FFP**	**45**	**83 FFP**	**468**	**479 FFP**

One of the project's industrial partners conducted a 4th field test without the assistance of the researchers. The feedback from this industrial partner is summarized as follows:

- Concepts and measurement procedures in the FFP measurement manual were relatively clear and easy to understand. It was not difficult to measure without the assistance of an FFP specialist.

- FFP measured 79 processes out of the 81 they expected were there to be measured with an adequate functional size measurement method.
  - This was because FFP did not take into account processes containing only internal algorithms.
  - From a practical perspective, the development of such algorithms in terms of software was not a problem. The real problem was related to engineering, specifically figuring out the algorithm that would solve their engineering problem.
- The FFP size coverage rate was therefore 97% of their optimal coverage target, and was considered "good enough" from their perspective.

Based on feedback from the field tests, the following observations were made about the quality of the measurement prototype designed.

11.5.2.1   Quality 1: Ease of Understanding.   One criticism often made of FP is that it constitutes a set of complex definitions and time-consuming procedures, and that it takes an FP expert to produce an accurate FP size.

The new function types were designed to be simpler to learn and master.

- This simplicity was confirmed during the field test measurement sessions. Once the application specialists understood the definitions of the new function types, they had no problem identifying them. After a full day of FFP measurement, they were able to measure with limited assistance.
- According to application specialists participating in the measurement sessions, this is mostly due to the fact that:
  - it is much easier to identify function types that only refer to one type of action (for example, receiving data) as in FFP,
  - than it is to identify function types that potentially refer to more than one action, as in FP (some mandatory and some optional, and multiple possible combinations, some of which qualify and others that do not).
- In addition, application specialists believed that the definitions, measurement procedures, and rules were clear and detailed enough that different individuals would be able to come up with relatively similar results. They also believed that the proposed concepts, measurement procedures, and rules were based on current practices of what was documented at the time.

11.5.2.2   Quality 2: Measurement Effort.   Regarding the effort required to measure an application, the FFP and FP measurement efforts were found to be similar.

Even though more function types had to be measured with FFP, they were easily identified and therefore the effort required to measure them was no greater. In fact, the application specialists seem to require less counting assistance from FP experts when measuring with FFP than with FP, so the identification of more function types did not increase the measurement effort.

To summarize, the results of the field tests were positive: according to the real-time specialists present at the field tests, FFP met its stated objective of measuring the user's functional requirements adequately:

- They believe that this was done objectively, precisely, and in an auditable manner, and that someone else with the same set of rules would come up with more or less the same results.
- They also believe that FFP measurement procedures and rules are based on current practices of what is really being documented at the present time.

11.5.3   Limitations of the Initial Prototype

Of course, there were some limitations to the evaluation of this measurement prototype, and to the generalization of the evaluation results:

- The designers of this prototype were very involved, not only throughout the design process, but also in its evaluation. They could not, therefore, be totally objective in their evaluation of the prototype.
- The field tests were carried out in a small number of organizations, and without a sufficient number of field tests to make them significant for statistical purposes. The results could be considered only as anecdotal, and without generalization power per se.

It was recongized that more people would need to be brought on board to strengthen the prototype of the proposed measurement method to ensure that the prototype would reflect a broader consensual basis and find a broader application domain.

11.6. FIRST-YEAR FEEDBACK FROM INDUSTRY

The FFP method was first presented at the IFPUG Fall Conference in Phoenix (Arizona) in 1997, at which time it was put into the public domain and, it was hoped, be integrated as an improvement to the original FP method.

Two different kinds of feedback were received from industry, within and outside the IFPUG organization.

11.6.1   Feedback from Outside the IFPUG Community

Strong interest was voiced from organizations that used and tested FFP.

Within a year, a new international users group was set up to foster the scaling up and deployment of the prototype:

- The "Common Software Measurement International Consortium"— COSMIC was founded in 1998 as a voluntary initiative of software

measurement experts, which included practitioners and academics from the Asia/Pacific region, Europe, and North America.
- Participating measurement experts were drawn from Australia, Canada, Finland, Germany, Ireland, Italy, Japan, Netherlands, and the UK.

The aim of the COSMIC group is to design and bring to market a new generation of functional size measurement methods for software. The work done by the COSMIC group to scale up the COSMIC method is presented in Chapter 12.

In 2010, the COSMIC group includes representatives from at least 19 countries.

11.6.2   Feedback from the IFPUG Organization

Interest from the IFPUG organization was next to nil. When asked specifically why this was the case, the organization reported that the feedback received from their own community indicated:

- no interest in significantly modifying the FP method, and
- a vested interest in protecting the relevance of their historical data on projects measured with the traditional IFPUG FP method. This type of feedback can be understood in particular in terms of the fact that active membership in the IFPUG organization comes mostly from the MIS community, and those members were satisfied with the method for their MIS applications.

ADVANCED READINGS: KEY DIFFERENCES BETWEEN FP AND THE PROPOSED EXTENSION

Audience

This Advanced Reading section is of most interest to researchers and industry practitioners interested in understanding some of the fundamental differences between the traditional Function Points method and the COSMIC method.

To illustrate the key difference between a Function Points (FP) function types and the extension proposed in the prototype, Figure 11.2 presents the *External Control Entry transactions* proposed in the extension and Figure 11.3 presents the traditional *Input transactions* from FP:

- An Entry refers to a group of control data received by a process from a user outside the application boundary (Figure 11.2): that is, the action (or sub process) of receiving a group of data from the user.

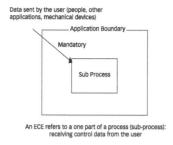

Figure 11.2. External Control Entry (in the proposed extension)

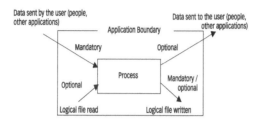

Figure 11.3. External Input transaction in IFPUG

- An Input, in contrast, refers to a whole process that receives a group of data from the user *and* updates a logical file in some cases (depending on the type of data).
  - An Input, as defined by IFPUG, can also read a logical file and send information to the user (Figure 11.3).
  - In the extension proposed initially, the sub processes of updating logical files, reading logical files, and sending information to the user are counted as separate function types.

In summary, the extension (and later, the COSMIC measurement method) takes into account a finer level of granularity, the sub process level, while FP only considers the process level.

A finer level of granularity is important in real-time software, since its processes have a variable number of sub processes compared to MIS software, and this is an important element to consider in the measurement of the functional size of real-time software.

EXERCISES

1. List the project steps in the design of the initial prototype of the COSMIC measurement method.

2. List some of the key findings from the analysis of previous attempts to adapt Function Points to the measurement of real-time software?

3. List some of the weaknesses of Function Points that have been addressed in the design of COSMIC?

4. Why would you consider the first design of COSMIC as a prototype?

5. What were the lessons learned from the field results?

6. What criteria were used to analyze the field results?

7. What were the limitations of the initial design?

TERM ASSIGNMENTS

1. Identify three metrology criteria which were not addressed in the initial design of COSMIC. Propose an empirical approach to study how COSMIC performs on these criteria.

2. Compare the design approach for the COSMIC method with the previous approaches to designing functional size methods for real-time software. Document comparative strengths and weaknesses in these approaches.

COSMIC: SCALING UP AND INDUSTRIALIZATION

This chapter covers:

- The objectives of the design scale up
- Design decisions
- Independent field trials in industry
- Design outcomes
- Fit within international software measurement infrastructures

12.1. INTRODUCTION

In this chapter, we describe the process for scaling up the development of the prototype of the new COSMIC measurement method presented in the previous chapter to a method which is:

- internationally designed,
- supported by an international user group, and
- endorsed by an international standards organization—ISO.

If this scale up does not occur, then most of the software measures proposed by researchers (or practitioners) will typically:

Software Metrics and Software Metrology, by Alain Abran
Copyright © 2010 IEEE Computer Society

- stay within the realm of their authors and that of a few researchers who use them for research purposes only, or
- be identified by other researchers as having weaknesses, and partial solutions will be proposed by those researchers to address them, and so on.

This leaves the industry with a continuously shifting foundation, consisting of:

- local optimizations (documented in a number of individual papers, but still suffering from other weaknesses), and
- at times, very different designs put forward for the alternatives proposed.

We outline in this chapter the steps deliberately taken to scale up the design of the COSMIC measurement method, both to make that design more robust from a measurement perspective, and to broaden its consensual basis to bring it up to what should be considered as the ultimate reward for a measure in terms of recognition, that is, its adoption as an International Standard by the ISO.

Such a scaling up is very important for an organization, as well as for the industry as a whole:

- An organization typically wishes to measure something right away with a measurement method already widely recognized in the industry.
  - It does not want to spend time and monies going through an evaluation of a large number of alternatives measurement methods.
  - They typically do not have the skills and expertise to evaluate a number of distinct measurement methods.
- An organization does not want to adopt a measurement method which could rapidly become obsolete, either through of a lack of support in industry or through rapid successive improvements without due consideration to past investments in data collection and training.

This chapter is organized as follows:

- Section 12.2 presents the scaling up objectives set up by the COSMIC group.
- Section 12.3 presents the design decisions made for this scaling up.
- Section 12.4 presents an overview of the field trials in industry.
- Section 12.5 presents the outcome of this process, i.e. the design of the COSMIC measurement method.
- Section 12.6 presents some of the strengths of this design.
- Section 12.7 presents the actions taken to position COSMIC within the international metrology infrastructure.
- Section 12.8 summarizes the competitive advantages of COSMIC from a measurement perspective.

12.2. SCALING UP OBJECTIVES

The members of the COSMIC group defined the following objectives for the process of scaling up the measurement prototype to ensure its robustness over time as a measurement method capable of meeting industry needs:

- To meet the constraints of the many new and complex types of business and real-time software, as well as the business application software served by first generation functional sizing methods.
- To be easy to train, understand, and use with consistency (with key concepts and measurement models which are well structured and described to facilitate understanding without recourse to numerous interrelated rules and exceptions).
- To fully meet the data collection rules of the established measurement repositories.
- To facilitate the development of approximate size estimation on the basis of requirements as they emerge early in a project's life.
- To meet all feasible metrology criteria to ensure robustness for its use in industry.
- To meet the requirements of correct application of numerical rules to facilitate its adoption by academia.
- To fit into the international regulatory environment (as an ISO standard).
- To facilitate automated sizing (that is, make it simple enough to define the interpretation rules for tool specifications, and for a variety of development paradigms).
- To be independent of methodologies and technologies.
- To be provided with free access through the Web.

To meet these objectives, the following key decisions were taken to improve the design of the prototype:

- The aspects of the IFPUG method that did not meet the metrology criteria were dropped. This included dropping the assignment of weights and the corresponding ambiguous mix of numerical scales[1].
- A more generic model of software functionality was designed which captured the key concepts of functionality that cut across most of the previous functional size measurement methods and were embedded in them.
- As many as possible of the metrology concepts described in the ISO VIM (International Vocabulary on Metrology) were implemented[2];

[1]See chapter 8.
[2]See chapter 3.

- The design would be in full conformity with the mandatory requirements of ISO 14143-1 on functional size measurement methods, including the key one: what is to be measured is a "functional requirement" of the software, independently of its quality and technical (non-functional) requirements, and of the effort associated with it[3].

12.3. DESIGN DECISIONS

To meet the objectives of the COSMIC group, the prototype version—see chapter 11—was reviewed and a number of changes were made.

Among the important changes were the following:

- The concepts integrated within the addition of the control transaction types were reviewed and generalized to a higher level of abstraction. This meant that they could apply to all types of software, and not only to real-time software.
- The adoption of a generic description of functionality in software, independently of its functional domain:
  - The key concept of functionality at the highest level of commonality that is present in all software was identified as the "data movement."
  - This data movement concept was then assigned to the metrology concept of a size unit.
- The IFPUG transaction types were dropped, for the following reasons:
  - The data movement concept was more generic and superceded the IFPUG transaction types.
  - The data movement concept was simpler and required less intricate rules to specify a measurement method.
  - The assignment of 1 unit to a data movement did not require recourse to arbitrarily (or somewhat arbitrarily) defined weights.
  - The absence of weights and the use of a single unit ensured a proper use of measurement scale type and, correspondingly, correct additivity of measurement results.
- The adoption of a generic description of a level of granularity for the measurement of this functionality in software: that is, at the data movement level, without taking into account data manipulation with the simplifying assumption of an average number of data manipulations for each data movement).

---

[3]See chapter 3: Avanced Readings section.

- The recognition of distinct phases for quantifying the functionality of software:
  - a *strategy phase*, where the purpose and scope of measurement are determined;
  - a *mapping phase*, where the documentation of the piece of software to be measured is analyzed and modeled to the generic model of the software described by the scale up, that is, the COSMIC generic model of that software;
  - A *measurement phase* for the application of the numerical assignment rules of the COSMIC method.
- The recognition of layers of functionality, and the adoption of the same model of functionality for each layer, as well as the same size unit.

The design was scaled up in an iterative manner and benefited from the vast expertise of the participants, many of whom were long-time contributors to ISO working groups for the development of international standards in systems and software engineering.

- For instance, in ISO standards, the set of concepts (and the interrelationships across these concepts) that constitute the foundation of standards is embedded in the set of definitions adopted for any specific ISO document.
- Of course, the establishment of a consensus on these definitions is a very difficult exercise, since the participants in the design of a standard invariably come from different individual backgrounds and levels of expertise, and many of them from very different cultural backgrounds.
  - Ensuring common understanding on terms, and on relationships across terms, is, on the one hand, a very time consuming effort, but,
  - on the other hand, it leads to a very robust, unambiguous, and coherent set of definitions.
- Once agreement had been reached on these definitions, the measurement principles were developed to provide for a measurement method which would lead to reproducibility, repeatability, and reproducibility. These are criteria that reflect the metrological strengths expected from a measurement method.

Again, this was a highly iterative process with a large number of back and forth discussions and clarifications, and redocumentation whenever a team member had interpreted a concept and a rule differently.

Overall, close to 40 experts from 8 countries participated in the design of the prototype and of the scale up of this measurement method.

> **Implicit/Explicit Testing of a Design by a Group of Experts**
>
> Throughout the scale up process, the contributing experts tested the application of the measurement rules based on their own expertise at working with requirements from different functional domains and verifying what the measurement results would be if the rules were applied:
>
> - to software they had measured with previous measurement methods, or
> - to requirements which could not have been measured adequately before such methods were used.

12.4. INDEPENDENT INDUSTRIAL FIELD TRIALS

Another key aspect of the COSMIC measurement method is the conducting of another field trial period designed to demonstrate that the method could withstand being scaled up to industrial software from multiple and varied contexts.

A 12-month period was allocated for conducting industrial field trials of the COSMIC measurement method in a significant number of organizations around the world.

- During this period, each participating organization received training on the application of the measurement method.
- Multiple software projects were selected from each organization's portfolio and their functional size was measured.

The results, along with some key data on the effort and scheduling involved in delivering each software project, were registered and centralized for analysis.

Once analyzed, a specific report was prepared for each participating organization, offering:

- guidelines for applying the method based on that organization's software engineering standards, and
- some preliminary benchmarking information allowing the organization to leverage its investment in the new data and put it to use immediately.

From the perspective of the participants in the field trials, the benefit of this approach lay in the availability, at the end of the field trial period, of a database of historical data useful for jumpstarting the implementation of the measurement method within their own organizations while respecting the confidentiality of the sources.

12.5. OUTCOME: THE DESIGN OF THE COSMIC MEASUREMENT METHOD

12.5.1 Allocation of Functional User Requirements

From the perspective proposed by COSMIC, software is part of a product or service designed to satisfy functional user requirements. From this high-level perspective, functional user requirements can be allocated:

- to hardware,
- to software, or
- to a combination of the two.

The functional user requirements allocated to software are not necessarily allocated to a single unit of software. Often these requirements are allocated to pieces of software operating at different levels of abstraction and cooperating to supply the required functionality to the product or service in which they are included.

This is illustrated in Figure 12.1.

In the context of the COSMIC measurement method, which is aimed at measuring the functional size of software, only those functional user requirements allocated to software are considered.

As illustrated in Figure 12.2, the functional user requirements in this example are allocated to three distinct pieces of software, each of which exchanges data with another through a specific organization:

- One piece of the software lies at the application level and exchanges data with the software's users and with a second piece lying at the operating system level.
- In turn, this second piece of software exchanges data with a third piece lying at the device driver level.
- This last piece then exchanges data directly with the hardware.

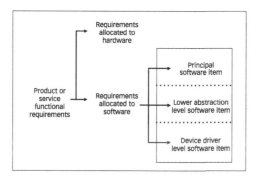

Figure 12.1. Allocation of functional user requirements [COSMIC2009]

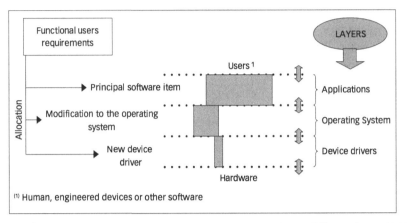

Figure 12.2. Example of functional user requirements allocation to different layers [COSMIC 2009]

The COSMIC measurement method associates each level with a specific layer—each layer possesses an intrinsic boundary for which specific functional users are identified.

The functional size of the software described through the functional user requirements is thus broken down into three pieces, each piece receiving some of the functional user requirements.

12.5.2 Representation of Functional User Requirements in Software

The functional user requirements in the subset allocated to one or more pieces of software are represented by functional processes.

Each functional user requirement is thus represented, within the piece of software to which it has been allocated, by one or more functional processes. In turn, each functional process is represented by sub processes:

- A sub process can either be a data movement type or a data transform type.
- By convention, the COSMIC measurement method recognizes only data movement type sub-processes in its numerical assignment rules.

The Common Concept: A Data Movement

Taking into account data movements is a common feature of many previous methods of measuring functional size, on which there is quite broad consensus that it is a fair representation of the concept of the functional size of software.

Of course, each method will have its own way of assigning a number to such a concept, leading to variations in that respect.

Lack of Consensus on the Size of Algorithms

By contrast, while it is often said that algorithms also contribute to functionality, there is **no consensus in the industry:**

- on how to represent such functionality, or
- on how to assign a quantitative value to it.

Although imperfect, most methods of functional size measurement do not take algorithms into account directly, and assume that, in general, this does not have a significant impact on size.

Of course, there are exceptions when there are many algorithms in a piece of software: any organization can easily recognize these exceptions and treat them as exceptions for whatever purpose they are measuring, be it for productivity analysis or estimation.

This approach is illustrated in Figure 12.3.

12.5.3 COSMIC Model of Generic Software

A key aspect of the COSMIC measurement method is the explicit definition of the attributes of software relevant to the measurement of its functional size and their arrangement in a coherent model of generic software.

The COSMIC measurement method defines an explicit model of software functionality derived from the functional user requirements. Based on this explicit model of functionality, relevant functional attributes of software are identified, that is, the four data movement types recognized by the COSMIC measurement method (Entry, Exit, Read, Write)—see Table 12.1.

Taken as a whole, these functional attributes form a generic model of software offering a universal basis for measuring software functional size. Furthermore, the COSMIC software model was designed to comply with the ISO-14143 standard for the measurement software functional size.

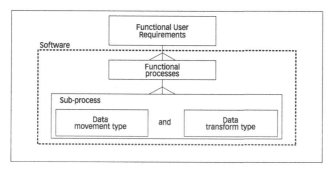

Figure 12.3. COSMIC representation of functional user requirements [COSMIC 2009]

TABLE 12.1. Definitions of COSMIC Data Movement Types

Type	Definition
ENTRY	A *data movement* type that moves a *data group* from a *functional user* across the *boundary* into the *functional process* where it is required.
EXIT	A *data movement* that moves a *data group* from a *functional process* across the *boundary* to the *functional user* that requires it.
READ	A *data movement* that moves a *data group* from *persistent storage* within reach of the *functional process* that requires it.
WRITE	A *data movement* that moves a *data group* lying inside a *functional process* to *persistent storage*.

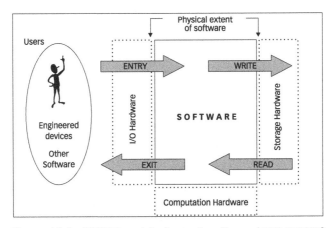

Figure 12.4. COSMIC model of generic software [COSMIC2009]

The COSMIC model of generic software is illustrated in Figure 12.4.

It is to be noted that each data movement type is considered to include a certain number of associated *data manipulations*—see the COSMIC Measurement Manual for details—www.cosmicon.com/portal/dl.asp

12.6. STRENGTHS OF THE COSMIC DESIGN

12.6.1 Conformity with Metrology Design Criteria

The COSMIC measurement method has been designed to conform to the metrology design criteria embedded within the set of definitions in the VIM.

For instance, two elements characterize the COSMIC measurement rules and procedures:

- the base functional components that constitute the arguments of the measurement function, and

- the standard unit of measurement, which is the yardstick defining one unit of functional size.

12.6.1.1   Base   Functional   Components. The COSMIC measurement method uses only four base functional components: Entry, Exit, Read, and Write.

What about Data Manipulation?

Data manipulation sub processes are not used as base functional components.
   The method assumes, as an acceptable approximation for many types of software, that the functionality of this type of sub process is already embedded among the four types of sub process defined earlier.

12.6.1.2   Standard Unit of Measurement. The standard unit of measurement, that is, 1 CFP (COSMIC Function Point) is defined by convention as equivalent to one single data movement at the sub process level.

Standard Unit of Measurement in COSMIC

1 COSMIC Function Point unit or CFP, in version 3.0

12.6.1.3   Aggregation Function. Using the standard unit of measurement, base functional components are thus assigned size units.

The functional size of the base functional components can then be combined to obtain the size of higher-level functional structures like functional processes or layers.

This is done by arithmetically adding the functional sizes of the constituent functional structures using an aggregation function.

The measurement system proposed by the COSMIC measurement method offers a scalable result, which means that the functional size figure can be constructed at the desired level of abstraction.

12.6.2   COSMIC Measurement Method

According to ISO-14143-1, a functional size measurement method is based on the perspective provided by the functional user requirements of the software to be measured.

- In practice, functional user requirements do not often exist in a "pure" form, as a stand-alone document.
- Therefore, very often, functional user requirements constitute a relatively abstract view of the software which needs to be extracted from other documents generated by the software engineering process.

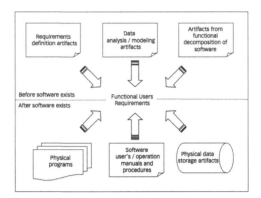

Figure 12.5. Extracting Functional User Requirements—COSMIC [2009]

Essentially, functional user requirements can be extracted:

- from software engineering documents which are produced before the software exists (typically from architecture and design artifacts), or
- after the software has been created (typically from user documentation, physical programs, and storage structure layouts).

This is illustrated in Figure 12.5. Thus, the functional size of software can be measured:

- prior to its creation, or
- after its creation.

The effort to extract the functional user requirements will obviously vary, depending on the quality of the documents used but, as long as the focus is placed on extracting them, the functional size of software can be measured.

Experience with other functional size measurement methods has shown that there are two distinct activities involved in measuring the functional size of software:

- identify some base functional components within the software, and
- assign size units to each of these components.

The COSMIC measurement method recognizes this practice explicitly by proposing a measurement process where:

- the software to be measured is first mapped to the generic software model, and then

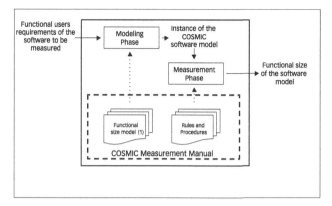

Figure 12.6. COSMIC measurement procedure [COSMIC 2009]

- a measurement function is applied to this software model in order to generate a numerical figure representing the functional size.

This measurement process is illustrated in Figure 12.6.

12.6.3   Applying the Measurement Function

This step consists of applying the COSMIC measurement standard to each of the data movements identified in each functional process.

The COSMIC measurement standard, 1 CFP, is defined as the size of the data movement of a single data group.

According to this measurement function, each instance of a data movement of one data group (Entry, Exit, Read, or Write) is assigned a numerical size of 1 CFP.

The final step consists of aggregating the results of the measurement function, as applied to all the identified data movements, into a single functional size value:

For each functional process, the functional sizes of individual data movements are arithmetically added:

$$\text{Size}_{\text{CFP}}\left(\text{functional process}_i\right) = \sum \text{size}\left(\text{entries}_i\right) + \sum \text{size}\left(\text{exits}_i\right) + \sum \text{size}\left(\text{reads}_i\right) \\ + \sum \text{size}\left(\text{writes}_i\right)$$

Note that the minimum size of a functional process is 2 CFP (there must always be one Entry and either a Write or an Exit) and there is no upper limit to the size of any one functional process.

For any functional process, the functional size of changes to the Functional User Requirements is aggregated from the sizes of the corresponding modified data movements according to the following formula:

$$\text{Size}_{\text{CFP}}\left(\text{Change}\left(\text{functional process}_i\right)\right) = \sum \text{size}\left(\text{added data movements}\right) +$$
$$\sum \text{size}\left(\text{modified data movements}\right) +$$
$$\sum \text{size}\left(\text{deleted data movements}\right)$$

Measuring a Software Enhancement

A requested change to a piece of software might be:

- add 1 new functional process of size 6 CFP, and
- add 1 data movement to another functional process, make changes to 3 other data movements, and delete 2 data movements.

The total size of the requested change is:

$$6 + (1 + 3) + 2 = 12 \text{ CFP}.$$

Can You Have a Size of 1 CFP?

The minimum size of *a functional process* is 2 CFP; there must always be one Entry and either a Write or an Exit.

However, **an enhancement may be to a single data movement of size = 1 CFP**

The size of such an enhancement is then equal to 1 CFP.

12.6.4 COSMIC Method vs. Procedure

Another key aspect of the COSMIC measurement method is the distinction made between a measurement method and a measurement procedure. As defined by ISO VIM, in relation to metrology:

- a measurement method describes the concept and generic principles pertaining to a measure, while
- a measurement procedure describes how to apply the method in specific instances.

In the COSMIC measurement method, the concepts, the generic principles, and a unit to measure the functional size of software are described in detail in a measurement manual containing the measurement standards adopted by the COSMIC group.

- The method is designed to be applicable to a wide range of software types, including MIS and real-time software.

- A generic process, applicable to this range of software types is also described, but the specifics of measuring one particular type of software are left to a specific measurement procedure.

From the perspective of measurement practitioners, the benefit of this approach lies in the combination of the relative universality of the functional size unit and the specificity of a measuring tool (the procedure) adapted to the particular type of software to be measured.

In addition, COSMIC documentation has been placed in the public domain and is available at http://www.cosmicon.com/portal/dl.asp

This documentation has been translated into many languages, including Japanese, Chinese, French, Arabic, Turkish, Dutch and Spanish.

Measurement of Temperature

A **method** for measuring temperature would define temperature, the unit of measurement of temperature, and what principles govern the reading of temperatures.

Based on this method, one **procedure** can be designed to measure the temperature of the human body for medical purposes, and another to measure the temperature of the lava inside a volcano.

Obviously, the two procedures will be quite different, but both will measure the same concept, namely temperature, and using the same units of measurement, that is, degrees Celsius.

12.7. SCALING UP—METROLOGY INFRASTRUCTURE

12.7.1 International Standards

What is the ultimate recognition for a measurement method—and for its designer(s)?

- Is it to be published in the most prestigious academic journal?
- Is it to be extensively referenced by other researchers in the academic literature?
- Is it to be copyrighted?
- Is it to be assigned a patent?

In the field of measurement in the sciences and in engineering, the ultimate recognition is to be adopted by the largest community on the one hand, and to be adopted within an international recognized legal framework on the other.

In practice, this is achieved by being recognized, for instance, as an ISO standard.

In the COSMIC design process, one of the criteria had been that its design meet all the criteria specified in the ISO meta standard on functional size measurement—ISO 14143-1. Therefore, the COSMIC design and its measurement manual had to:

- meet all the technical and editorial requirements of ISO standards; and
- have its content widely accessible (that is, understandable) across the many cultures and languages of the national standards organizations with voting rights at the ISO international level.

Since many of the experts who contributed to the design of COSMIC had a vast experience of working in ISO standardization groups in software engineering, they used this expertise in both the design process itself and in submitting the COSMIC measurement method to the ISO voting process.

With both these advantages, in addition to the submission to ISO of a document that had been already been extensively reviewed (and adapted) to an international community, the COSMIC method was easily adopted as ISO standard 19761 in 2003.

- This gave it official international recognition which could be used in both national and international trade contexts.
- Since then, it has been adopted as a national standard in various countries, such as in Japan, for example.

In addition, the ISO guide to ISO 9001 for software organizations, that is, the ISO 90003 document, specifically includes COSMIC as a recognized measurement method—see *ISO 90003—Guide to the implementation of quality system in software.*

12.7.2 International Data Collection Practices—ISBSG

The International Software Benchmarking Standards Group (ISBSG)—see www.isbsg.org—maintains the largest publicly available repository of software projects. This ISBSG repository included over 5,000 projects by mid-2009.

The COSMIC group has obtained recognition for COSMIC as one of the ISBSG's functional size standards for data collection. Since then:

- The ISBSG has developed a tailored data collection questionnaire for projects measured using COSMIC.
- COSMIC projects are now being collected and stored in this repository; similarly, COSMIC projects are being used in benchmarking studies.

This makes available to both industry and researchers a number of COSMIC measured projects for productivity studies and for the development of estimation models.

As of mid-2009, the Release 11 of the ISBSG repository contains over 300 projects measured with the COSMIC standard.

12.8. COMPETITIVE ADVANTAGES

The competitive advantages of COSMIC can be summarized as follows:

- It is in the public domain, and so, as with any classic measure in the sciences and in engineering, it is available free of charge.
- It has full ISO recognition.
- Its design is simple.
- Its flexibility allows it to be applicable to a very wide range of software.
- It has the ability to capture size from multiple software viewpoints.
- Its underlying concepts are compatible with modern software engineering concepts.

The COSMIC measurement method is designed to be applicable to domain software:

- Business application software which is typically needed to support business administration, such as banking, insurance, accounting, personnel, purchasing, distribution, and manufacturing. Such software is often characterized as "data rich", as its complexity is dominated largely by the need to manage large amounts of data about events in the real world.
- Real-time software, the task of which is to keep up with or control events happening in the real world. Examples would be software for telephone exchanges and message switching, software embedded in devices to control machines such as domestic appliances, elevators, and car engines, for process control and automatic data acquisition, and in the computer operating systems.
- Hybrids of the above, as in real-time reservation systems for airlines and hotels, for example.

It is possible, to define local extensions to the COSMIC measurement method software, which:

- is characterized by complex mathematical algorithms or other specialized and complex rules, such as may be found in expert systems, simulation software, self-learning software, weather forecasting systems, etc.
- processes continuous variables, such as audio sounds or video images, as found, for instance, in computer game software, musical instruments, and the like.

Visit www.cosmicon.com for further information about COSMIC, and for free downloads of:

- COSMIC Implementation Guide to ISO 19761:2003,
- measurement bulletin updates,
- case studies,
- publications,
- certification information, etc.

In addition to the COSMIC measurement manual providing the principles and rules to improve the accuracy and repetitiveness of the measurement results, the COSMIC group has documented a number of guidelines for related issues in their Advanced Topics document, such as:

- Local extensions for contexts not addressed in the initial design.
- Derivation of an approximate size early on, when not all the functional requirements have been fully described.
- Convertibility to other functional size measurement methods[4], etc.

EXERCISES

1. What were the objectives for the scaling up of the COSMIC measurement method?
2. Which levels of experts contributed to the scaling up of COSMIC?
3. List some design decisions and their related rationale.
4. What is the generic model of software adopted in the COSMIC design?
5. What is "functionality" in the COSMIC design?
6. What has been considered, in designing the functional size measure in COSMIC, and what has not been taken into account?
7. What is the unit of measurement in COSMIC?
8. How can you obtain a single unit of measurement in COSMIC?
9. What is the measurand in the COSMIC measurement method?
10. Do you measure this measurand directly?
11. When you apply the COSMIC numerical rules, which scale types are being handled mathematically?
12. How is the COSMIC measurement method integrated within the international framework for this type of technology?

[4]See chapter 13.

13. Discuss the advantages of a measurement method recognized as an ISO standard.

TERM ASSIGNMENTS

1. Document a measurement procedure for measuring with the COSMIC method for implementation in your own development environment.

2. Use the measurement procedure designed in the previous step to measure software in your own development environment. Did your measurement procedure work well? Document what should be improved, either in terms of measurement procedure or in terms of your own development environment to facilitate measurement.

3. Take the same *software implemented in a specific environment*, and, with three of your classmates, independently measure the COSMIC size of this software. Next, compute the differences in measurement results across measurers at the total Function Points level and at the detailed level for each function measured. Discuss the findings and compare the error rates. Explain the differences. Is the difference at the total level meaningful?

4. Take the same *set of requirements for software not yet developed*, and, with three of your classmates, independently measure the COSMIC size of these requirements. Next, compute the differences in measurement results across measurers at the total Function Points level and at the detailed level for each function measured. Discuss the findings and compare the error rates. Explain the differences. Is the difference at the total level meaningful?

5. Take the documentation of the requirements before review and inspection and measure it with COSMIC. Take the documentation for the same set of requirements and, this time after review and inspection, measure them again with COSMIC. Compare the measurement results and discuss the differences in them.

6. Measure, with COSMIC, software developed and implemented for which the documentation of the approved requirements still exists, on the basis of those requirements and again on the basis of the software as implemented. Compare the measurement results and discuss the differences in them.

7. Select an automation tool for COSMIC. Analyze it and propose improvements to it. Continue to evolve and improve this tool that supports software measurement.

PART 4

OTHER ISSUES IN THE DESIGN OF SOFTWARE MEASURES

Part 1 of this book (chapters 1 to 5) looked into the key characteristics of measurement from a metrology perspective and discussed how to design a software measure.

Part 2 (chapters 6 to 10) presented analyses of the design of a few of the most popular measures proposed to the industry, such as the Cyclomatic complexity number, Halstead's metrics, Function Points, and Use Case Points.

Part 3 (chapters 11 and 12) presented the design process of the software measurement method that became ISO 19761: the COSMIC functional size measurement method. These two previous chapters illustrated:

- how to design a software measurement method, and
- how to introduce metrological strengths into the design of a software measurement method in order to bring a software measurement method to market.

Part 4 presents two other topics which, although not often discussed in connection with the design of software measurement methods, are fundamental to measurement in general:

Software Metrics and Software Metrology, by Alain Abran
Copyright © 2010 IEEE Computer Society

- convertibility across different methods to measure the same attribute (chapter 13), and
- the design of a software standard etalon to ensure comparability across measurement results and traceability of measurement to internationally recognized reference material in measurement (chapter 14).

13

CONVERTIBILITY ACROSS MEASUREMENT METHODS[1]

This chapter covers:

The issue of convertibility across measurement methods of the same attribute by looking into issues of convertibility from Function Points to COSMIC measurement results. This includes:

- Overview of related convertibility studies.
- A convertibility study of an industrial dataset.
- FP to COSMIC convertibility: issues and discussion.

13.1. INTRODUCTION

Sometimes in the field of software measurement, a large number of measures are proposed for the same attribute, such as software complexity, cohesion, and coupling, as well as the various characteristics of software quality, such as maintainability, reliability, etc.

This leaves practitioners with a number of alternatives, but without much information about how to compare the results obtained from such alternatives.

---

[1]See also: Jean-Marc Desharnais, Alain Abran, and Juan Cuadrado-Gallego, "Convertibility of Function Points to COSMIC-FFP: Identification and Analysis of Functional Outliers," MENSURA2006, Cadiz, Spain, Nov. 4–5, 2006, Editor: University of Cádiz Press <www.uca.es/publicaciones>, pp. 190–205.

Software Metrics and Software Metrology, by Alain Abran
Copyright © 2010 IEEE Computer Society

Even in the three technical reports of ISO 9126, it is often the case that different measures are proposed to measure the same quality characteristics or sub characteristics[2], without any documentation as to convertibility across those measures.

This is a bit like measuring temperature using different units of measurement, but without knowing how to convert from one system of measurement to another.

There is one software measurement domain where convertibility across methods has long been a concern, that is, functional size measurement.

This chapter presents, for illustrative purposes, work done on convertibility in the functional size measurement community.

- For instance, several organizations are interested in using ratios of convertibility ratios between the COSMIC measurement method and first-generation functional size measurement (in particular, the traditional Function Points method), in order to leverage data from their historical databases of software measures.
- Previous convertibility studies have indicated that the convertibility of Function Points (FP) to COSMIC can be simple, with a very good correlation for most MIS projects, but that there are some outliers for which convertibility is less straightforward.

This chapter provides further insights into this issue of convertibility between traditional FP and COSMIC.

It analyzes a dataset of 14 projects measured with both sizing methods, and for which measurement results are available at the detailed level. The analysis reported in this chapter identifies reasons why, for some MIS projects, convertibility is not so straightforward. It also provides lead indicators to identify outliers for convertibility purposes.

This chapter is organized as follows:

- Section 13.2: Overview of previous convertibility studies.
- Section 13.3: A convertibility study of an industry dataset.
- Section 13.4: Convertibility issues and discussion.

13.2. OVERVIEW OF PREVIOUS CONVERTIBILITY STUDIES

The following preconditions exist in all studies reported in this chapter:

- All functionalities inside the boundary of the software being measured are included in the measurement.

[2]See chapter 10.

- Measurements have been taken from the human end-user's viewpoint.
- All convertibility studies reported here were carried out with duplicate measurements using both COSMIC and FP (or the NESMA equivalent) on the same set of functional user requirements.
- The specific versions of methods used in each convertibility study are documented for each study.
- The FP result is considered not to include the value adjustment factor (VAF) which means that the result, in conformity with ISO 14143-1 and ISO 20926, is unadjusted function points (UFP).

13.2.1 Fetcke [1999]

In the [Fetcke 1999] study, four software applications of a data storage system were measured. These are business applications with few data entities.

The linear regression model of Fetcke's data provides the following convertibility formula, where CFP represents COSMIC functional size units and UFP represents unadjusted function points, with a very high coefficient of determination (R^2) of 0.97:

$$Y(CFP) = 1.1 * (UFP) - 7.6 \tag{1}$$

Of course, because the number of data points is small (that is, only four in this dataset), care must be exercised in extrapolating the results:

- to larger datasets, and to
- datasets from different contexts.

To summarize, in this study, the duplicate measurement of software containing few data files and from the human end-user's viewpoint gave fairly similar results, and a convertibility formula with a slope fairly close to 1.

13.2.2 Vogelezang [2004]

In the [Vogelezang and Lesterhuis 2003; Vogelezang 2004] study, the COSMIC measurements were carried out on 11 projects already measured with the NESMA FP method [ISO 24570].

The linear regression model of this dataset provides the following convertibility formula, with a coefficient of determination (R^2) of 0.99:

$$Y(CFP) = 1.2 * (UFP) - 87 \tag{2}$$

Vogelezang and Lesterhuis postulate that the figure 87, the constant in equation (2), probably owes its existence to the counting of the logical files of data (ILFs and EIFs) in FP [Vogelezang 2004] that are not directly included in COSMIC.

This interpretation suggests that the high value of 87 might not be due entirely to the error term in this model.

13.2.3   2005 Dataset

The duplicate measurement results reported in [Abran *et al.* 2005c] were collected in 2005 using FPA version 4.1 and COSMIC version 2.2. This dataset of 6 projects comes from a single governmental organization and was measured using the documentation of completed projects.

The linear regression model of this 2005 dataset provides the following convertibility formula, with a coefficient of determination (R^2) of 0.91:

$$Y(CFP) = 0.84*(UFP) + 18 \tag{3}$$

Again, a large difference in convertibility results for one project was noted, both in absolute and in relative terms. This means, again, that there must be some peculiarities in the way functionality is measured that lead to non straightforward convertibility for this project.

In FP, the data are taken into account from multiple perspectives, once as logical data files (ILF—Internal Logical Files, and EIF—External Interface Files) and again whenever there are references in FP transactions (the transaction types Input, Output, and Enquiries). This has already been noted in [Vogelezang 2003], where it is reported that, in FP-like methods, 30 to 40% of functional size comes from the data files.

By taking into account only the FP data file points from the FP transaction-type points, it was investigated next whether or not a better convertibility ratio could be derived by excluding the FP data files, that is, by taking into account only the size from the transactions (UFP-TX).

With the FP for the transactions only (TX), the linear regression model provides the following convertibility formula with a coefficient of determination (R^2) of 0.98:

$$Y(CFP) = 1.35*(UFP\text{-}TX) + 5.5 \tag{4}$$

Thus, there is a slight improvement in the (R^2) for the convertibility formula when using only the results of the transactions for UFP, instead of the total size derived from both data and transactions. Again, with such a small dataset, this result should be taken as indicative only, and be investigated with larger datasets.

13.3.   A CONVERTIBILITY STUDY OF AN INDUSTRY DATASET

13.3.1   Context

In 2006, another set of 14 MIS projects was measured using UFP version 4.1 and COSMIC version 2.2 [Desharnais *et al.* 2006].

- The UFP and COSMIC measurements were taken concurrently, using the same documentation, by a single expert in both measurement methods.
- All 14 projects come from a single governmental organization (different from the one reported in the [Abran *et al.* 2005c] study).
- As for the datasets reported in the literature review, the measurements were taken from the user's viewpoint that is, taking into account that most of the software functionalities involve interaction with a human, which is typical of business software applications.

13.3.2 Distribution of Functional Size at the Transactional and Data Movement Levels

Analysis of the distribution of the transactions in FP and the distribution of data movements in COSMIC is one way to identify discrepancies in the measurement results.

Figure 13.1 presents the distribution of function-type sizes for the UFP measurement results:

- the total size (expressed as a percent) of the Input and Output function types is the same, at 36%,
- while the total size of the Inquiry function type is lower, at 28% (Figure 13.1).

The distribution of the function-type size for this set of 14 projects is reasonably comparable to the distribution of function types of the 3,161 UFP (IFPUG version) projects in the February 2006 edition of the International Software Benchmarking Standards Group—ISBSG—repository (Figure 13.2).

13.3.3 Convertibility Using Total UFP Size

The first convertibility analysis investigates the relationship of UFP to COSMIC based only on total UFP, that is, only on the summation of all the UFP, without looking into the details of the measurement results.

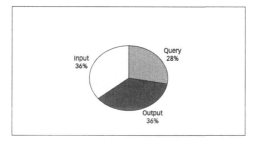

Figure 13.1. FP transaction size distribution (N = 14) **[Desharnais *et al.* 2006]**

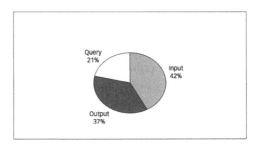

Figure 13.2. ISBSG 2006 FP transaction size distribution (N = 3,161)

TABLE 13.1. Convertibility Comparison on *Total UFP Size* (N = 14)

Project number	UFP Total points	COSMIC 2.2 (2)	With convertibility formula (3)	% diff (4) = (3) – (2)	(5) = (4)/(2)
1	383	364	379	15	4%
2	647	565	643	78	14%
3	400	398	396	−2	0%
4	205	188	202	14	7%
5	372	448	368	−80	−18%
6	126	88	123	35	39%
7	111	115	108	−7	−6%
8	287	298	284	−14	−5%
9	500	579	496	−83	−14%
10	344	291	340	49	17%
11	317	294	314	20	7%
12	258	252	255	3	1%
13	113	114	110	−4	−4%
14	447	467	443	−24	−5%

The measurement results of the duplicate measurement of the 14 applications are reported in Table 13.1 and presented graphically in Figure 13.3, with the UFP data on the x-axis and the COSMIC data on the y-axis.

The linear regression model of the data in Figure 13.3 provides the following convertibility formula, with a coefficient of determination (R^2) of 0.93:

$$Y(CFP) = 1.0 * (UFP) - 3 \tag{5}$$

This convertibility formula represents a convertibility ratio of almost 1-to-1. This does not mean, however, that the results produced will be entirely accurate, as can be seen in columns 4 and 5 of Table 13.1:

- For 9 projects out of 14, the relative difference is less than 7%;
- For 4 projects, the relative difference is between 14% and 17%; and
- For 1 project, the relative difference is 39%.

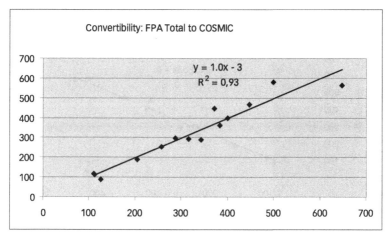

Figure 13.3. Convertibility model on *Total UFP Size* (N = 14)

TABLE 13.2. Convertibility Comparison on *FP Transaction Size Only—TX* (N = 14)

Project number	UFP TX points	COSMIC 2.2 (2)	With convertibility formula (3)	% diff (4) = (3) − (2)	(5) = (4)/(2)
1	271	364	369	5	1%
2	430	565	585	20	4%
3	302	398	411	13	3%
4	144	188	196	8	4%
5	295	448	401	−47	−10%
6	73	88	99	11	13%
7	55	115	75	−40	−35%
8	217	298	295	−3	−1%
9	404	579	549	−30	−5%
10	239	291	325	34	12%
11	212	294	288	−6	−2%
12	209	248	284	36	15%
13	87	114	118	4	4%
14	342	467	465	−2	0%

13.3.4 Convertibility Using FP Transaction Size—TX

The next convertibility analysis is based on the sizes of the three FP transaction types (Inputs, Outputs, and Inquiries)—that is: *Excluding* the sizes from the Internal and External logical files of the IFPUG method.

The measurement results of the duplicate measurement of the 14 applications are reported in Table 13.2 and presented graphically in Figure 13.4, with the UFP transaction sizes (TX) on the x-axis and the COSMIC data on the y-axis.

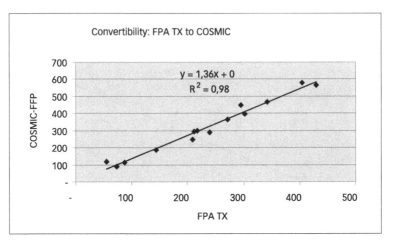

Figure 13.4. Convertibility model on *FP transactions size only—TX* (N = 14)

The linear regression model of the data in Figure 13.4 provides the following convertibility formula, with a coefficient of determination (R^2) of 0.98:

$$Y(CFP) = 1.36 * (TX) + 0 \qquad (6)$$

This convertibility formula is, of course, different from (5), since it is derived from a distinct basis (FP transaction size rather than total FP size) and its R^2 (0.98) is slightly better than the previous one (0.93).

- Again, this does not mean that entirely accurate results are produced for all projects converted, as can be seen in column (4) of Table 13.2, which represents the difference between the results of the convertibility and direct measurements in COSMIC.
- In column (5), the same difference is presented as a percentage. Some significant improvements can be observed:
  - 9 projects out of 14 have a very small relative difference of less than 5%;
  - 4 projects have a relative difference of between 10% and 15%; and
  - 1 project has a relative difference of 35%.

13.4. FP TO COSMIC CONVERTIBILITY: ISSUES AND DISCUSSION

13.4.1 Convertibility at the Data Level

The measurement of data is particular to the traditional FP method[3]. In FP, the sizes of the files (ILF and EIF) are added to the sizes of the transactions (Input, Output, and Enquiry) to obtain the FP total size in UFP. This is equivalent to

---

[3]See chapter 9.

adding together distinct entity types (analogous to adding the sizes of tables to the sizes of TV sets), leading to totals without a clear interpretation of the summation results, and thereby leaving end results which are difficult to interpret from a size viewpoint.

In COSMIC, there is no equivalent to adding two different entity types, only data movement types—Entry, Exit, Read, and Write—are added together.

Therefore, *it is expected that convertibility at the transaction level be more meaningful.*

13.4.2   Convertibility at the Transactions (TX) Level

The concept of the functional process in COSMIC is, in practice, equivalent to the concept of the functional transaction type in Function Points. When identifying a COSMIC functional process in the documentation of a project, it was observed that there is an equivalent FP elementary process.

While the mapping of the total size at the total level is reasonably direct from FP to COSMIC CFP for this sample, there are differences at the lower levels (sub-totals at the function type level and individual measurement results at the functional process level).

Notwithstanding this, there is still a difference between measuring the size of COSMIC functional processes and measuring FP transactions:

- the COSMIC functional process is based on the number of data movements in a functional process, while
- the FP transactions (Input, Output, and Inquiries) are based:
  - on the number of Data Element Types (DET) and File Type References, (FTR), and
  - on sets of weights (from 3 to 7) provided in different FP weight tables.

In addition, when analyzing the results for each functional process and each transaction, it was observed that the COSMIC sizes of all the functional processes are, in this dataset, systematically equal to or higher than the FP size of corresponding transactions.

There are at least two explanations for this:

- The weights in the FP tables for the transactions are limited to 7 points, while there is no such upper limit to the number of data movements in a COSMIC functional process.
- The measurement of the error messages:
  - On the one hand, FP version 4.1 rules includes error messages as a part of a transaction without assigning it additional points;
  - On the other hand, COSMIC recognizes an error message as one additional data movement in a functional process.

- The result is that a simple functional process has one more COSMIC size units (e.g. the data movement that takes into account the error message in the measurement process).

13.4.3 Summary of Findings

This 2006 study replicated the 2005 study (six projects from a single, but different organization) with a larger dataset (14 projects from a single organization), and the findings were similar at the total UFP size and UFP transaction size levels.

They were also comparable to the findings of previous studies:

- The convertibility formula is within the same range and works for most of the software measured with both methods.
- However, there are a few projects for which the convertibility formula provides poor results.

To summarize, this analysis, together with the findings highlighted in the literature review, indicates that:

- A relatively reasonable convertibility formula can be obtained for each MIS data set.
- However, there are some variations in the convertibility formulas across organizations.

These variations could be caused by extraneous factors, such as:

- non homogeneity in the distribution of FP function types (ratio of data files to transactions sizes), or
- variation in the quality of such documentation across the organizations where the measurements were derived,
- or both.

These analyses also indicate that convertibility can be straightforward, either based on total UFP size or on UFP transaction size for the majority of the projects in a dataset, even though there are larger variations for a few projects.

This means that the convertibility of a full portfolio of software applications could be reasonably accurate overall, but that a few individual projects would show some larger deviation from the values predicted by the convertibility formulas.

This study has also identified some candidate lead indicators to explain these greater variations, such as:

- a large deviation of the UFP file ratio from the sample average, and
- the size of the ratio of FP processes, which is constrained by the upper limits in the FP tables of points.

This study did not investigate more complex contexts, such as those having projects with more algorithm-rich processes and those involving software users other than software or engineered devices, such as in the case of real-time software.

Under these latter conditions, of course, backward convertibility (from COSMIC CFP to FP) is not of much interest, nor is it an issue, since functionality related to non-human users (such as interactions with sensors or controllers in embedded software, or in multi-layered software) is not usually taken into account and not measured by first-generation measurement methods.

EXERCISES

1. If different measurement methods are proposed in ISO 9126 to measure the same quality characteristic (or sub characteristic), how is convertibility handled when different designs of measures are selected?

2. How do you handle the convertibility of measured lines of code measured from different programming languages & from the *same* programming paradigm?

3. How do you handle the convertibility of measured lines of code written in different programming languages and from *different* programming paradigms?

4. What is the convertibility between COSMIC Function Points and conventional Function Points?

5. What is known about the convertibility of the newest ISO standard on functional size measurement, FISMA—ISO 29881, with respect to the other functional size measurement methods already recognized as ISO standards?

TERM ASSIGNMENTS

1. Conduct your own study to analyze the convertibility of the newest ISO standard on functional size measurement, FISMA—ISO 29881, with respect to the other functional size measurement methods already recognized as ISO standards.

2. Select three different measures of cohesion and coupling and analyze convertibility across them.

3. Select three different designs of Use Case Points and analyze convertibility across them.

4. In the ISBSG data repository, there are projects to which distinct sizing methods have been applied to measure functional size. Identify the convertibility studies already documented across these various methods and prepare

recommendations on procedures to take into account the convertibility issue across them. Identify in particular those that can be combined (using known convertibility ratios) and those that should not.

5. Analyze ISO TR 14143-5 and use it to document the functional domain of the software in your organization. If you do not have access to industry software, select a variety of open-source software. Discuss when this standard has an impact on convertibility.

6. Measure the functional size of two sets of Reference User Requirements in ISO TR 14143-4 with both Function Points and COSMIC. Identify and discuss the difficulties inherent in measuring these two sets of requirements and in analyzing convertibility across the measurement results.

14

DESIGN OF STANDARD ETALONS: THE NEXT FRONTIER IN SOFTWARE MEASUREMENT[1]

This chapter covers:

- An introduction to the concepts of measurement standard etalon
- Related work in software functional size measurement
- A (draft) methodology to design a software measurement standard etalon
- Advanced Readings: An example of an initial draft of a measurement standard etalon for COSMIC—ISO 19761.

14.1. INTRODUCTION—MEASUREMENT STANDARD ETALON

Measurement standards are designed to make life easier. In disciplines such as physics, chemistry, and biology, the reference to a measurement standard etalon is critical to ensure the correctness and consistency of measurement results across contexts and countries.

According to the International Vocabulary of Basic and General Terms in Metrology a *measurement standard etalon* is: "The realization of the definition

[1]See also: Adel Khelifi and Alain Abran, "Software Measurement Standards Etalons: A Design Process," International Journal on Computers, North Atlantic University Union—NAUN Press www.naun.org, Vol. 1, No. 3, 2007, pp. 41–48.

Software Metrics and Software Metrology, by Alain Abran
Copyright © 2010 IEEE Computer Society

of a given quantity, with stated quantity value and associated measurement uncertainty, used as a reference" [VIM 2007].

The [VIM 2007] provides a number of examples which illustrates a number of ways to implement a measurement standard etalon. It is noted in particular in the VIM the following:

- A "realization of the definition of a given quantity" can be provided by a **measuring system**, a **material measure**, or a reference material.
- A measurement standard is frequently used as a reference in establishing **measured quantity values** and associated measurement uncertainties for other quantities of the same **kind**, thereby establishing **metrological traceability** through **calibration** of other measurement standards, **measuring instruments**, or measuring systems.

In sciences, as well as in many economic activities, it is most relevant to develop, for both measurers and users of measurement results, a system of references made up of software measurement standards.

Measurement standard etalons are essential elements of an adequate metrological structure, in that they provide measurement users with a common reference and give them greater confidence in the measurement process.

Indeed, standards facilitate the realization of measurement results on common bases.

Using a standard etalon can improve competitiveness by reducing the cost of both manufacturing and market transactions; a producer does not need to reinvent the specifications or performance criteria incorporated in the standard, and can therefore concentrate resources elsewhere.

Furthermore, a standard etalon can contribute to the propagation of innovations, and consequently enhance the economic benefit to be derived from them.

It is difficult to develop measurement standard etalons:

- They are created through an iterative process in which each iteration represents an improvement over the previous ones, in terms of both accuracy and stability.
- Each iteration may span years, if not decades.

Ideally, the design of standard etalons is an activity which must be undertaken at the international level by groups of experts from several countries in order to obtain a broad consensus.

The structure of this chapter is as follows:

- Section 14.2 presents some concepts about calibration, testing and uncertainty.
- Section 14.3 presents related work in the design of measurement standards, in software functional size measurement (FSM) in particular.

- Section 14.4 presents a proposal for a methodology to design a software measurement standard etalon.
- The Advanced Readings section presents its application for defining an initial draft of a set of etalons for ISO 19761—COSMIC.

14.2. CALIBRATION AND TESTING: REFERENCE MATERIAL AND UNCERTAINTY

A measurement method is first defined in terms of:

- its objectives,
- a meta-model of the entity to be measured, and
- the characteristics of the attribute to be measured.

This definition is then realized by means of a measurement unit and a corresponding assignment of numerical rules—see Part 1 of this book, Chapters 3 and 5.

Next, to ensure that measurements across a community are performed in a consistent manner, a baseline should be established as a primary reference.

Any specific measurement results using such a measurement method (or typically a measuring instrument in traditional science) can be compared with the primary measurement reference by means of calibration and testing; calibration determines the performance characteristics of a measurement instrument or the reference material.

There are three main reasons for calibrating a measuring instrument:

1. to ensure that the instrument readings are consistent with other measurements,
2. to determine the accuracy of the instrument readings, and
3. to establish the reliability of the instrument, i.e. that it can be trusted.

Reference procedures can be defined as testing, measurement, or analysis procedures, which are:

- thoroughly characterized and proven to be under control, and
- intended for the quality assessment of:
  - other procedures for comparable tasks,
  - the characterization of reference materials, including reference objects, or
  - the determination of reference values.

The uncertainty of the results of a reference procedure must be adequately estimated and appropriate for the intended use.

According to this definition, reference procedures can be used to:

- verify other measurement or test procedures used for a similar task, and determine the level of uncertainty associated with them,
- determine reference values for the properties of materials which can be compiled in handbooks or databases, or
- determine reference values which are embodied in reference material or a reference object.

Uncertainty is a quantitative measure of the quality of a measurement result enabling the measurement results to be compared with other results, references, specifications, or standards.

14.3. RELATED WORK IN SOFTWARE MEASUREMENT

14.3.1   Related Issues in Software Measurement

In the information technology domain, and more specifically in software engineering, concepts of units and etalons have seldom been used, and this is a symptom of the immaturity of software measurement.

Up to now, some characteristics of software have made it challenging to measure:

- It is an atypical product when compared to other industrial products, in that it varies greatly in terms of size, complexity, design techniques, test methods, applicability, etc.
- There is little consensus on specific measures of software attributes, as illustrated by the scarcity of international measurement standards for those attributes, such as software complexity and quality.

Because of these challenges, some have claimed that software "metrics" are to some extent unique, and, as such, cannot be constrained to meet all the metrological properties as defined in the ISO document on metrology.

- However, the fact that there is currently no standard etalon for software does not imply that one cannot be created.
- There is, indeed, a lack of documented attempts to do so, and a lack of a methodology for doing so for software.

In this chapter, it is postulated that it is feasible to create a standard etalon for software and that a methodology for doing so could be designed.

If measurement reference material in the form of standard etalons were available to software practitioners, it could:

- be used as a common baseline for measurement,
- offer a point of reference for software measurers to verify their measurement results and their ability to measure the same reference material, and
- allow measurers to use the related reference concept, and thus to speak at the same level.

Material measurement standard etalons are widely recognized as critical for accurate and repeatable measurements in any field. However, none of the designers of software measures has yet included any of them in their design.

To verify measurement results and ensure unambiguous comparability across contexts and measurers, researchers in software measurement should design standard etalons and incorporate them into the design of every measure proposed.

Lack of Standard Etalons in Software Measurement

In software engineering, most measurement proposals:

- do not refer to any references (primary or other),
- do not suggest any measuring instrument, and
- do not design or adopt any measurement standard etalon.

The absence of standard etalons in software measurement is most probably having a negative impact on software developers and managers when they come to use measurement results in decision making.

While it is difficult to determine the effect of measurements on software quality, for instance, it is clear that using standards of measurement would provide software measurers, developers, and managers with much better indicators of that quality, as well as more time to react, and could reduce the number and seriousness of software failures.

Since the design process for establishing standard etalons for software measures has not yet been investigated, this chapter tackles that issue and illustrates the application of such a process for one of the international standards for software functional size measurement, ISO 19761: COSMIC.

The focus of this chapter is on a proposal of a design procedure for developing a standard etalon for a software Functional Size Measurement (FSM) [Khelifi *et al.* 2004, 2005].

The motivation for proposing an initial software measurement standard for functional size is the need for a traceable and widely recognizable standard etalon in software measurement, as exists for measurement in other human endeavors.

14.3.2   ISO Pioneered Work on FSM Reference Material

Of the hundreds of proposals to measure various attributes of software, only in functional size measurement has there emerged a broad enough consensus to lead to software measurement methods as international standards.

ISO 14143 Meta-standard for Functional Size Measurement Methods

Part 1: Definition of Concepts

Part 2: Conformity Evaluation of Software Size Measurement Methods

Part 3: Verification of Functional Size Measurement Methods

Part 4: Reference Model

Part 5: Determination of Functional Domains for use with Functional Size Measurement

Part 6: Guide for Use of ISO 14143 Series and Related International Standards

Parts 1 and 2 are recognized International Standards.

Parts 3 to 6 are Technical Reports only, *published by the ISO.*

Related ISO FSM International Standards

- ISO 19761: COSMIC
- ISO 20926: Unadjusted Function Points
- ISO 20968: Mk II
- ISO 24570: NESMA
- ISO 29881: FISMA

Of these five specific FSM methods recognized by the ISO:

- none explicitly addresses the concept of a standard etalon;
- only COSMIC specifically specifies and documents the concept of a measurement unit for size.

The ISO community has directly recognized the need for reference material on FSM:

- ISO TR 14143-4 provides a set of Reference User Requirements (RUR), which were put together to provide FSM communities with material intended to be used for convertibility studies across specific measurement methods.
- Such reference material in ISO TR 14143-4 was intended to be used to test some of the metrological properties of a specific measurement method, such as the accuracy, repeatability, and reproducibility criteria quoted in ISO TR 14143-3.

In practice, however, ISO TR 14143-4 suffers from a number of important limitations, and in its current state it cannot be used to assess an FSM method against some standard reference points to determine whether or not it yields expected results in a given situation:

In 14143-4, all the sets of Reference User Requirements (RURs) are *described in a non standardized textual format.*

- There is, therefore, great variation in the description of these RURs within a given set, and, of course, across sets.
- In particular, none has been reviewed for quality control.

Therefore, trial use of reference material in 14143-4 by both experts and beginners has highlighted a number of ambiguities and a lack of completeness, leading to different interpretations of these ambiguous functional requirements, and, of course, to various measurement results. This, of course, defeats the purpose of the publication of this document, and the ISO should return it to the drawing board.

Observations from Trial Usages of ISO 14143-4

Distinct measurers produce different measurement results when they need to make assumptions, and these will often vary from one person to another based, in particular, on their work experience.

Of course, in the presence of incomplete or ambiguous requirements, distinct developers would also produce distinct software designs and related software implementations.

The measurement of software functional size generally relies on the functional documentation of the software to be measured:

- It has been illustrated in [Nagano *et al.* 2001] that the quality of the documentation has an impact on both the quality of the measurement results and the effort required to perform the measurements.
- Several researchers and practitioners have also noted that the software documentation is often either incomplete or obsolete, and even sometimes erroneous.

This issue has not been addressed in ISO 14143-4, which leads to similar difficulties in measurement practice, where the application of software functional measurement requires:

- knowledge of the specific software measurement method being used, and
- sufficient experience in the interpretation of software artifacts.

For instance, in the measurement process with the COSMIC method, the measurer must determine the following, from the available artifacts:

- software layers to be measured,
- software boundary,
- functional users,
- triggering events,
- functional processes,
- data groups, and
- data movements.

Should the documentation be complete and accurate, these measurement steps are easy.

Unfortunately, in practice, the documentation is often incomplete, and, to measure software, the measurer has to supplement the information provided on some requirements which is either incomplete or ambiguous.

The availability of a standard etalon for FSM would help improve the quality of FSM results on a practical level. Using a standard etalon can therefore help reduce the time spent addressing inconsistency issues in measurement results.

14.3.3   Case Studies as Reference Material in FSM

Up to now, the ISO-recognized FSM communities have developed case studies as reference material for training purposes.

- These case studies are very specific in terms of teaching some of the peculiarities of individual FSM methods.
- However, they are not generic enough to be used as reference material for calibration and testing purposes.

These case studies suffer from a number of limitations:

- there is no normalized input to their design process;
- they have been drafted based on the judgments of experts within their own communities;
- they are limited in scope;
- they most often address only a limited number of measurement rules, sometimes in peculiar contexts;
- they cannot be used as generic reference material.

14.3.4   Related Work on COSMIC

The topic of a standard etalon for ISO 19761—COSMIC was initially discussed in [Khelifi *et al.* 2004] and initial drafts were published in [Khelifi 2005].

A limitation of this pioneering work is that it is an individual effort and does not benefit from international recognition or worldwide dissemination.

Official international recognition of a standard etalon for software measurement would be of practical interest to both industry and researchers.

The next section builds on the drafts of a standard etalon in Khelifi [2005] and extends its use to any FSM, and, by extension, potentially to any software size measurement method.

14.4. A (DRAFT) METHODOLOGY TO DESIGN AN FSM STANDARD ETALON

The challenge is how to design a standard etalon for software which is not a material product.

The generic process described next is based on the lessons learned from the preparation of case studies for training purposes and from work done to explore the design of an initial draft version of etalons for the COSMIC method.

This generic process includes the following seven steps—see Figure 14.1.

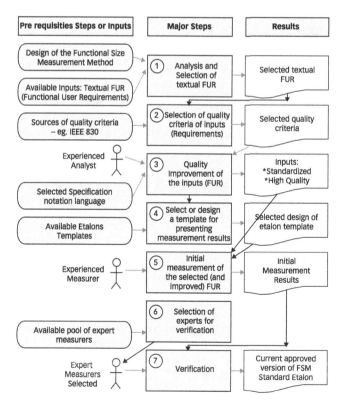

Figure 14.1. A Methodology to Design a Software Measurement Standard Etalon

1. Analysis and selection of textual descriptions of candidate Functional User Requirements (FUR); the input is the literature survey of previous work on the design of a specific measurement method and available descriptions of FUR. It has been noted that these sets of FUR are often available in non-standardized textual format.

2. Identification and selection of quality criteria for the inputs to the measurement process. For FSM, the inputs are usually expressed in the form of textual descriptions of requirements, and related quality criteria are defined, for instance, in the IEEE standards on Specifications Requirements [IEEE 830]. These quality criteria then become inputs to Step 3.

3. Quality improvement to the set of FUR by transforming the selected set of textual FUR into the selected specification language, and, in parallel, analysis of the quality of the requirements and correction of requirement defects (for instance, to remove ambiguities and inconsistencies in the requirements). The output of this step is then FUR described in the selected notation specification language which meet the specified quality criteria.

4. Selection or design of an etalon template for presenting the measurement process and measurement results. This step can be skipped if a template already exists.

5. Initial measurement of the requirements documented in the adopted specification notation by an experienced measurer to produce an initial draft of measurement results using the adopted output format for the standard etalon.

6. Selection of a group of experts to review the initial measurement results. Ideally, these measurement experts should be internationally recognized by industry for their specific FSM expertise. Of course, it would add credibility if these experts were also active participants in the ISO standardization program on FSM.

7. Verification by expert measurers of the initial measurement results and correction of either the inputs (the requirements themselves if they were incomplete or ambiguous) or the outputs (the measurement results).

14.5. DISCUSSION

This chapter has presented a methodology for developing a standard etalon for software measurement.

A specific example is provided in the Advanced Readings section using ISO 19761—COSMIC. In summary, the example includes:

- Verification of the quality of the FUR in inputs and the addition of UML diagrams, use cases, and sequence diagrams, and their verification by UML developers, enhances the description of the software functionalities by providing greater understandability, accuracy, and completeness to the reference set of FUR for the measurement exercise.

- The application by COSMIC experts to this reference set of FUR has generated a reference set of COSMIC measurement results.

It is the verification of every part of the standard etalons by recognized experts that makes them more accurate.

Of course, the example referred to the design of the first draft on an initial design of a software measurement etalon based on the knowledge available in the late 2000s: this has not yet provided a single standard etalon, as would typically be the case in conventional metrology.

The designers of software measurement methods must learn how to build standard etalons for software.

Notwithstanding this, it is important that the software measurement community come to appreciate that the development of a standard etalon for the measurement of software may take many decades.

After all, it took two centuries for the definition of the meter to become established.

ADVANCED READINGS: THE DEVELOPMENT OF AN (INITIAL) DRAFT OF A MEASUREMENT STANDARD ETALON FOR COSMIC

Audience

This Advanced Reading section is of most interest to researchers and industry practitioners interested in a specific example of the development of a standard etalon for the COSMIC measurement method.

This Advanced Reading section illustrates the process used to design the initial draft of a standard etalon for COSMIC (Khelifi, 2005).

1. *Analysis and selection of candidate FUR as input.*
   This step included the prerequisites for beginning the process of designing a standard etalon for COSMIC. In this specific instance, it consisted of the output of the literature survey of previous work on the design lessons learned from COSMIC case studies, as well as on the identification of a set of candidate inputs for measurement.

   - In this specific instance, the ISO work on FSM was selected (that is, *ISO TR 14143-4 2000—Reference User Requirements (RUR)*, since it contains an inventory of textual descriptions of requirements collected for measurement purposes.

   - Since the input to this step contained multiple sets of requirements, one specific set was selected as the basis for the work reported here, which was *RUR B9—Valve Control System* (from ISO 14143-4).

2. *Identification of the quality criteria of the inputs (i.e. of the requirements).*
   The quality criteria selected as prerequisites were selected from the IEEE standard on software requirements, that is, IEEE 830.
3. *Quality improvement of the inputs.*
   In ISO TR 14143-4, all the sets of RUR are described in a non standardized textual format. There is, therefore, great variation in the description of these RUR within this specific B9 set. This is typical of most inputs for the measurement of the functional size of software, in particular when the measurements are taken early in the software life cycle. As a result, it was necessary to verify the quality and completeness of these requirements.

   The RUR were therefore analyzed, verified, and improved using the quality criteria identified in the previous steps, that is, the quality criteria from IEEE 830.

   In this step, a specification language was selected as an input, and the selected set of textual FUR was transformed into a specification language.

   To improve the consistency of the documentation to be used as input to the FSM, the decision was made to adopt the UML notation, such as use cases and sequence diagrams, for the software to be measured.

   - The UML Use Case diagram is a tool for representing the entire functionality of a system; a sequence diagram is a structured representation of software behavior as a series of sequential steps over time.
   - Developing such diagrams can improve the comprehension of software functions and provide the measurer with more consistent and precise documentation as input to the measurement process.

   This allows the measurer to have his measurement inputs documented in a consistent manner, which in turn allows him greater transparency in the intermediate steps of the measuring process, as well as more repeatable results. For illustrative purposes, Figure 14.2 presents the sequence diagram for one of the case studies measured for the design of an initial version of a standard etalon.

   An analyst with expertise in UML notation carried out this step, which consisted of analyzing the textual description of the requirements and their transformation into UML notation, and, within this process, correcting defects (for instance, to remove ambiguities and inconsistencies in the requirements).

   The outcome is the verified set of FUR to be measured, that is, the measurand.
4. *Template for presenting the measurement results.*
   The step consists of the selection of a template (or design when there is no template) for presenting the measurement process and measurement results. Since there had already been documented case studies for COSMIC, these were reviewed and tailored for the purpose of document-

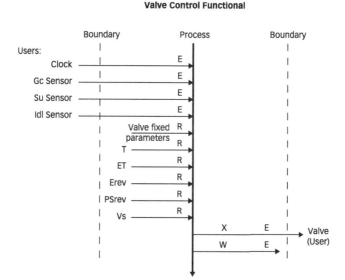

Figure 14.2. Valve Control Application—Sequence Diagram

ing the intermediate steps of the measurement process, as well as for the outcome in terms of measurement results.

For an example of a template for a COSMIC standard, see box. This template is an evolution of the reports developed by the COSMIC group for documenting case studies.

5. *Initial measurement*

An experienced measurer performed the initial measurement of the requirements documented in the adopted specification notation to produce an initial draft of the measurement results, while the detailed inputs and outputs were documented with the output format selected (see box).

Box: Template for a COSMIC Standard Etalon

1. Overview
    1.1 Introduction
    1.2 Measurement viewpoint, purpose, and scope
2. Requirements as documented in ISO 14143-3-4: 2000
    2.1 Context
    2.2 Input
    2.3 Output

3. COSMIC measurement procedure
   3.1 Identification of layers
   3.2 Identification of users
   3.3 System boundary
   3.4 Identification of triggering events
   3.5 Identification of data groups
   3.6 Identification of functional processes
4. Identification of data movements
   4.1 Message sequence diagram
   4.2 List of data movements
   4.3 Observations on the requirements' clarity
5. Analysis of measurement results
6. Summary, including observations
7. Questions & answers

6. *Selection of experts*
   In this step, a group of experts was selected to review the initial measurement results.

   • The selection of experts for the draft COSMIC standard etalon was made through the researchers' contacts. It includes international experts in software measurement in the COSMIC group, constituting a group of international volunteer experts in software measurement. Some of these experts were also members of the ISO working group specializing in software FSM.

   • However, this work was not done in an official context, and the credibility of the measurement outcomes derived from their individual expertise, and not from an official international process recognized by national institutions.

7. *Verification cycle*
   In this step, the initial measurement results were corrected, and even the requirements themselves if they were incomplete or ambiguous.

   The verification process illustrated in Figure 14.3 involved individual verification, FSM expert verification, and systematic verification by the COSMIC measurement practice committee.

   The final output constituted the initial version of a standard etalon for COSMIC. It is to be noted that, for traceability purposes, the output for establishing the standard etalon in software measurement must include both the inputs and the outputs of the measurement process.

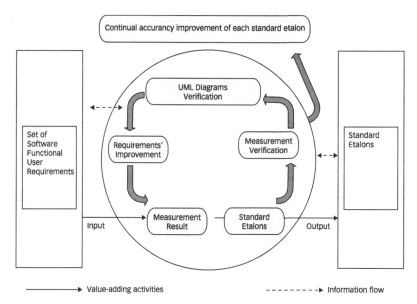

Figure 14.3. Iterative verification process for the design of a software standard etalon

In summary, the end-result of the design of a standard etalon for the COSMIC method consists of a detailed report using a template documenting the inputs, and the outputs of the measurement process on a set of software FUR.

The iterative verification process is highly relevant at the international level; in practice, this process will go through an iterative cycle.

EXERCISES

1. What is a standard etalon in metrology?

2. Name three standard etalons.

3. What is the relationship between a primary reference etalon and calibration and testing?

4. In software engineering, what is currently closer to a software standard etalon for measurement?

5. What key metrology concepts were introduced in the ISO 14143 series for functional size measurement?

6. Which part of ISO 14143 partially deals with standard etalons?

7. There are five international standards for functional size measurement:

    a. Which has (have) documented its (their) standard etalon(s)?

    b. Which have documented their measurement unit?

8. Illustrate how you would verify the design of a software measurement standard etalon.

TERM ASSIGNMENTS

1. Analyze an object-oriented measure and design a standard etalon for it.

2. Select a measure of cohesion and design a standard etalon for it.

3. Select a measure of complexity and design a standard etalon for it.

Appendix A

LIST OF ACRONYMS

Acronym	Description
AFP	Adjusted Function Points
API	Application Programming Interface
BFC	Base Functional Component
BIPM	Bureau International des Poids et Mesures—International Bureau of Weights and Measures
CFP	COSMIC Function Points
CMMi	Capability Maturity Model Integrated
COCOMO	Constructive Cost Model
COSMIC	Common Software Measurement International Consortium
DET	Data Element Type
EF	Environment Factor
EIF	External Interface File
FCD	Final Committee Draft
FFP	Full Function Points
FISMA	Finish Software Measurement Association
FP	Function Points
FPA	Function Points Analysis
FTR	File Type Referenced
FSM	Functional Size Measurement
FUR	Functional User Requirement
GSC	General System Characteristics

Software Metrics and Software Metrology, by Alain Abran
Copyright © 2010 IEEE Computer Society

Acronym	Description
IEC	International Electrotechnical Commission
IEEE	Institute of Electrical and Electronics Engineers
IFCC	International Federation of Clinical Chemistry and Laboratory Medecine
IFPUG	International Function Points Users Group
ILF	Internal Logical File
IS	International Standard
ISBSG	International Software Benchmarking Standards Group
ISO	International Organization for Standardization
IUPAC	International Union of Pure and Applied Chemistry
IUPAP	International Union of Pure and Applied Physics
KA	Knowledge Area
MIS	Management Information System
MMRE	Mean Magnitude of Relative Error
MR	Mean Resources
NESMA	Netherlands Software Measurement Association
OF	Overhead Factor
OIML	International Organization of Legal Metrology
OO	Object Oriented
OOP	Object Oriented Programming
PMBOK	Project Management Body of Knowledge
PMI	Project Management Institute
R^2	Coefficient of determination (for example: in a statistical regression model)
RUP	Rational Unified Process
SWEBOK	Software Engineering Body of Knowledge
TCF	Technical Complexity Factor
TR	Technical Report
TX	Transactions
UCP	Use Case Points
UFP	Unadjusted Function Points
UML	Unified Modeling Language
UUCP	Unadjusted Use Case Points
VAF	Value Adjustment Factor
VIM	Vocabulary International of Metrology

Appendix B

GLOSSARY OF TERMS IN SOFTWARE MEASUREMENT

In Chapter 3 on Metrology, the measurement concepts have been presented as defined in classical metrology and used throughout the sciences and in engineering. However, software has defined its own measurement terminology; for instance, while the widely "quantity," "base quantity" and "derived quantity" are the terms adopted in metrology, the corresponding terminology in software would be "attribute," "base attribute" and "derived attribute."

To help practitioners and researchers in the software engineering and metrology communities bridge the cultural gap between them, this Appendix presents the terms, and their definitions, that would be the most familiar to each culture, while not specifically recommending their use.

B.1 SOME MEASUREMENT TERMS IN SOFTWARE ENGINEERING

Attribute: the property of an entity that can be determined quantitatively, that is, for which a magnitude can be assigned. In the metrology vocabulary, this is called a *measurable quantity*, or *quantity* for short.

> Some quality attribute models, such as in ISO 9126, use the terms *quality characteristic* and *sub-characteristic*.
> ISO 15939 considers an attribute to be a property related to information needs.

Software Metrics and Software Metrology, by Alain Abran
Copyright © 2010 IEEE Computer Society

Measurand: the name given by standards like the VIM to label the attribute to be measured.

Attributes of the same type: attributes which can be placed in order of magnitude relative to one another.

Base attribute: a simple property defined by convention, with no reference to other attributes, and possibly used in a system of attributes to define other attributes. In the metrology vocabulary, this is called a *base quantity*.

Derived attribute: a property defined in a system of attributes as a function of base attributes. In the metrology vocabulary, it is called a *derived quantity*.

The distinction here between a base attribute and a derived attribute is based on the way the attribute is defined, which is independent of the way it will be measured. That is, in a system of attributes, an attribute is a base attribute if it is defined by convention as functionally independent of the other attributes, but it can also be used to define other attributes.

Whether the attribute, length, for example, is determined by using a tape measure or a king's arm, the definition of a meter depends only on how we want to define it.

To avoid any confusion in the marketplace, it is mandatory to develop an international consensus on the definitions of the base attributes in software engineering (such as the base quantities that correspond to the base units in the International System of Units, SI).

Making the distinction at the concept definition level, rather than later at the measurement level, is a more precise way to do it, even though this is not explicitly the case in the software measurement standards.

ISO 15939 uses *base measures* and *derived measures* to illustrate the application of measurement methods to attributes.

The ISO's VIM uses *base quantity* and *derived quantity* to refer to a property to which a magnitude can be assigned. This corresponds to the base attribute and the derived attribute above.

Entity: refers to any distinguishable object in the empirical world for which a measurement can be applied. Fenton and Pfleeger [1997] distinguish three kinds of entities: *products*, *processes*, and *resoFurces*. An entity is characterized by a set of attributes, each corresponding to one observable simple property.

Examples of Software Entities to Be Measured

A piece of code, a design artifact, a database, a programming task, a maintenance process, or any other intermediate software product or process.

Entity Population: defined as a set of empirical entities having similarities. This concept designates the set of objects (entities) usually considered to be characterized through the same set of attributes and for which we try to design one measurement method. Indeed, measurement is a way to compare entities within a set of similar ones, that is, within an entity population.

> In the software domain, applying a measurement method outside the entity population for which it was originally designed is uncommon.
>
> It would be inappropriate, for example, to apply a measurement method designed for Fortran programs to measure the attributes of a Java program.

Entity Population Model: defined as a model describing the measurement of an attribute on some entity population in order to identify a reference value (i.e. a conventional value of an attribute). Therefore, the entity population model allows the definition of a value as the reference needed to analyze and interpret data for software experimentation.

> This concept is not explicit in measurement knowledge documents like the VIM, because, like other ISO international standards, the VIM:
>
> - focuses on the measurement design and its application through measuring instruments, but
> - does not take into account the interpretation of the measurement results.

Measurement of an attribute: the characterization of that attribute in terms of numbers or symbols. This general definition is consistent with most of the standards and with the literature. However, beyond this general definition, it is sometimes useful to distinguish, as does the measurement literature for the most part, two complementary viewpoints: operational and theoretical.

> **From an Operational Viewpoint**
>
> Measurement is the process of mapping empirical entities to numbers (the process of measuring).
>
> More precisely, the measurement of an attribute of an entity is the process of experimentally obtaining information about the magnitude of that attribute; that is, to establish an association between the attribute of the entity and a value.
>
> Note that the concept of value in VIM extends beyond numbers, including as it does the number (an element of R) and the underlying reference, such as the unit (see below).

From a Theoretical Viewpoint

Measurement is the mapping between an empirical relational structure (roughly the entity population set with its associated ordering and operations) and a numerical relational structure (typically the reals of **R**, but other numerical structures as well, and, more generally, any structure of symbols).

This view corresponds to the representational approach of measurement. The three components of this theoretical view of measurement:

- the empirical structure, say E,
- the numerical structure, say N, and
- the mapping, say □,

which are defined next.

Sometimes the measurement refers to the whole triplet <E, N, □>.

It can be observed that these two viewpoints are complementary, and that they do not present any contradiction: the operational view focuses on the act of mapping (how to map), while the theoretical one focuses on the properties of the mapping.

Value: refers to the magnitude assigned to an attribute of an entity represented by a number and a reference (VIM 2007). A reference is generally a unit, but it could also be the unit 1 in particular cases or in a measurement procedure acting as a reference.

Note that several authors talk about the value assigned to an attribute as only a number, disregarding the underlying reference. Though this may be acceptable when the underlying reference is obvious, it should be remembered that a value is both a number *and* a reference.

B.2 SOME MEASUREMENT TERMS IN METROLOGY—VIM 2007

Calibration: operation that, under specified conditions, in a first step, establishes a relation between the quantity values with measurement uncertainties provided by measurement standards and corresponding indications with associated measurement uncertainties and, in a second step, uses this information to establish a relation for obtaining a measurement result from an indication.

Conventional reference scale: quantity-value scale defined by general agreement. In the software domain, agreement is still a long way off. Such agreement would help software measurement to mature as a discipline.

Measurement method[1]: generic description of a logical organization of operations used in a measurement.

Measurement procedure: detailed description of a measurement according to one or more measurement principles and to a given measurement method, based on a measurement model and including any calculation to obtain a measurement result.

Measurement result: set of quantity values attributed to a measurand together with any other available relevant information. As mentioned above, a measurement result is generally expressed as a single measured quantity value and a measurement uncertainty (see below).

> The term *measurement* in everyday language has different meanings:
> It can, for instance, label the mapping of entities to values or the action of applying that mapping. It is also used to designate the result of the application of the mapping.
> To avoid confusion in this text, more explicit terms, such as *measurement result*, *applying the measurement*, *measuring*, or *to measure* are preferred.
> The term *measurement*, referring to the mapping with its dual meaning described above, will be avoided where possible.

Measurement standard (etalon): According to [VIM 2007], an etalon is the realization of the definition of a quantity (an attribute), with a stated quantity value and associated measurement uncertainty, used as a reference. Note that this corresponds to a more common view than the one that considers an etalon as defining the unit.

Measuring instrument: device used for making measurements, alone or in conjunction with one or more supplementary device(s).

Measuring system: set of one or more measuring instruments and often other devices, including any reagent and supply, assembled and adapted to give information used to generate measured quantity values within specified intervals for quantities of specified kinds.

Metrological traceability: property of a measurement result whereby the result can be related to a reference through a documented unbroken chain of calibrations, each contributing to the measurement uncertainty.

Quantity-Value Scale: ordered set of **quantity values** of **quantities** of a given **kind of quantity**[2] used in ranking, according to magnitude, quantities of that kind.

> From the mathematical viewpoint, this structured set corresponds to the relational structure N alluded to above.
> Sometimes the scale is viewed more generally as the whole triplet: <E, N, □>.
> In the VIM, this concept is related to a display device.

[1]From "International Vocabulary of Basic and General Terms in Metrology," International Organization for Standardization, Switzerland, 3rd edition, 2007.
[2]The use of bold characters in this definition is "as is" from the VIM 2007.

Measurement Uncertainty: non-negative parameter characterizing the dispersion of the quantity values being attributed to a mesurand, based on the information used.

Measurement Unit: real scalar quantity, defined and adopted by convention, with which any other quantity of the same kind can be compared to express the ratio of the two quantities as a number.

A number of these metrology concepts are seldom used in the software domain. This reflects an incomplete view, and an incomplete understanding, of measurement in software engineering when compared to the generally accepted view of the field of measurement in science and engineering.

Appendix C

REFERENCES

Abd Ghani, A.A.; Hunter, R. (1996) "An Attribute Grammar Approach to Specifying Halstead's Metrics," *Malaysian Journal of Computer Science*, Vol. 9, no. 1, pp. 56–67.

Abran, A.; Al-Qutaish, R.E.; Desharnais, J.M.; Habra, N. (2005a) "An Information Model for Software Quality Measurement with ISO Standards," International Conference on Software Development—SWEDC-REK, Reykjavik, Iceland, University of Iceland, pp. 104–116.

Abran, A.; Al-Qutaish, R.E.; Desharnais, J.M. (2005b) "Harmonization Issues in the Updating of the ISO Standards on Software Product Quality," in Metrics News, Vol. 10, no. 2, December, 2005, pp. 35–44.

Abran, A.; Desharnais, J.M.; Azziz, F. (2005c) "Measurement Convertibility: From Function Points to COSMIC," 15th International Workshop on Software Measurement—IWSM 2005, Montréal (Canada), Shaker Verlag, Sept. 12–14, 2005, pp. 227–240.

Abran, A.; Moore, J.; Bourque, P.; Dupuis, R.; Tripp, L. (2005d) Guide to the Software Engineering Body of Knowledge—SWEBOK—Version 2004, IEEE-Computer Society Press: www.swebok.org, Los Alamitos (USA), p. 206.

Abran, A.; Lopez, M.; Habra, N. (2004) "An Analysis of the McCabe Cyclomatic Complexity Number," 14th International Workshop on Software Measurement—IWSM-Metrikon-2004, Magdeburg, Germany: Springer-Verlag, pp. 391–405.

Abran, A.; Sellami, A.; Suryn, W. (2003) "Metrology, Measurement and Metrics in Software Engineering," 9th International Software Metrics Symposium—METRICS'03, IEEE Computer Press, Sydney (Australia), September 2003, pp. 2–11.

Abran, Alain (1998) "*Software Metrics Need to Mature into Software Metrology*," NIST Workshop on Advancing Measurements and Testing for Information Technology (IT), Gaithersburg (Maryland), October 26–27, 1998.

Abran, A.; Robillard, P.N. (1996) *Function Points Analysis: An Empirical Study of its Measurement Processes*, IEEE Transactions on Software Engineering, Vol. 22, pp. 895–909.

Abran, A.; Maya, M.; Desharnais, J.M.; St-Pierre, D. (1997) "Adapting Function Points to Real-Time Software," American Programmer, Vol. 10, Issue 11, November 1997, pp. 32–43.

Abran, Alain; Robillard, P.N. (1994) "Function Points: A Study of Their Measurement Processes and Scale Transformations," *Journal of Systems and Software*, Vol. 25, Issue 2, p. 171.

Albrecht, A.J. (1983) "Software Function, Source Lines of Code, and Development Effort Prediction: A Software Science Validation," *IEEE Transactions on Software Engineering*, Vol. 9, Issue 6, November.

Albrecht, A.J. (1979) "Measuring Application Development Productivity," Proceedings of Joint Share, Guide and IBM Application Development Symposium, October 1997, pp. 83–92.

Al Qutaish, R.; Abran, A. (2005) "An Analysis of the Designs and Definitions of Halstead Metrics," 15th International Workshop on Software Measurement—IWSM 2005, Montréal (Canada), Shaker Verlag, Sept. 12–14, pp. 337–352.

Bach, J. (1997) "Good Enough Quality: Beyond the Buzzword," *Computer*, Vol. 30, no. 8, August 1997, pp. 96–98.

Berge, C. (2001) *Theory of Graphs*, Dover Publications.

Boehm, B.W. (1981) *Software Engineering Economics*, New York, Prentice Hall.

Boehm, B.W.; Abst, C. (2000) *Software Cost Estimation with COCOMO II*, Prentice Hall, pp. 502.

Booth, S.P.; Jones, S.B. (1996) "Are Ours Really Smaller Than Theirs," Glasgow Workshop on Functional Programming, Ullapool, Scotland, UK, pp. 1–7.

Card, David; Glass, Robert L. (1990) "Measure software design quality," Prentice Hall.

Carnahan, L.; Carver, G.; Gray, M.; Hogan, M.; Hopp, T.; Horlick, J.; Lyon, G.; Messina, E. (1997) "Metrology for Information Technology," *StandardView*, Vol. 5, no. 3, pp. 103–109.

Carroll, Ed (2005) "Software Estimating Based on Use Case Points," The Cursor, Software Association of Oregon, Website: http://www.sao.org/newsletter

Chen, P. (1976) "The Entity-Relationship Model–Toward A Unified View of Data," *ACM Transactions on Database Systems*, Vol. 1, no. 1, March 1976.

Chidamber, S.R.; Kemerer, C.F. (1993) A Metrics Suite for Object Oriented design. M.I.T. Sloan School of Management E53–315.

Christensen, K.; Fitsos, G.P.; Smith, C.P. (1981) "A perspective on Software Science," *IBM Systems Journal*, Vol. 20, no. 4.

Chuan, C.H.; Lin, L.; Ping, L.L.; Lian, L.V. (1994) "Evaluation of Query Languages with Software Science Metrics," IEEE Region 10's Ninth Annual International Conference on Frontiers of Computer Technology TENCON'94, Singapore, pp. 516–520.

Conte, S.D.; Dunsmore, H.E.; Shen, V.Y. (1986) *Software Engineering Metrics and Models*, Menlo Park, California: Benjamin Cummings.

COSMIC (2009) The COSMIC Functional Size Measurement Method Version 3.0.1, Measurement Manual (The COSMIC Implementation Guide for ISO/IEC 19761: 2003), Published by the COSMIC Group, p. 80. Available at www.cosmicon.com/portal/dl.asp

Desharnais, JM.; Abran, A.; Suryn, W. (2009) "Attributes and Related Base Measures within ISO 9126: A Pareto Analysis," BSC SQM-2009 Conference.

Desharnais, J.M.; Abran, A.; Cuadrado, J. (2006) "Convertibility of Function Points to COSMIC-FFP: Identification and Analysis of Functional Outliers," MENSURA2006, Conference Proceedings, Publication Service of the University of Cádiz www.uca.es/publicaciones Nov. 4–5, 2006, Cadiz (Spain), pp. 190–205.

Desharnais, J.M.; Morris, P.M. (1996) "Post Measurement Validation Procedure for Function Point Counts," IEEE Forum on Software Engineering Standards Issues, Montréal, Québec, Canada, Oct. 21–25, 1996.

Dikici, P. (2009) "Error Message Effectiveness Measurement," Term Session Paper, Graduate Course "SM517 Software Measures," Professor JM Desharnais, METU Informatics Institute, Ankara, Turkey.

Evans, M.W.; Marciniak, J. (1987) Software Quality Assurance and Management, John Wiley and Sons.

Fenton, N. (1994) "Software Measurement: A Necessary Scientific Basis," *IEEE Transaction on Software Engineering*, Vol. 20, no. 3, March 1994, pp. 199–206.

Fenton, N.; Kitchenham, B. (1991) "Validating Software Measures," *J. of Software Technology, Verification and Reliability*, Vol. 1, no. 2, pp. 27–42.

Fenton, N.E.; Pfleeger, S.L. (1997) *Software Metrics: A Rigorous and Practical Approach*, 2nd Edition, PWS Publishing Co., London, pp. 638.

Fetcke, T. (1999) "The Warehouse Software Portfolio, A Case Study in Functional Size Measurement," Technical Report no. 1999–20, Département d'informatique, Université du Quebec à Montréal, Canada.

Galea, S. (1995) "The Boeing Company: 3D Function Point Extensions, V2.0, Release 1.0," Boeing Information and Support Services, Research and Technology Software Engineering, June 1995.

Gray, M.M. (1999) "Applicability of Metrology to Information Technology," *Journal of Research of the National Institute of Standards and Technology*, Vol. 104, no. 6, pp. 567–578.

Gruber, T.R. (1993) "Toward Principles for the Design of Ontologies Used for Knowledge Sharing in Formal Ontology," Conceptual Analysis and Knowledge Representation, Kluwer Academic Publishers.

Habra, N.; Abran, A.; Lopez, M.; Sellami, A. (2008) "A Framework for the Design and Verification of Software Measurement Methods," *Journal of Systems and Software, Elsevier*, Vol. 81, Issue no. 5, May 2008, pp. 633–648.

Halstead, M.H. (1977) *Elements of Software Science*, New York: Elsevier North-Holland.

Hamer, P.G.; Frewin, G.D. (1982) "M. H. Halstead's Software Science—A Critical Examination," 6th International Conference on Software Engineering—ICSE-1982, Tokyo, Japan, pp. 197–206.

Harel, D.; Rumpe, B. (2000) "Modeling Languages: Syntax, Semantics and All That Stuff," Technical Chapter, No. MCS00-16, The Weizmann Institute of Science, 2000. (http://www.cs.york.ac.uk/puml/).

Henderson-Sellers, S.; Tegarden, D. (1994a) "The Theoretical Extension of Two Versions of Cyclomatic Complexity to Multiple Entry/Exit Modules," *Software Quality Journal*, 3, pp. 253–269.

Henderson-Sellers, B.; Tegarden, D. (1994b) "Clarifications concerning Modularization and McCabe Cyclomatic Complexity," in *Technical Correspondence, Communications of the ACM*, April 1994, Vol. 37, no. 4, pp. 91–94.

Henderson-Sellers, B. (1996) *Object-Oriented Metrics—Measures of Complexity*, Prentice Hall.

Illingworth, V. (1991) (editor), *Dictionary of Computing*, Oxford University Press, 3rd edition, 1991, 510 pages.

Jacobson, Ivar (1987) "Object Oriented Development in An Industrial Environment," OOPSLA'87 Proceedings, Oct. 4–8, 1987, pp. 183–191.

Jones, Capers (1988) "Feature Points (Function Point Logic for Real Time and System Software," International Function Points Users Group—IFPUG Fall 1988 Conference, Montreal, Québec, October 1988.

Jones, Capers (1991) "Using Functional Metrics to Evaluate CASE," International Function Points Users Group—IFPUG Spring Conference, Baltimore, Maryland, April. 2–5, 1991.

Karner, Gustav (1993) "Resource Estimation for Objectory Projects," Objective Systems SF AB.

Khelifi, A.; Abran, A.; Buglione, L. (2004) "A System of References for Software Measurements with ISO 19761 (COSMIC)," 14th International Workshop, IWSM 2004, Berlin, Germany, November 3–5, 2004.

Khelifi, A. (2005) "A Set of References for Software Measurement with ISO 19761 (COSMIC): An Exploratory Study," PhD thesis, École de Technologie Supérieure, Montréal, p. 495.

Kiricenko, V.; Ormandjieva, O. (2005) "Measurement of OOP Size Based on Halstead's Software Science," 2nd Software Measurement European Forum—SMEF-2005, Rome, Italy.

Kitchenham, B.; Pfleeger, S.L.; Fenton, N. (1995) "Towards a Framework for Software Measurement Validation," *IEEE Transactions on Software Engineering*, Vol. 21, n. 12, December, pp. 929–944.

Knaff, F.J.; Sacks, J. (1986) "Software Development Effort Prediction Based on Function Points," COMPSAC'86.

Li, D.Y.; Kiricenko, V.; Ormandjieva, O. (2004) "Halstead's Software Science in Today's Object Oriented World," *Metrics News*, Vol. 9, no. 2, pp. 33–40.

Lister, A.M. (1982) "Software Science—The Emperor's New Clothes," *Australian Computer Journal*, Vol. 14, no. 2, pp. 66–70.

Lopez, M.; Paulus, V.; Habra, N (2003) "Integrated Validation Process of Software Measure," International Workshop on Software Measurement, IWSM2003, Montreal, September 2003.

Lopez, M.; Habra, N. (2005) "Relevance of the Cyclomatic Complexity Threshold for the Java Programming Language," Software Measurement European Forum—SMEF 2005, Rome (Italy). http://www.fundp.ac.be/recherche/publications/page_view/58160/

McCabe, T. (1976) "A Software Complexity Measure," *IEEE Transactions on Software Engineering SE*, 2(4), pp. 308–320.

MacDonell, S.G. (1991) "Rigor in Software COmplexity Measurement Experimentation," *Journal of Systems and Software*, October 1991.

McGarry, J.; Card, D.; Jones, C.; Layman, B.; Clark, E.; Dean, J.; Hall, F. (2001) Practical Software Measurement: Objective Information for Decision Makers, Addison Wesley Professional.

Melton, A.C.; Gustafson, D.M.; Bieman, J.M.; Baker, A.L. (1990) "A Mathematical Perspective for Software Measures Research," in *Software Engineering Journal* 5, 5, September 1990, 246–254.

Menzies, T.; Stefano, J.S.D.; Chapman, M.; McGill, K. (2002) "Metrics That Matter," 27th Annual NASA Goddard Software Engineering Workshop, Greenbelt, Maryland, USA, pp. 51–57.

Mohagheghi, Parastoo (2005) "Effort Estimation of Use Cases for Incremental Large-Scale Software Development," IEEE International Conference on Software Engineering—ICSE-2005, May. 15–21, St.Louis, MI, USA, pp. 303–311.

Mukhopadhyay, T.; Kekre, S. (1992) "Software Effort Models for Early Estimation of Process Control Applications," *IEEE Transactions on Software Engineering*, Vol. 18, no. 10, October 1992, pp. 915–924.

Nagano, Shin-Ichi; Mase, K.I.; Watanabe, Y.; Watahiki T.; Nishiyama, S. (2001) "Validation of Application Results of COSMIC to Switching Systems," ACOSM-2001, 17 Nov., 2001, Australian Government—Department of Employment and Workplace Relations. 6 Jan., 2004, www.cosmicon.com

Nageswaran, Suresh (2001) "Test Effort Estimation Using Use Case Points," Quality Week 2001, San Francisco, CA, USA, June 2001.

Ouwerkerk, J.; Abran, A. (2006) "Evaluation of the Design of Use Case Points (UCP)," MENSURA2006, Conference Proceedings Edited by the Publish Service of the University of Cádiz www.uca.es/publicaciones Nov. 4–5, 2006, Cadiz (Spain), pp. 83–97.

Ozcan Top, O. (2009) "Measurement Method for CASE," Term Session Paper, Graduate Course "SM517 Software Measures," Professor JM Desharnais, METU Informatics Institute, Ankara, Turkey, 2009.

Reifer, D.J. (1990) "Asset-R: A Function Point Sizing Tool for Scientific and Real-Time Systems," *Journal of Systems and Software*, Vol. 11, no. 3, March 1990, pp. 159–171.

Samoladas, I.; Stamelos, I.; Angelis, L.; Oikonomou, A. (2004) "Open Source Software Development should Strive for Even Greater Code Maintainability," *Communication of ACM*, Vol. 47, no. 10, pp. 83–88.

Sellami, A.; Abran, A (2003) "The Contribution of Metrology Concepts to Understanding and Clarifying a Proposed Framework for Software Measurement Validation," 13th International Workshop on Software Measurement—IWSM 2003, Montréal (Canada), Springer-Verlag, Sept. 23–25, 2003, pp. 18–40.

Smith, John (1999) "The Estimation of Effort Based on Use Cases," Rational Whitepaper, Rational Software.

Szentes, S. (1986) QUALIGRAPH User Guide, Budapest: Research and Innovation Center.

Vincenti, G.W. (1990) *What Engineers Know and How They Know It—Analytical Studies from Aeronautical History*, Johns Hopkins University Press, pp. 326.

Vogelezang, F. (2004) *Implementing COSMIC as a replacement for FP*, 14th International Workshop on Software Measurement—IWSM-Metrikon 20043, Konig-Winsterhausen, Germany.

Vogelezang, F.; Lesterhuis, A. (2003) "Applicability of COSMIC Full Function Points in An Administrative Environment: Experiences of an Early Adopter," 13th International Workshop on Software Measurement—IWSM2003, Shaker Verlag, Montréal.

Watson, A.H. (1995) "McCabe Complexity," Software Development Systems Management Development, Auerbach.

Watson, A.H.; McCabe, T.J. (1996) "Structured Testing: A Testing Methodology Using the Cyclomatic Complexity Metric," NIST Special Publication.

Whitmire, S.A. (1997) *Object-Oriented Design Measurement*, John Wiley & Sons.

Whitmire, S.A. (1995) "An Introduction to 3D Function Points," *Software Development*, April, 1995, pp. 43–53.

Whitmire, S.A. (1992) "3-D Function Points: Scientific and Real-Time Extensions to Function Points," *1992 Pacific Northwest Software Quality Conference*, June 1, 1992.

Zuse, Horst (2005) "Resolving the Mysteries of the Halstead Measures," METRIKON Conference, Fall of 2005, DASMA, Germany.

Zuse, Horst (1997) *A Framework for Software Measurement*, Walter de Gruyter, Germany, Berlin, pp. 755.

ISO and IEEE Measurement Related Standards

IEEE 610.12 (1990) IEEE Standard Computer Dictionary: A Compilation of IEEE Standard Computer Glossaries, The Institute of Electrical and Electronics Engineers, Inc., New York, NY, 1990.

IEEE 982.1-1988 IEEE Standard Dictionary of Measures to Produce Reliable Software.

IEEE 90, Institute of Electrical and E. Engineers. An Empirical Evaluation (and Specification) of the all-du-paths. *IEEE Standard Computer Dictionary: A Compilation of IEEE Standard Computer Glossaries*, 1990.

ISO GUM. *Guide to the Expression of Uncertainty in Measurement (1993 amended 1995):* published by ISO in the name of BIPM, IEC, IFCC, IUPAC, IUPAP and OIML.

ISO/IEC 9126-1: 2001. *Software Engineering–Product Quality–Part 1: Quality Model*, International Organization for Standardization—ISO, Geneva, 2001.

ISO/IEC TR 9126-2: 2003. *Software Engineering–Product Quality–Part 2: External Metrics,* International Organization for Standardization—ISO, Geneva, 2003.

ISO/IEC TR 9126-3: 2003. *Software Engineering–Product Quality–Part 3: Internal Metrics*, International Organization for Standardization—ISO, Geneva, 2003.

ISO/IEC TR 9126-4: 2004. *Software Engineering–Product Quality–Part 4: Quality in Use Metric*, International Organization for Standardization—ISO, Geneva, 2004.

ISO/IEC 12207: 2008, Systems and software engineering—Software life cycle processes, International Organization for Standardization, Geneva (Switzerland).

ISO/IEC 14143-1: 1998, *Information technology—Software measurement—Functional size measurement—Part 1: Definition of concepts*, International Organization for Standardization–ISO, Geneva, 1998.

ISO/IEC 14143-3: 2003, *Software Engineering–Functional Size Measurement–Part 3: Verification of Functional Size Measurement Methods*, International Organization for Standardization–ISO, Geneva, 2003.

ISO/IEC 14764:2006, *Software Engineering—Software Life Cycle Processes—Maintenance, Geneva*: International Organization for Standardization.

ISO 15288:2008, Systems and software engineering—System life cycle processes. International Organization for Standardization, Geneva (Switzerland).

ISO/IEC 15939: 2002, *Information Technology—Software Engineering—Software Measurement Process*, International Organization for Standardization–ISO, Geneva, 2002.

ISO/IEC 19761: 2003, *Software Engineering—COSMIC-FFP—A Functional Size Measurement Method*, International Organization for Standardization—ISO, Geneva, 2003.

ISO/IEC 20926: IFPUG *Function Point Counting Practices Manual'*, International Organization for Standardization—ISO, Geneva, 2001.

ISO/IEC 20968: MK II. *Function Point Analysis: Counting Practices Manual'*, software Metrics Association, International Organization for Standardization—ISO, Geneva, 2001.

ISO/IEC 24570: NESMA Definitions and Counting Guidelines for the Application of Function Point Analysis: A Practical Manual: version 2.0, International Organization for Standardization—ISO, Geneva, 2001.

ISO 24765, Systems and Software Engineering Vocabulary, International Organization for Standardization, Geneva (Switzerland).

ISO 25000:2005 Software Engineering—Software product Quality Requirements and Evaluation (SQuaRE)—Guide to SQuaRE, International Organization for Standardization, Geneva (Switzerland).

ISO/IEC 26514 Systems and Software Engineering: Requirements for Designers and Developers of User Documentation, International Organization for Standardization, Geneva (Switzerland).

PMBOK, "A Guide to the Project Management Body of Knowledge (PMBOK® Guide)," Project Management Institute, Third Edition.

VIM ISO/IEC Guide 99 International vocabulary of metrology—Basic and general concepts and associated terms (VIM), International Organization for Standardization— ISO, Geneva, 2007.

INDEX

Software Metrics and Software Metrology, by Alain Abran
Copyright © 2010 IEEE Computer Society

.

Printed in the United States
By Bookmasters